off~white

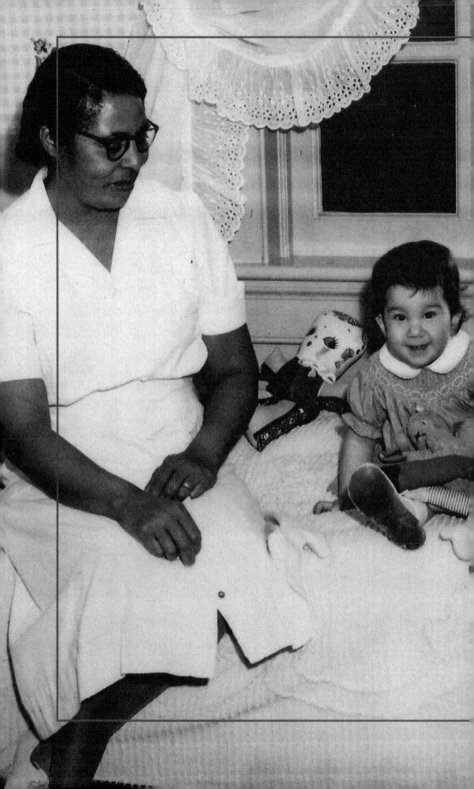

LAURIE GUNST

off~white

a memoir

For Jane – sister Virginian!
Laurie Gunst

SOHO

Published by
Soho Press Inc.
853 Broadway
New York, NY 10003

Library of Congress Cataloging-in-Publication Data

Gunst, Laurie.
Off-white : a memoir / Laurie Gunst.
p. cm.
ISBN 1-56947-400-1 (alk. paper)
EAN 978-1-56947-400-6
1. Gunst, Laurie. 2. Jews—North Carolina—Wilmington—Biography.
3. Gunst, Laurie—Relations with African Americans.
4. Lloyd, Rhoda, 1894–1986. 5. African Americans—
North Carolina—Wilmington—Relations with Jews.
6. Wilmington (N.C.)—Biography. I. Title.
F265.J5G86 2005
975.6'27004924—dc22
2005042471

Designed by Pauline Neuwirth, Neuwirth & Associates, Inc.

10 9 8 7 6 5 4 3 2 1

For Jonathan

author's note

The past is a foreign country; they do things differently there.
—LESLIE POLES HARTLEY

*W*ell . . . yes and no.

The past of which this book tells is not another country, for as long as some women (mostly white) give over the love work of raising their children to other women (mostly of color and from other cultures), this story will remain.

It is not the story of a wannabe. My southern Jewish parents instilled much too strong a sense of who we were, and Rhoda gave me far too deep a respect for who she was, for me to have grown up ever wanting to be someone other than who I am.

And yet . . . can one have a soul that does not match the color of one's skin? I don't know. Reader: This is for you to decide, as you walk this road with me, from the past into the present of what Alice Walker has so justly named "the American race."

hoodoo child

one

RHODA STRODE INTO our lives on an August day in 1921, on the beach at Wrightsville, North Carolina. It was nearly thirty years before I was to be born. But that hardly mattered; to her way of thinking, the two of us were destined for each other.

"I came to work for your grandmother way back in the days . . . ," Rhoda liked to tell me when I was a child. "Before you were even thought of." Then she'd give me one of her Gioconda smiles, secretive and all-knowing, as if *she* knew I was going to come along even if God Almighty hadn't figured it out yet.

I feel as if I was born knowing the story of the first encounter between Rhoda and my grandmother; it's my origin myth, you might say, a haunting blend of accident and fate. The image it conjures for me is of these two utterly dissimilar women, poised at a moment in time before my own life was imagined. When I see them on that blazing hot beach, they live again, though they've been dead for decades: my red-hot Roaring Twenties flapper of a grandmother, and Rhoda, the sedate, beautifully mannered, and self-contained woman of color—two figures of equal magnitude to me, no matter that they sprang from opposite sides of a South both belonged to.

On that day so long ago, on a wide stretch of hot sand just like the one at Virginia Beach, Virginia where Rhoda and I would one day spend hours together, she was trundling another white child by the hand, a little girl from Savannah, where Rhoda was then living. The child's parents had taken a cottage at Wrightsville for a couple of weeks and had brought Rhoda with them.

My grandmother, Alice Einstein, was there for the season. Her family owned a gingerbread cottage on the dunes, a beautiful little whitewashed Victorian that Alice's father had built at the turn of the century, when he was Wilmington, North Carolina's high-rolling mayor. The Einsteins would come and go, all summer long, between this cottage and their home in Wilmington, an hour's trolley ride away. When June came and the heat descended on Wilmington like punishment for the sins of its too-glorious spring, Alice Einstein and the children made their annual pilgrimage to the beach at Wrightsville; her husband, Arthur, would join them on weekends if he could leave his store. Their daughter Evelyn—who would become my mother—was then a little girl, and she counted the days leading up to her family's departure from Wilmington to Wrightsville. Well before the trolley arrived at the Lumina station, she would be waiting breathlessly for her summer's first glimpse of the ocean, rising suddenly beyond the dunes like a blue-gray mirage. Evelyn was ten when her baby sister, Alice, was born; when the family reached the cottage, Evelyn would mind the baby while her mother and a maid swept and cleaned, being ever so sure to look before they reached an arm into the cabinets and closets where black widows lurked.

Arthur Einstein owned a dry-goods store on Front Street, the mercantile district on the Cape Fear River. Along the riverfront stood the handsome brick warehouses where stevedores weighed the bales of cotton and factors sold it for the Carolina oligarchs

My grandmother, Alice Fishblate, and my grandfather, Arthur Einstein, on their wedding day in Kinston, North Carolina, 1909. Their first child—my mother, Evelyn—was born one year later.

My grandmother on her honeymoon in Atlantic City.

whose fortunes King Cotton had made. The Einstein brothers were not among them; they were the sons of Jewish peddlers who'd come down from the North in the years just after the Civil War. Black people had a perfect phrase for brothers like the Einsteins: They called the peddlers "rolling-store men" because of their horses and wagons heaped high with shiny tin, starched calico, and pretty ribbons for a girl's hair. Now, half a century later, the store the Einstein men had built was doing very well. But that was mostly due to the acumen of Arthur's partners; he had no head for business. He was a quiet, thoughtful man and not all that strong, his heart having been weakened by the rheumatic fever he'd had as a child.

Was it his delicacy, his sensitive face and shy demeanor, that made him all the more appealing to my strong-willed, self-indulgent grandmother? Because no two people could have been less alike than Alice Fishblate and Arthur Einstein. When I consider them, I think of Scarlett O'Hara and Ashley Wilkes, and of Scarlett's father warning his headstrong daughter: "Only when like marries like can there be any happiness." I wonder if my great-grandfather, the blustering ex-mayor of Wilmington, ever issued a similar warning to his daughter; if he did, she listened about as long as Scarlett did. Alice Fishblate married Arthur Einstein in the summer of 1909, and even in their wedding pictures, I can see trouble brewing. Oh, yes: They were very much in love; I can tell that from the way their eyes lock. But Arthur has this slightly puzzled look, as if he is wondering what he's going to do next with this handful of a woman. And my future granny is perched seductively on the arm of her bridegroom's wicker chair, gazing down into his sleepy eyes as if to say, "Gotcha!"

By the time Rhoda sauntered down the beach at Wrightsville, Alice and Arthur had two little girls, Evelyn and Alice; a third daughter, Barbara, would be born in 1925. Evelyn was already showing signs of growing up to be a beauty, with hair as black and glossy as a raven's plumage and eyes to match. But she had a chipped front tooth, her tomboy's badge of honor from roller-skating at breakneck speed on the rippling brick sidewalks of downtown Wilmington.

◔

A PERFECT DAY for the beach, that August afternoon of 1921. Rhoda and "her" white child were slowly making their way along the water's foamy edge. The little girl was ecstatic, running back and forth, chasing the shore birds on their stiltlike legs and planting her bare feet in the wet sand. She was fascinated by how it captured and then erased the print of her heel, her toes.

Rhoda would not have been similarly barefooted. Because she was this child's nurse, she was dressed accordingly, wearing heavy white shoes and a white uniform with a pinafore apron and a cap. Even on the beach, in this heat, she wore stockings, and they pinched the hair on her unshaven legs into dark whorls. Rhoda never shaved because she considered the practice to be for "loose" women, like the ones she glimpsed there on the beach, sunning themselves like so many turtles on a rock. Rhoda smiled to herself at the irony of this: Why, when white folks so prized their paleness, would these women be trying to turn several shades darker than they were?

Alice Einstein was one of the women turning her face up to the sun. Her body, still well covered, was poured into a striped wool bathing costume that only accentuated the fullness of her breasts, the roundness of her belly. She was a handsome woman and she knew it, with glittering black eyes and hair like coal, vain just like her mother, my great-grandmother Fannie, who used to take a pencil and outline her features in photographs of herself, never pleased enough with what the camera's eye had captured. Never mind that Alice Einstein was married now and the mother of two little girls. She still lived for parties, and this was surely the era for them: tea dances and dinners and late-evening soirees. Her passion for baubles and beautiful clothes drove her husband to distraction, but what could he do? Alice just smiled winningly when he complained about the bills, said it was a stroke of great good fortune that he was in dry goods, because he could afford to buy her all the latest styles from New York. And Arthur turned a blind eye to her endless flirting, the adulatory glances from her former beaux, and the way she delighted in the whispered sweetness of their blandishments.

At this moment on the beach, Alice Einstein was smoking a cigarette, staring out at the glistening ocean, and aimlessly watching her two-year-old build a drip castle at the water's edge. To tell the truth, Alice was never much on children, especially her own. But this was the maid's day off; otherwise she would have been the one down here on the beach, watching out for the baby, and Alice would have been up at the cottage, playing bridge for serious money with "the Girls," as she still called her crowd from the confirmation class of 1903 at Wilmington's Temple of Israel. (They would go on calling each other that until they began to die, one by one, half a century later.) The Girls played cards for high stakes, and Alice Einstein always won. She never rose from the table at the end of an afternoon without a hundred or so dollars, in twenties, folded into her silver money clip, which was shaped like a dollar sign.

Alice was taking a deep drag from her Lucky Strike when, out of the corner of her eye, she spied a light-skinned Negro woman walking toward her with a white child in tow. The Negro woman had caught a whiff of that tobacco from way down the beach, and she wrinkled her nose in distaste. She had gone to work in a cigar factory in Charleston when she was only ten, sitting at a long table with the other girls and women who sorted the foul-smelling leaf. The memory of how it stank could still set her stomach heaving. So don't ask Rhoda what her opinion of tobacco was. She would tell you that it was the nastiest plant God ever made.

Rhoda was a lady, with stature to match. She was tall and queenly, built strong, with long bones and smooth skin of coppery brown. Her jet hair, tucked into a net beneath her nurse's cap, was almost straight and it gleamed like oiled string. Rhoda was fond of saying, "A lady's hair is her crowning glory." She had inherited hers from one of her Cherokee ancestors, a lineage she did not particularly like to be reminded of, even though it had given her those high, proud cheekbones and a complexion only a few shades darker than what her people called "high yaller." Rhoda was proud of her beauty. And she wasn't above admitting that there were certain advantages to being lighter, in this color-struck Jim Crow South.

Little Alice Einstein glanced up from the drip castle she was building and saw the child Rhoda was shepherding along the shore. She raced up with her bucket full of sand and asked if this other girl wanted to help with the castle. This was the moment when Granny and Rhoda greeted each other for the first time, and the next three-quarters of a century in the lives of these two women and their people began to unfold. They introduced themselves, Alice Einstein and Rhoda Lloyd. Lloyd wasn't Rhoda's last name—yet—but she used it because her fiancé was named Willie Lloyd. Rhoda first met Willie when she was a girl of twelve and he was past thirty, and he had waited for her to grow up. Now they were husband and wife in all things except the law, and they would have been legally wed if it wasn't for the fact that Willie's aged mother refused to let her son marry Rhoda. "You can wait to marry that girl till after I'm gone," Clarissa Lloyd told her son. Willie was not about to cross her.

The conversation that Rhoda Lloyd and Alice Einstein struck up on the beach went on for hours, since the two little girls they were with weren't willing to part. I imagine that my grandmother asked Rhoda to sit down with her under the umbrella and that Rhoda politely declined. Not her "place." She remained standing, which had the advantage of giving her the edge, allowing her to be as tall and upright in her stance as in her spirit. The two women chatted as if they'd known each other for years, and Rhoda found herself laughing along with this other woman, in spite of her own better judgment, because she knew not to be overly familiar with white folks. But there was something so unusual about this chance-met woman; she was so forthright and friendly and warm that the distance between them closed. As much as it ever could, in this time and in this place.

Rhoda and Granny on the front steps of our house in Richmond, 1940. By then, they had known each other for almost twenty years, and though their body language and attire reveal their disparate roles, the fondness of their gaze tells another story.

They were still talking when all the other nurses and mothers on the beach began rounding up their children, shaking out the sodden, sandy towels and heading up to their cottages for dinner. Quickly, before she even knew that she was going to do this, before the moment could slip away, my grandmother offered Rhoda a job.

"Would you consider leaving Savannah?" she asked. "Would you come to Wilmington and work for us?"

Before Rhoda answered, an idea flashed into her thoughts. Down in Savannah, Willie Lloyd was hanging fire, too cowed by his mother to ask Rhoda to be his wife. Maybe, Rhoda opined, if she left for a while, showed that she wasn't to be taken for granted, that man just might see the light and realize he had better make his move.

"You know, Miz Einstein," Rhoda said, "I think that might work out fine."

Rhoda was right about Willie Lloyd; a few years of being with his mother and without Rhoda in Savannah lit a fire under him. In 1925, he finally asked Rhoda to be his wife. But they did not have long together. Willie died less than two years later, and then Rhoda left Savannah for good. She moved to Richmond, where her older sister, Lizzie, lived.

❧

THE EINSTEINS HAD also moved to Richmond. Evelyn Einstein, the child Rhoda had helped to raise, had grown up to marry a blue-eyed boy from Richmond, Richard Gunst, on whom she'd first set eyes when she was seven and he was twelve. Evelyn, who had been visiting her aunt in Richmond at the time, was outside on Monument Avenue, playing jacks beneath the stony-eyed gaze of the Confederate statues that rose above the gray cobblestones every couple of blocks, and Richard Gunst was sitting on the balustrade of his family's mansion across the street, bored to tears now that his friends had gone home after their daily drill with broomsticks against the Hun—the year was 1917. With nothing better to do, he was watching the little girl playing jacks across the

Mother at sweet sixteen, when she and my father were courting.

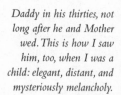

Daddy in his thirties, not long after he and Mother wed. This is how I saw him, too, when I was a child: elegant, distant, and mysteriously melancholy.

avenue when he saw her ball go bouncing out into the street. He was a fine runner—the hundred-yard dash was his best event in track and field—so he untangled his legs from the balustrade and cut a graceful figure as he sprinted across Monument Avenue to retrieve Evelyn Einstein's errant ball.

"Here, little girl," he said. "Here's your ball back."

My mother looked up into his sparkling blue eyes and said to herself, *This is the boy I'm going to marry.*

Which she did, on a sweltering June afternoon in 1930, when she was nineteen and Richard Gunst had turned into a spoiled, lady-killing playboy of twenty-five. He had left the University of Virginia after four years with no degree but a fair amount of experience in the bordellos of Charlottesville. He drank a fifth a day of anything he could get his hands on, but so did everyone else in their crowd. You could have said that whiskey ran in his blood: His father, Emmanuel, had inherited the distillery founded by the family in 1887. The Gunsts were German Jews who'd been in Virginia since before the Civil War, and the fortune they had made could pass for old money in the tight-knit community to which they belonged. And they had a history just racy enough—the whiskey business was always a slightly shady enterprise, after all—to excite the admiration of a warm-blooded girl like Evelyn Einstein. Yes, Richard Gunst was definitely a catch.

I WAS BORN in 1949, the last of their four children, and I came late and unexpected. Mother was thirty-nine and Daddy was forty-five; my brother, Dickie, was thirteen, and my sisters, Susan and Mary, were ten and eight. Placed around our house, on mahogany end tables and desks and dressers, were family photographs in silver frames, but these elegant presentations did not reveal the anguish that underlaid the posed images. My brother had been schizophrenic from early childhood, and my two sisters had grown up beneath the cloud of fear and unpredictability that hovers over all siblings of disturbed children. By the time I was born, Dickie was somewhat better, but the scars lay thick upon everyone's hearts.

The pictures I remember most vividly from my childhood—the ones I would dig out on rainy afternoons from the piles of loose snapshots tossed haphazardly into huge lavender coat boxes from Bergdorf Goodman that were stashed on shelves in every closet of our house—were of my father with Dickie as a toddler at Richmond's Acca train yards, where my brother loved to watch the steam locomotives. There is my handsome, tweed-coated father, kneeling in front of one of these shiny black engines hissing steam, with my three-year-old brother, beautiful as Christopher Robin, huddled in front of him in his own wool coat and matching leggings. Dickie is trying to smile, holding one of his toy train cars in a gloved fist, but his little face is screwed tight in what I know was terror, and my father looks as if he is about to cry. His only son, his firstborn, is damaged. Mysteriously, irrevocably impaired. Less than perfect, in a world where perfection matters more than anything, for we are Jews in a hostile gentile society: ever so closely watched, cruelly scrutinized, and all our failures glaring like sun on broken glass.

WHEN MOTHER DISCOVERED that she was carrying another child, she was overcome with both delight and dread. At that time, my father's relentless drinking and my brother's sickness were giving her such terrible anxiety attacks that she often fainted in public places, elevators, and escalators in department stores downtown. She took to carrying a bottle of smelling salts in her purse and often came to with some kind stranger's face bent over hers. Sometimes her headaches were so unbearable that she went to see the sinus doctor, who swabbed pharmaceutical cocaine high up into her nostrils. This she adored, loving the oblivion it induced and driving home in the Pontiac sedan feeling as if she hadn't a care in the world.

Rhoda was far away, in New York City, at that time. She was working for my grandmother there, and hating it. Rhoda was forced to share not only a room, but also a bed, with another maid named Florence, who, Rhoda said, rarely washed. It was therefore no wonder that when my mother called Rhoda in New York, begging her to return to Richmond and help take care of this baby about to be born, Rhoda did not reject the request out of hand. But she was reluctant all the same.

"You must think I'm ageless!" she said to Mother. "You're forgetting that I'm all of fifty-five. Now you know that's too old to be staying up all night with a newborn baby and then chasing after a toddling child." But Rhoda had known Evelyn since she was a child of ten, and now she heard the desperation in her voice.

"Please, Rhoda. Please," my mother entreated. "I can't do this alone. I just know I can't." The tears began to rise in her throat.

"All right, Miz Evelyn," Rhoda finally said. "I'll come back."

@

BUT WHEN RHODA arrived, she had to reestablish her primary position in the household: There was someone else working for us, taking care of my sisters and my brother. Her name was Sophia Norrell, and she was barely out of her teens. Sophia had just graduated from high school, a tall, slim, high-spirited young woman who cut a fine figure in the nightclubs along Second Street, Richmond's tiny facsimile of the Harlem that Rhoda had come to know while she was living in New York. Sophia would leave work at our house almost every night in the company of one good-looking fellow or another, while Rhoda—a stern matron of fifty-five—seemed to have put her dancing shoes away forever. She had no time for foolishness. Rhoda arrived in our household to take charge of me, with all the respect and authority this role entitled her to. Furthermore, she had a history with the family that went back nearly thirty years, and she was not about to take any sass from an upstart like Sophia Norrell.

As Sophia was to tell me, many years later, "We two caught up on each other like a shirttail on barbed wire." Rhoda had every Wednesday off, and when she came back to work on Thursday morning, all hell would break loose.

Sophia Norrell as Queen of the May for her high-school graduation in 1943. She began working for us not long after this picture was taken.

Rhoda, at left, and Sophia, second from right, with two unidentified women one summer in the late 1940s. This was a moment of rare camaraderie between Sophia and Rhoda, on their night off at Buckroe Beach, where African Americans swam and had their own clubs. They were barred from nearby Virginia Beach, where my family was vacationing.

"Sophia Norrell!" Rhoda would bark. "You come here this minute! Look at this child's hands. Her nails are black with dirt. Did you even bother giving her a bath last night? Or were you in too much of a hurry to get out of here? You don't fool me, girl, with that dyed red hair of yours! I can see right through you. And I don't like what I see."

After a year of this, Sophia left. She couldn't take it anymore. But there was another reason for her departure. She had been in our house long enough to see things that no one else saw. Certain things that even if my mother had seen, she would never have believed, or understood. But Sophia was watching, and she knew: Rhoda was working roots over me. Lighting candles in the maid's room and sprinkling powder across the doorsill of my nursery. Anointing my infant head with oil-of-leave-me-not, thick and slick as axle grease, praying to Jesus and to other, equally reliable, deities. Casting a spell so that I would never leave her. So that I would be hers for life.

◎

THIS WAS WHAT Sophia told me many years later, when Rhoda was long dead and Sophia and I were women together, she in her sixties and I in my middle forties. On the spring afternoon when she imparted this story to me, we were sitting in the sunny yellow kitchen of Sophia's house in Richmond, but I felt the warm air in that room turn icy as she told her tale. She said she awakened to what Rhoda was doing on a March morning when I was no more than a month old and Rhoda brought me downstairs to the kitchen after my bath. She had rubbed some kind of potion onto my head and when she set me in Mother's lap, Mother started trying to clean it off, frowning in consternation. Sophia knew what it was, but Rhoda threw her a look that said, *Keep your mouth shut*, and Sophia didn't dare speak.

"But I knew," Sophia told me that spring afternoon. "Of course I did. Only there wasn't any way I was going to take on Rhoda right there, in front of your mother and all. To tell you the truth, I was afraid of her."

The question is: Was Sophia telling the truth? Was I really Rhoda's "hoodoo child," as she put it? Did she know for a fact that Rhoda worked roots on me, used the lore that Sophia herself believed in and often spoke to me about: the ways of healing and punishing and preserving power that were handed down from generation to generation?

"My grandmother used to tell me about this," Sophia recalled. "She said her mother told her that, in the slavery times, people would steal away at night, into the woods. That was the only way they could go on worshipping their own gods. The whites would kill them if they knew what was going on, so my grandmother said they would take a big iron pot along with them, turn it upside down on the ground to catch the sound of the drum and the singing, keep it from traveling out of those woods."

This was the power, the knowledge, that Sophia said Rhoda had. And she swore it was the truth. But I will never know. All I have by way of proof is the ties that bound me to Rhoda, for they were indeed not entirely of this world. They transcended mother and child, black and white, and made me into the person I have become. Our bond has outlasted death—just as I believe Rhoda intended, on that night when she altered the course of our two lives.

$$\wp$$

I HAVE IMAGINED it countless times. The maid's room in our house would have been the only safe place for Rhoda to have worked her roots. For this was her domain, the one room in our house where she knew that, late at night, she would not be disturbed.

It was March, and a fierce spring wind soughed in the high branches of the trees around our house, the tall pines and the pin oaks and the brush that rambled down the hill to the banks of the James River. I was a month old, if you count my age from birth—which Rhoda did not do; she said I was an Old Head, "born with those black-black eyes of yours wide open, like you've seen it all before. Like you got here from somewhere else where you'd been living for some time. . . ."

This is what she told my mother. And Rhoda knew whereof she spoke. She knew that Mother thought I was the reincarnation of her grandmother, my great-grandmother Fannie, a spiritualist who never doubted for a minute that souls were reborn again and again. Rhoda had known Fannie very well and had heard her prophesy that after she was gone, my mother would have one last child, and it would be a girl, and this baby would be Fannie come back to life. So that when Rhoda said I was born with my jet-black eyes wide open, looking like I'd been around a time or two before, this struck a note of deep delight in my mother's heart. Comforting, to believe that Fannie was somehow still alive. But also frightening, when you came to think about it: the way Rhoda seemed to have that insight, hers and hers alone, into the world beyond this one.

On that night, she would have sat alone in the maid's room, wrapped in a plaid wool robe, rocking to and fro in the spindly rocking chair, deep in a reverie. I feel certain that she was pondering her thirty years with us, considering how many of us she had diapered and wiped and cleaned up after, put up with and solaced, mourned and comforted and told the truth to . . . and lied to. Her white folks. Her "place" with us was so carefully circumscribed by southern convention, yet even so it was constantly breached, impossible to maintain, because, after all, she was the nurse, the raiser of young ones, and there was no position open to a woman of her race in domestic work more powerful than that. She had known this family through four generations already, and I would be the last child of my mother's that Rhoda would see. Of that she was certain; I was the baby who Rhoda's people in South Carolina might have called "the wash-belly pickney"—the child who finally empties its mother's womb.

And so, Rhoda may have asked herself: What was she owed for all this time, and labor, and love both false and true? All this sacrifice and salvation? If this debt were ever to be repaid, this was the moment. God had dropped a newborn baby right into her waiting arms. At fifty-five, a chance like this wasn't likely to come again.

Meanwhile, several rooms away, I would have been sleeping soundly in my white-painted nursery, lying on my stomach with one fist balled into my mouth. Full of my mother's milk and dreaming the intense infant dreams none of us can ever remember later. Mother would have gone back to sleep, lying next to my father in their twin beds pushed together, the taste of that long-anticipated midnight Marlboro she always smoked when nursing me growing sour now in her mouth. Daddy would have been snoring loudly, as he always did, sleeping off the day's uncounted drinks.

Rhoda would have turned off all the lamps in the maid's room, so that she would not attract the attention of my mother or father or siblings, should one of them have awakened. There would have been a candle burning on the dresser, reflected in the oval mirror, and next to the candle two things: a piece of folded paper with a lock of my hair inside and a vial of powdered roots. I do not know exactly which ones, but I've imagined that it was the ginger-looking root black people call High John the Conqueror, used in many a spell to bind a lover or to seal a pact.

Perhaps these roots had been sent to Rhoda by her best girlhood friend from South Carolina, a woman named Mamie, of whom she often spoke. Mamie would have known where to find High John the Conqueror. Into that root would have been coiled the ancestral memory of West Africa, of the men and women who stood on the shores of South Carolina's Low Country sea-grass inlets and looked away across the endless ocean, never forgetting whence they had come.

I can see Rhoda tiptoeing down the long hall from the maid's room and softly turning the knob of the nursery door. She has the lock of my hair and the powdered roots in her bathrobe pocket, waiting to work their magic. Now, she shakes a little of the powder out onto the doorsill, smiling to herself. The powder will draw an invisible circle of power around her, and me. It is not intended to ward off my mother, but to keep Sophia out of this business. Away from me. The powder will make me cleave to Rhoda, make me holler blue murder if Sophia tries to take me into her arms. And no one but Sophia will know what it is, if she even sees it; my mother will just think it's baby powder that got spilled.

Rhoda closes the door to my room, pads soundlessly down the back stairs to the kitchen, and out the garage door. She prays that my father's bird dogs won't hear her and set up a racket in their pen. And, sure enough, they don't even growl as she walks by. The dead leaves crunch beneath her slippers, the shriveled husks of garden plants flutter in the wind. She kneels, knee joints cracking, puts my lock of hair into the earth, and pats the dirt back over it.

"Lord," she whispers fervently. "Fasten this child to me! Bind her to me for life."

two

WHATEVER DID OR did not happen on that night long ago, the truth is that I belonged to Rhoda before I belonged to myself. And from the moment when I came to know who I was, I believed that our two skins were only the thinnest of membranes, the casings for our bound-together hearts.

The connection between Rhoda and me had as much to do with my family, with our anomalous and ambivalent positioning in our world, as it did with her and me. For even though we were southerners, and privileged, we were also Jews, and this gave us a peculiar slant on things. We were "Members of the Hebrew Persuasion," which quite a few of our First Family of Virginia (FFV) friends thought was a polite way of referring to us, and our religion set us well apart from the gentile majority. Also, Mother and Daddy came of age during the Great Depression and the New Deal, and they would have eaten barbed wire rather than vote Republican. Mother came this close to joining the Communist

Party in the thirties, and she was fiercely proud of her affiliation with the NAACP and the Women's International League for Peace and Freedom. When one of our FFV neighbors accused her of being "nothing but a bleeding heart," Mother didn't miss a beat.

"You're damn right I am," she shot back. "And this world would be a better place if there were a few more of us, I'll tell you that."

As a child, I was both proud and scared about what our different values boded for me: If childhood has an Eleventh Commandment, surely it is "Thou Shalt Fit In." I knew that I did not fit in and never would, that I shared my mother's passionate politics, and that as the civil rights struggle intensified in the fifties, when I was a little girl and Rhoda was my beloved, I had no choice but to take sides.

Rhoda was the towering presence in my life as a child. Her power and authority had been felt by four generations of my family, and many of the ways in which she cared for and defended me were invisible to others, but I knew that without her protection, I would have been utterly lost. Rhoda was the only person I could count on. Mother and Daddy were physically present and I adored them, admired them, longed for their love. But I understood, without ever having to be told, that they were not to be bothered with my troubles—or my joys—and this I sensed almost from the first moment I can remember. Daddy's drinking made him volatile and quixotic, yet the alcoholic aura that shrouded him made him all the more compelling to me. Mother could be warm and inviting one moment and then treacherous the next, turning cool and dismissive if I displeased her in some way I could never predict or avoid. My two older sisters were teenagers by the time I was five, and they were as capricious as the grown-ups I knew, by turns indulgent and mockingly cruel. And my brother, Dickie—my terrifying schizophrenic brother—bullied me with sadistic antics that brought me to the edge of hysteria. One of his favorite tortures was putting spiders in my bed so that when I turned down the sheets, there they'd be, shiny bodies with way too many legs scurrying frantically in the sudden light.

"Dickie!" Rhoda would holler above my screams, while I buried my face against her hip and tried to stop trembling. "Will you tell

This is one of those photographs where everyone in it is the distilled essence of themselves. Mother's beamingly beautiful, as usual. Granny—at the ripe age of sixty-five—wears a two-piece like the red-hot mama she still aspires to be. Daddy looks bemused. My aunt Barbara isn't exactly scowling but she isn't smiling, either, and it looks like she's relating to Fella, the family dog, better than to anyone else. Meanwhile, Rhoda kneels in the sand behind them, with a smile that says, "What couldn't I tell you about these people, if I chose!" The year was 1949. I was six months old.

me why you want to frighten this child so bad? What's wrong with you? Sometimes I think you got the devil in your bones."

Against these terrors, these shadows, Rhoda stood as my bulwark. Not only did she attend to my heart, she took sole charge of my body. It was she who woke me, wiped the crust she tenderly called "sleepywinks" from my eyes, washed and dressed and fed me every morsel of food I ate, walked hand in hand with me through the neighborhood, and perched on the edge of the sandbox while I played with friends. At night, when Daddy had passed out from the day's drinking and Mother was out at school—she was working toward a degree in psychology—Rhoda put me to bed. She slept in the room next to mine, and the two of us would take turns singing to each other the spirituals she had taught me. "Swing Low, Sweet Chariot" and "Go Down, Moses" were the ones I loved best. Moses I knew from the Bible stories Rhoda also read to me, and sometimes I pretended I was like him, discovered in a basket in the bulrushes by Pharaoh's beautiful, dark-skinned daughter, who I imagined must have looked a little like Rhoda.

BEGINNING WHEN I was five or six, Mother started letting me go home with Rhoda on Saturday, to spend the night and go to church with her on Sunday. I counted the days; by Wednesday, I had chosen which dress I was going to wear and packed my small overnight case. Toothbrush, pajamas, the slippers with the bunny head on the front. Patent leather shoes, white socks, clean underwear. My toy rabbit, whom I'd named Salami—why I didn't know, but I liked the way it sounded—sat propped on my bed, waiting for Saturday, too.

Mother knew I was spending almost every Sunday at Third Street Bethel African Methodist Episcopal, singing gospel hymns and praying to Jesus and having the first authentic religious experiences of my life. She wanted this for her child, and a part of her went with me. Not only to Bethel but also to Rhoda's neighborhood, Idlewood Avenue, and the Negro families who lived there.

These sojourns among people of color—"going home with the help," to be with the maid and her neighbors—had been part of my mother's own childhood, and that of her younger sisters, my aunts Alice and Barbara. This was something many other white children did, of course, but for most of them, these visits, along with the innocent ease they felt in the company of black people, vanished with adulthood. But not for me.

When I was invited to Rhoda's house, I knew I was being given something infinitely precious, ushered into Rhoda's life and allowed to honor it. I found acceptance and welcome there, which was a miracle to me, because I knew that segregation was the iron-clad system under which we lived our daily lives, and thus these Saturday nights and Sunday mornings were a privileged time. And a minor crime as well; a little murder of the forced separation I had come to question and resent. My time with Rhoda was a transgression we two shared.

My mother knew about all of this, and I always knew she did. It was there in the things she told me about her own childhood. Wilmington, where she grew up, was one of those southern towns where blacks and whites lived close to each other, sometimes on the very same streets. This did not spring from any vision of equality or justice on the part of whites, but (ironically) from their wish to have "the help" close by. This was one of those southern anomalies that persisted in the teeth of Jim Crow, and sometimes it had the unintended consequence of bringing individuals from both races closer together. My mother was one of those people.

When she sent me home with Rhoda for the weekend, she was not only reliving a part of her own childhood and wanting me to grow up the same way. She was also rebelling, in the present, against another kind of prejudice she knew all too well: my father's German Jewish snobbery about the "other" Jews, the ones from Russia or Poland or God-knows-where—just any place other than Germany, which he and many of our highborn friends from Beth Ahabah (our synagogue) still secretly thought produced a better breed of Jew.

This sentiment drove Mother crazy. "Richard," she would say to my father—with her characteristic mixture of sly humor, sadness, and thinly veiled contempt—"all your family ever cared about was money. And noses." The former large and the latter—hopefully—pert and small and upturned. When I was little, she told me about her own childhood friendship with a Russian Jewish child, Isidore Goldstein, whose family lived just around the corner. Mother's grandmother, Fannie, lived with the Einsteins and she was forever admonishing my mother not to play with Isidore because his family was not "like us."

"Have you ever?" Mother would say to me indignantly. "Telling a child she can't play with someone because he's another kind of Jew?"

Her political lights were reflected in the books she read, the shelves in our den sagging beneath their weight. I'd stand on the couch and study their important-sounding titles: George Bernard Shaw's *The Intelligent Woman's Guide to Socialism and Capitalism* and another that mystified me, *Jews Without Money*.

"Are there any Jews without money?" I asked her, since all the ones we knew from Beth Ahabah were very well-off. (The word I was taught to use was "comfortable.")

"Yes," Mother answered, "there are." This was how I learned about the Jews who came from Russia, from Poland, from those distant places where someone named the czar instigated massacres called pogroms, from which Jews by the hundreds of thousands fled. Many came to the Lower East Side of New York City, which sounded to me, from Mother's description, as if it could well have been on the other side of the world from the German Jewish neighborhood called Yorkville on the Upper East Side where my grandmother Alice now lived.

I became intrigued with this figure known as the czar not only because I was horrified by what he had done to the Jews, but also because the Virginia Museum had a phenomenal collection of Faberge. I was so fascinated by these treasures—by the sheer, outlandish splendor of the enameled, jewel-encrusted eggs and the diamond frames around the haunting portraits of Nicholas, his beautiful, sad-eyed wife, and their five doomed children—that I was forever begging Mother to take me to see them.

Even more than the jewels, it was the incredibly lifelike flowers that astonished me. They were carved from semiprecious stones with gold and diamonds used for the stamens and pistils, and the stems were set into rock-crystal vases with what looked exactly like water in them. The drama of these objects was heightened by the way they were displayed, in three small chambers with walls covered in red velvet, so that stepping into them was like entering a jewel box. Enchanted and terrified, by these sparkling objects and my awareness of the cruelty that had been the backdrop to their making, I would stand, scarcely breathing, before the iconlike photographs of those five exquisite children, whose fate I knew. I was smitten with Anastasia—she had been the youngest, so I identified with her—and I wondered if, as the legend had it, she might have survived. I was also captivated by the boy, Alexei, sick with hemophilia, who bore an uncanny resemblance to my brother, Dickie.

On the way out of the museum, I always had to use the restroom. There were two, one marked Colored and the other White. When the Colored door opened and a woman came out, I caught the same whiff of scent that dwelled in the closet in the maid's room at our house—the tang of skin and sweat and Evening in Paris that I associated with Rhoda and with her house, too.

This made me want to go into the restroom marked Colored, but I didn't dare. Instead, I took a surreptitious sip from "their" water fountain, which was also marked with a sign. Mother stood guard in case one of the watchmen strolled by.

"Does it taste any different?" she asked, when I rejoined her.

"Nope," I answered. I knew she knew it didn't.

MOTHER WOULD COME into my room on Saturday morning, as I was putting my white gloves into the tiny black patent-leather pocketbook I would be taking to church when I accompanied

Rhoda there on Sunday. Into it I also put money for bus fare, a clean white handkerchief—like Mother always carried, even though mine was only for show—and a fat wad of Kleenex, because I knew I was going to need it; I always cried at some point or points in the service, usually when the gospel choir sang.

"Here's a dollar for the collection plate," Mother said. Then she thought about it. "Wait a sec." She came back with a ten. "Reverend Walker is going to ask everyone to give extra, because of what's been happening. You know . . . for all the people in jail."

The Montgomery bus boycott of 1954 was going on, but its effects had not yet begun to ripple through white Richmond. Our buses were still segregated, although black maids could ride up front with their white children if the maids were in uniform. But on Saturdays, when I went home with Rhoda, and on Sundays when we went to church, she'd wear her own clothes. This meant she and I had to sit apart. I was always afraid I'd lose her.

"Don't you worry, sugar," Rhoda said. "I won't leave you. Just watch me, and when I pull the string, you stand up, too."

I spent most of the ride craning my neck, to make sure she was still there.

Having to separate from her was something I never got used to; it only happened when we left our house on Wilton Road and ventured into the outside world, where everything suddenly changed. We could not eat together in restaurants. So we always took sandwiches and ate them sitting in the car by the side of the road. Then we would go into the woods to wee-wee, Mother and Rhoda and me, because the three of us couldn't use a restroom marked White Only together, and you never knew if there was going to be one marked Colored for Rhoda to use.

But predictable separation was easy compared to the other kind, when someone ordered us to split up. This happened once when Granny was visiting from New York and she took me and Rhoda to see a movie. Rhoda wasn't wearing her uniform. It was a Saturday matinee of *Anastasia*, starring Ingrid Bergman, one of Granny's favorite stars, and for some reason she thought the usher

would let Rhoda sit with us because—even without her uniform—it was obvious that she was with Granny and me. Granny
had been living in New York City for so long that she'd forgotten
how things were in Richmond.

"Excuse me, Ma'am," the usher said as we were on our way
through the baroque lobby of the Byrd Theater. "Colored upstairs."

Rhoda made a move toward the staircase before Granny could
gather her wits to say something. "Don't make a to-do, Miz Alice,"
Rhoda whispered. "I'll be fine in the balcony."

I began silently to cry. Tears of rage as much as anything else,
because I had my heart set on sitting between my grandmother
and Rhoda. When Granny saw me crying, she lit into the usher
like a lioness protecting her young.

"Are you crazy?" she hissed at the pimply kid in his organ-
grinder's monkey costume. "You can see this lady is with us."

"That don't matter," the boy said smugly. "I don't make the rules."

"I don't give a damn about the rules!" Granny's voice rose. The
crowd in the lobby began to stare. "Tell your manager to step out
here."

The boy went into an office off the lobby. Rhoda had already
disappeared in the gloom at the top of the steps and I knew I
would not see her again till after the movie was over. The manager
came out of his office, a fat, balding man with sweat glistening on
the top of his head. He took Granny off into a corner and the two
of them began to talk. She kept her voice down now, but I could
read anger in every line of her body, the hands on her hips, the jut
of her chin, and the hunch of her shoulders. I could see it was useless, and I knew who was going to win.

"The law's the law, lady," the manager said. It was the way he
smiled that made me sick.

☙

I'M ALWAYS RELIEVED when the Saturday morning bus drops
Rhoda and me at the corner of Lady Street and we walk, hand in
hand, the two blocks from there to Idlewood Avenue. Rhoda's

Rhoda at home, in her backyard.

house is on the corner, a neat brick bungalow with metal awnings over the two front windows and a glider on the porch. Her front steps are banked with blue and purple hydrangeas. Rhoda calls them "high geraniums."

"You be careful on those steps," she warns, because the bricks are sharp and I'm already running, having seen Rhoda's sister, Lizzie, waiting for us at the front door. She's a little bit shorter than Rhoda and her hair is grayer because she's older, and she kind of keeps to herself. But now she stoops and gives me a big hug and I dash through the front door into my other home.

Here's the brick fireplace with the oil painting above the mantel, a country scene, with cows and trees and a river. The tall brass shell casing on the hearth, which Lizzie's husband, Berry Quivers—the perfect name for this gentle man, who is quiet and shakes a bit, with "nerves"—brought back from France, where he was a soldier in World War I.

I kick off my shoes and leap onto the chintz sofa, printed with huge red and green flowers. Folded on its arm is my favorite thing of all in Rhoda's house, a satin quilt, maroon on one side and pale pink on the other. I unfold it reverently, and then wrap myself in its slithery softness. Rhoda and Lizzie smile indulgently, shaking their heads.

"It's not bedtime yet!" Lizzie teases me. I know, but I can't resist curling up on that sofa in this quilt, in this room. I eye the dark mahogany coffee table topped with glass and festooned with candy dishes. Butterscotch! Hershey's kisses! (We don't keep candy at our house.) There are stiff white fluted doilies on all the tables, sticking out like ballerina skirts under every dish. In the corner is the tall mahogany shelf that Rhoda calls a whatnot, which holds all her china knickknacks and assorted treasures. Many of them are presents from me, or from my sisters, or from Mother. "What should we bring back for Rhoda?" we always ask, whenever we go somewhere.

I spy the little silk pincushion encircled by miniature Chinese men with pigtails hanging down their backs. I bought it for Rhoda in New York's Chinatown, when I went there for dinner with Mother and her sister, my aunt Barbara, who loves poking around

Chinatown with me. The night I bought the pincushion, the ancient shop owner sat on a stool behind the counter while Barbara and I tiptoed up and down the narrow aisles, making sure not to knock anything over. When he wrapped my gift for Rhoda, he handed it to me with a sudden smile that showed his cracked, brown teeth.

"God!" Barbara whispered when we were back out on the street. "I bet he has an opium den in the basement!" I was thrilled by this hint of danger lurking just beneath my feet.

"Come on outside with me," Rhoda says now, standing by the couch where I am cocooned inside that satin quilt. "Let's go see Patsy."

Patsy is Rhoda's hound dog, part terrier, brown and white. We slip through the dining room—more doilies everywhere, and plastic flowers on the dining table, and a sideboard with a long mirror above it—and pass through the kitchen—red vinyl chairs—out to the backyard, which is swept clean, even though it's dirt. Lizzie's roses grow along the back fence, spilling into the yard. Patsy barks and whines and wee-wees ecstatically when she sees us, but Rhoda won't let her off her chain by the dog house.

"I know you wish I would," she says. "But she's a watch dog. And she has to earn her keep. I can't have her running all over creation like your daddy's dogs."

"But how can she bite a prowler if she can't get off that chain?" I ask. Rhoda shakes her head. "You and Patsy got some kind of plan I don't know about?"

Before supper, which I know will be Swanson chicken pot pies—my favorite—I go next door to play with the neighbor kids, Robert E. Lee and Carlene. I have brought with me the only baby doll I own, whose skin is a rich chocolate brown. As a general rule, I reject every baby doll I am ever given. I can't stand their rubbery bodies and the way they moo "MaaaMaaa" when I lay them down. I have no interest whatsoever in pretending to mother them. The dolls I adore are the grown-up Madame Alexanders from FAO Schwarz in New York that Granny gives me every Christmas. They are such heavenly figures, with china faces and velvet gowns. I dress them in their elaborate costumes, their beautifully detailed coats with little muffs made from real fur, and I concoct elaborate fantasies of their charmed, elegant lives.

But the colored doll I bring with me to Rhoda's was a gift from Claudine, our cook, and therefore I treasure it. I've named this doll Deanie, after her. The doll's skin is not at all like mine but our eyes are the same color—brown, not blue—and her hair is black and soft and fuzzy, which mine is, too. Carlene and I play with our dolls until she decides it would be fun for us to walk down the street to the corner store and get Cokes. Rhoda says not to buy anything else or I'll ruin my supper, but the man behind the counter gives Carlene and me each a Butterfinger, my favorite candy. On the way home, we stop and speak to the people on their porches, because every single one of them knows me and they know Carlene, of course, and we remember our manners.

After the chicken pot pies, Rhoda and I do the dishes together; she washes and I dry. Lizzie and Berry have gone upstairs to their bedroom. Rhoda sleeps in the big front room downstairs, where there is an old four-poster bed with a white chenille spread. She is the only person I know who has such a grand bed, and I covet it. Mother has promised to buy one for me when I am thirteen. On Rhoda's dresser are two photographs. We never come in here together that I do not take my time gazing at them. Each has a story, and these stories are my window into Rhoda's past.

"That's Willie Lloyd," she says, handing me the picture of her late husband. "The only man I ever loved." It is framed in gold and I hold it very carefully in my lap. Willie's face is so different from Rhoda's; he is the most African-looking man I have ever seen, with an enormous, wide nose and huge lips and skin that gleams against the clouded backdrop behind him. He is beautifully dressed in a pale linen suit with a little gold stickpin that holds his tie between the starched wings of his collar. But it is the expression in Willie's eyes that I find so haunting. He is gazing at a point somewhere beyond the camera, like he is seeing into the future or the past, and his eyes glisten as if he's about to cry.

"Maybe he knew," Rhoda says softly. "This was taken on our wedding day. But maybe he knew we weren't going to have much longer."

Then Rhoda tells me their story once more. I know that she's holding back some of it, though; I am too young to hear it all. Even if I am an Old Head, like she always says.

"Well, child, he was a good many years older than me," Rhoda would begin.

"How much older, Rhodie?"

"Old enough. We met when I wasn't much more than a girl, and I guess you could say he waited for me to grow up.

"I was living in Savannah by then. Lizzie and I together, we moved down there from Charleston, after our mother died. And she told Lizzie to take care of me, see, because I was the baby girl." Here, Rhoda smiles that Mona Lisa smile of hers. "Lizzie took that to heart. She turned into a mother hen, squabbling at me all the time to do this and not do that, till I thought I'd go crazy. She didn't like the idea of me being with an older man. And Willie's mother didn't like it, either. He lived with her, and she thought he oughtn't to get married at all, should just take care of her."

"So what did you do?"

"What didn't we do! Lizzie told me to quit seeing him. But I was mule-headed. Well, there came a night when Willie and I were going out to a dance. Lizzie said if I went, she'd throw all my clothes out the window. I didn't believe she'd do it, but she did, and when I came waltzing home at dawn, every single thing I owned was on the sidewalk, in the rain."

Rhoda shakes her head. "I went and stayed with a girlfriend of mine for a while. Eventually, Willie's mother died, so we could get married."

But there isn't a happy ending to this story.

"I had a baby," Rhoda goes on, her voice down to a whisper. "But she died. You know about that—she had her cord wrapped around her neck the same way you did, only that doctor of your mother's knew just what to do. I guess I wasn't so lucky."

I know she is not blaming me for her baby's death, but I still feel a stab of shame. I believe that white people have better doctors, so I think that maybe if Rhoda were white, her baby might not have died. And if she had lived, would Rhoda have wanted me?

"Losing that baby, sometimes I think it might have been even worse for Willie than it was for me. He was sick by then anyway, had the pressure something terrible. His head was hurting him all the time. Seemed like just about every night when he came home from work, he'd be so worn out from those headaches that he couldn't even eat his supper. And one evening, he just commenced to bleed. From his nose."

I can hardly bear to think of this; there is something so pitiful to me about nosebleeds. I have never had one, but when one of my friends at school does, they always look so frightened and they have to go to the nurse's office and lie flat until the red gush stops. But what if it doesn't? I think of Willie, bleeding to death.

"I couldn't get it to stop," Rhoda goes on. "I held him and I rocked him and I cried for someone to get a doctor. By the time someone brought a wagon to fetch him to the infirmary, he was all but gone. He died in my arms."

I sit next to Rhoda, on the edge of her bed, holding Willie's picture. I can't parse the thoughts reeling through my head. But one of them is that if Willie had had a doctor right away, he might not have died.

Rhoda seems to read my mind. "I don't know," she says, gazing down at Willie's picture with me. "Maybe it was just his time had come."

And then she reaches for the other photograph I love, the one of her. It, too, has a story. One that links Rhoda to my grandmother and to the time close to when I was born.

"I remember the day I had this picture taken," Rhoda says. "It was in Harlem, back when I was working for your grandmother up in New York. Hot? Child, I can still feel the heat coming up off that sidewalk when I got off the train. Don't tell me about summers in that city! I've had enough to last me a lifetime. Miz Alice had let me

Rhoda, in all her haunting beauty, photographed in Harlem sometime in the nineteen-forties.

William Lloyd, Rhoda's husband. Taken around the time of their marriage in 1925.

go early that day, so I went uptown to see this friend of mine. I was so hot and tired, I thought I might faint, right on those subway steps. I was holding onto the handrail, trying to catch my breath, when I looked up and saw a sign. Photography Studio, it said. I thought if I went in there, they'd let me sit down for a while."

But the photographer didn't let Rhoda sit. He posed her in front of one of those painted backdrops—I can see the faint outline of trees behind her—and draped her wide shoulders with a black velvet cape. He asked her to turn ever so slightly, so that her face was in three-quarters profile. Did he ask her to smile, too? Or did he just let her be, knowing how tired she was? Whatever he did, Rhoda gave the camera a half smile that was not of this world. In it, she is more regal, more mysterious to me, than the czar of all the Russias and his sad-eyed wife.

"Promise me," I say, "that you'll leave this picture to me. In your will."

Rhoda hesitates for just a moment. "But you'll be a big woman by then. Don't you think you'll have forgotten?"

"Never," I vow, shaking my head.

"Then you promise *me* something," Rhoda says. "That you'll keep the picture of Willie, too. You make sure the two of us are together, always."

"I promise, Rhodie."

"All right, sugar. Let's say our prayers and get into bed."

℧

THE FOLLOWING MORNING, we ride the Broad Street bus to Bethel African Methodist Episcopal. On the steep front steps, Rhoda's church sisters have gathered, admiring each other's best dresses and finest hats and chattering like a flock of glossy starlings. Between them flows a river of womanly wisdom, things I am still too young to understand.

"Girl!" someone exclaims, planting a kiss on the cheek of a robust friend decked out in a towering feathered hat. "I declare, you have never looked so well! That husband of yours must be doin' something right! Is he gonna show his face this morning?" This is delivered with a sly smile. "Or did you wear him *out* last night?"

Rhoda listens, off to one side, holding herself a little apart from this banter, maybe because I am here and she doesn't want me to hear anything I shouldn't. Her best friend, Pinckney—they've known each other since they were girls in Charleston—comes up the steps on her bandy legs and gives me a crushing, bony-chested hug. Pinckney is a cheek-pincher from way back—she does it so hard it hurts—so I smile firmly before her fingers get a grip because I've learned that it hurts less that way. I like Pinckney because she always exclaims, "Rhoda, this little girl of yours is getting prettier by the day!" although I know I'm not. I'm fat. The sleeves of my red velvet dress are so tight they cut into my arms, even though Rhoda let the seams out on Friday night. She sat sewing in my bedroom while I devoured the bedtime feast she fed me every night, a ritual we called "our party," even though I was the only one who partook of it.

For as long as I could remember, Rhoda had given me this bedtime treat. It was really a fourth meal, but one that was made up almost entirely of the luscious, forbidden things I knew I was not supposed to have. There were Oreos, which I separated into their black and white halves and ate methodically, saving the half with the sweet white frosting for last. There was a Dixie cup with two scoops of chocolate ice cream that Rhoda poured Coca-Cola over—just enough to melt the outside of the ice cream, so it formed tantalizing little crystals that melted in my mouth. And Lance peanut-butter crackers and saltines with American cheese on top, still warm from the oven where Rhoda had slid them to melt the cheese. There were potato chips and pretzels—for what binge is complete without the taste of salt to balance all that sugar? All this was brought up to me on a tray with a napkin, so that I could eat as I sat in bed. Rhoda never touched a morsel, no matter that I always asked her to share our party with me.

"Oh, I'm not hungry, sugar. You go ahead," she'd say, as she licked the thread for the needle she was using to stitch back the sleeves she had let out on my dress for church. Though I did not know it then, I ate for Rhoda as much as for myself, to feel the peculiar joy that emanated from her as she watched me devour the rich food that was so abundant in our home. This mysterious pleasure, all but sexual in its intensity, came out of her own childhood hunger, her memory of a gnawing belly, of being so empty that her back stuck to her front. In feeding me, she remade my body in the image of the child she wished she could have been, plump and sated and never knowing hunger.

This morning, on the steps outside Bethel African Methodist Episcopal, with Rhoda's friend Pinckney pinching my cheek, I stick out for another reason besides my weight. I am the only white person here. I wonder if everyone knows I'm Jewish, too. They might not because I follow the service very closely and can sing many of the hymns. I also know a fair amount about Jesus, from the Bible stories Rhoda reads to me, with pictures that make him look sort of Jewish, which I know he was. Only not the Son of God, as Mother has taken pains to tell me. But I cherish the fact that he was one of us—"one of our boys," is how Daddy would describe him. There wouldn't be a Jesus if it wasn't for the Jews.

Rhoda and Pinckney and I go into the church, which is a blur of bright dresses and dark suits, hands fluttering with fans from Chiles Funeral Home with pictures of Jesus on them. The choir is seated around the pulpit, men and women alike in maroon robes with satin borders, so they glow against the soft pink of the sanctuary. Bethel is an old church with a proud history; the program says it was built in 1856 "by artisans both slave and free."

Once the service starts I listen, rapt, to Reverend Walker's preaching, his voice rising and falling in a rhythm I hear nowhere else. Some members of the congregation talk back to him; some rock in their pews and whisper to themselves. I am awed by their unashamed display of feeling, cannot help but wonder what on earth would happen if I was suddenly to do the same at Beth Ahabah—holler something in the middle of one of Rabbi Goldburg's droning sermons. I have a feeling that the dome would fall in, that lofty, cream-colored dome with its soft lighting and the frescoes of green palm fronds in each of its four corners, reminding me of ancient Egypt and Let My People Go.

I am roused from my reverie by the choir's first hymn of the morning. Their robes rustle as they rise, like God's own nightgown. Once they start to sing, I am carried down the river of my soul, out to a sea that is boundless, where I become someone other than myself.

three

M Y LIFE WITH Rhoda seemed safe to me, but of course it wasn't. Even with all her protectiveness, her love and vigilance, she and I were always vulnerable. We were caught in the South's sticky web, waiting for the spider of segregation to pounce. All we had to do was leave our house on Wilton Road and board one of those Richmond buses, with Rhoda dressed in her own clothes instead of her maid's uniform.

What I remember most keenly about those moments was my shame at seeing how Rhoda's pride, her strength and grace and beauty, could be obliterated in an instant. She would be wearing her nicest dress and a hat—she never went out without a hat—with a pearl-tipped pin holding it in place. She would have a pretty handbag, like any Virginia lady, and yet . . . and yet, only I could see who she really was: a person who happened to be a Negro, rather than a Negro who was therefore not a person. How come the rest of the world did not see her the way I did?

Things were much the same in our manicured, miniature kingdom on Wilton Road in the heart of Richmond's lily-white,
almost-all-gentile West End. We lived there in a nervous state of
grace, surrounded by the homes of our mostly friendly neighbors,
girded by Mother's beautiful flower beds and the gardens where
Daddy grew his abundant vegetables. I took great pride and pleasure in his skill as a gardener; in my eyes, this lifted him from the
realm of the mundane to that of the magical. He was someone
who could bring forth food from the earth. There was something
sanctified about his sheer love of dirt, in the way he shouldered up
between the wooden handles of his plow and put all his strength
into the labor of digging straight furrows in the loamy soil. I'd
watch in fascination, hoping maybe he'd turn up an Indian arrow-
head like the ones my older sisters sometimes found. But like as
not, he would simply stand there in his shorts, bare chested, mop-
ping his brow, and then beckon me over to his side.

"Look at this, Laurie Girl," he'd say, opening his palm to reveal
the three or four kernels of Silver Queen he was about to plant.
"Imagine all the ears of corn that will grow from one of these.
There's something downright *holy* about that."

I could hear the sadness in his voice, and I knew what he was
thinking: that he should have been a farmer, a true tiller of the soil,
instead of a suburban gentleman playing in his garden. He'd grown
up in a Richmond where formal avenues turned into dirt roads a
stone's throw from his house, where he could still ride horseback
out Broad Street and hunt quail with the black farmers who'd settled a community just west of the city that they'd named Zion
Town, in honor of the freedom they had won after the Civil War.

I'd inherited my father's love for this history and for the nearness
of country things. Like him, I breathed deep of damp earth and
dead leaves, gloried in my rambles through the empty woods that
tumbled from our one and a quarter acre of land down to the banks
of the James River. It was a forest of scrub oak and pine that my
aunt Barbara called "the Confederate woods," where she swore she
could see the ghosts of gray-clad soldiers flitting through the trees.

But once we left our little kingdom on the James, my sense of own-ership, of true belonging, would vanish beneath the scrutiny, the ever-present judgment that I felt of us, by the gentiles, for being dif-ferent. For being not like them, for being stubbornly who and what we were. Barbara always said that Richmond had a dank, familiar odor all its own, "like the inside of an old oak chest," and that musty air of dust and death and cherished relics clung to everything in Richmond. I loved my town, but I loathed it, too, simply because I somehow knew that my love would always be unrequited. Being *different* has always been the affront the South has the least tolerance for, and those who are will never truly belong.

Nothing made me more aware of our vulnerability, our isolation, than my two sisters' attendance at the fanciest private girls' school in town, a Georgian brick Episcopal fortress named Saint Catherine's. Mary and Susan despised the school—they were its only Jewish students—and the sole reason Mother sent them was that she had caved in to pressure from my snooty Aunt Virginia—Daddy's brother's wife, and thus no blood kin of ours—who thought the Gunsts were too wellborn for public school. Daddy said Virginia put on more airs than the queen of Sheba, but we all kowtowed to her nevertheless. She had a way of making you feel you had to, with her chill beauty, her stylish manners, and her way with horses, dogs, and guns. Virginia was the only woman I knew who could shoot and didn't mind killing a bird or two every now and then.

Mary and Susan suffered through Saint Catherine's. They had to take a Bible class from a blue-haired Daughter of the Confederacy, Miss Coleman, and they came to the dinner table every night with stories about her that literally made my hair stand on end; I could feel the skin on the back of my neck tighten whenever Mary said the woman's name.

"You won't believe what Miss Coleman said today," Mary began one evening, her brow knitting in a frown beneath her shiny page-boy bangs.

"What, darling?" said Mother absently; she was holding out a plate for Daddy to put some roast chicken and gravy on for me.

"Well, we were doing the Gospels and all of a sudden she pipes up, looking right at Susan and me, 'Now, class, you know we have two students of the Hebrew persuasion here with us. Mary and Susan Gunst.'"

Mary was a born actress and knew how to do a perfect imitation of Miss Coleman's First Family of Virginia Tidewater drawl. "Now, girls," Mary went on, "we all know their people killed our perfect lord"—this my sister pronounced as "owuh puhfect lawd"—"but we're going to let that pass for the time being, aren't we?"

How considerate Miss Coleman was; so thoughtful, so kind. I looked down into my plate of chicken, a skin forming over the pool of gravy like the eye of a dead fish. Mary stared at Mother, accusing her with her eyes. "Please-please-please," she begged. "Let Susan and me go to TeeJay next year. Please?"

TeeJay was Thomas Jefferson, Richmond's best public high school. Mother did relent. She defied Virginia and enrolled my sisters in TeeJay the following fall. Mother told Virginia that Saint Catherine's was a torture chamber and that she should never have subjected her children to such a place to begin with. And that she was sending me to public school, now that I was done with kindergarten.

"As a matter of fact," I heard Mother say to Virginia—over the telephone, so she did not have to come face to face with her—"now that we've had the Supreme Court decision, Laurie may well have Negro children as her classmates at Mary Munford. And that's a wonderful thing, don't you think?"

For once, Virginia's elegant manners failed her. She hung up in a state of shock.

Miss Coleman and her ilk; the ever-so-slightly-askance glances from the FFVs who lived in the Georgian mansions up and down Wilton Road; the annual June Bal de Bois at the Country Club of Virginia, where Richmond's debutantes "came out" to society in their white ball gowns—these are some of my less-than-happy memories of growing up Jewish in the Richmond of the fifties. As was the time when Mary's best Saint Catherine's friend, Isabel Brawley, asked her to come and swim at "the club." But Isabel's mother made her withdraw the invitation, and when Mary asked why, Isabel squirmed and wrung her hands till finally she blurted out, "Mother says that Jews are dirty and shouldn't be allowed in the pool."

Is it any wonder that I felt . . . not quite white? Or that I felt an affinity for those who could not sit in the front of the bus, or eat at Woolworth's, or use the restrooms? It was a measure of my anguish, my confusion over my own identity, that I both loathed the debutantes and wanted to become one. I did not know where I fit, or belonged.

Mother told me a story from her own childhood, about the terror she had felt when she watched the Ku Klux Klan parade down Monument Avenue in the twenties, right after her family moved to Richmond from Wilmington. That story lodged itself like a clot in my seven-year-old heart. She told me that their house on the Boulevard was only a few blocks from Monument, so she could hear the shouting of the drunken crowd and see the horses and the sheets and the burning cross if she leaned out the front window. Which she rarely had the nerve to do.

"I was so scared that I ran and hid under my bed. We had a maid then named Nannie Robinson—Rhoda had gone back to Savannah, to marry Willie Lloyd. Nannie knew how frightened I was, so she came upstairs and got me. We had the house in darkness except for candles. Why, I don't know, but maybe that was our way of letting it seem that no one was home. Nannie had a room off the kitchen and she and I went down there. We hid together with the shades drawn until the shouting had stopped."

Mother was quiet for a moment. "I guess I knew that the crowd on Monument would have been happy to get their hands on me, too."

❧

LITTLE BY LITTLE, I created a moral code of my own to deal with this life, this Jim Crow South I grew up in. I wouldn't call what I made a truce for it never felt peaceful. What I did—consciously or not—was to start seeing things in absolutes: all black, all white, no shades of gray. Because my child's moral universe was so menaced, so threatened by the craziness of the racial realities around me, and because of the love and the loyalty I felt for Rhoda and the other women of color who worked in our home, I thought I had no choice but to see the world in this stark way. Otherwise, I would lose the only love I trusted, the only people whose care for me was abiding and sure.

I became a rigid little thing, vehemently certain of what I knew and angry if anyone tried to tell me otherwise. One thing I knew for sure: Black people were *better* than whites. They had to be. Because what they went through made them better. Any fool could see that. I clung to this delusion like the plush toy rabbit I cuddled up to in bed at night. Until the warm spring afternoon when I was eight and the rude awakening I was bound to get arrived.

©

CLAUDINE LEAKE, OUR cook—the same Deanie who'd given me that black baby doll I used to take to Rhoda's house—was the one who knocked some sense into me about Negroes being human, like the rest of us. And not invariably loving or forever kind.

Claudine's arrival in our lives coincided with an event that made her coming all the more significant to me. I was six when she began working for us, and at this time a new house had just been built on the property adjacent to ours. I loathed seeing it go up, because bulldozers had come and ripped into the pines, snapping them like matchsticks. The dozers flattened the hedges of sweet-smelling honeysuckle that had always been on that parcel of land, and now there was a fence that kept me from getting down to the river that way. So, in the long twilight before Rhoda called me in for supper, I'd sneak down to the construction site and sabotage it as best I could. I kicked apart the neat stacks of bricks and tiles left by the workmen, stole the rolls of copper electrical wire, and hid them in the bushes down the hill behind our house, below the little mountain of broken glass where Daddy threw his empty whiskey bottles. But it was no use. That house got built anyway, and then a couple, the Meadors, moved in.

They both drank heavily and Mother said they were trashy people even if they were rich. (She stopped short of calling them "white trash," an expression she despised and taught me never to use.) Mr. Meador had made his money from tobacco; Mother said he was "a sharecropping bastard," but Daddy would try to defend him every now and then, in a halfhearted way. He knew so many men like Mr. Meador; they were the landowners he hobnobbed with out in the country, the ones who owned the farms and fields where he had to ask permission to hunt or work his dogs.

"Oh, Ev," Daddy would say, "Roger Meador isn't such a bad fellow. He's just a little rough in his ways."

"Richard," Mother would shoot back, "he's an SOB and you know it."

Mrs. Meador was the one who really scared me, though. She looked like a witch, her unnaturally large head scrunched down onto her tiny, wizened body. She sped up and down Wilton Road in a white Cadillac, peering over the steering wheel like an evil child bent on destruction. Daddy yelled at her to slow down on account of his dogs but she never paid any attention to him.

On the night before Claudine came to our house to be interviewed by Mother for the cook job, another woman arrived, hoping for work. Her name was Alice Hagen and she lived way out in the country. Since there was no one at home to watch her children, she brought them with her and left them in her car, which she parked in front of the white gates that led to the Meadors' house. I was sitting with Mother in the den, waiting for Mrs. Hagen to arrive, and when she rang our bell we both went to the door.

Alice Hagen's forehead was shiny with perspiration; I could tell how nervous she was, and right away I knew that something bad was going to happen. I didn't know what, but I had a sure sense it was going to have something to do with the Meadors.

"Where did you park, Mrs. Hagen?" Mother asked, smiling and friendly, trying to put her more at ease.

"Just down there by the gates to that big white house," Alice Hagen answered. "I wasn't sure which house was yours."

I knew what Mother was thinking. "Why don't you park in our driveway? You're welcome to bring your children inside."

"Oh, that's all right," Alice answered, wearily. "They'll be fine down there in the car."

The three of us had just settled into chairs in the den when the telephone rang. Mrs. Meador's voice came crackling through the receiver so loud we could hear her every word. I knew she must be drunk as usual. "The nerve of you, Evelyn Gunst!" she hollered, beside herself with rage. "Who told you to let that car full of *niggers* park at my gate?"

Mother gripped the phone so hard her knuckles turned white. "Don't ever use that word to me, Mrs. Meador," she said, soft and menacing. But her voice shook and I thought maybe she was going to cry. "Do you hear me? *Ever.*" Then she hung up the receiver like she was dropping something vile into the trash. Alice Hagen had already disappeared into the night, running to the rescue of her children.

☙

CLAUDINE CAME THE following night. I was still jumpy from the scene with Mrs. Meador and scared we'd have a repeat perform-ance, so when I heard a car pull up in the driveway, I went outside to escort her into the house. I need not have worried; she'd gotten a ride with a gentleman friend by the beautiful name of Miles Darling, and it was he who handed her out of the car.

Claudine was in her midforties, short and plump and stylishly dressed in a soft sweater and a tweed skirt with a kick pleat in back. When she greeted Mother, her voice was melodious. Mother asked her if she'd had any trouble finding our house and Claudine answered, "Not at all. A friend of mine drove me and he knows this neighborhood."

It turned out that Mother knew Miles Darling because he chauffeured for my fearsome Aunt Virginia now and then. Mother

Claudine Leake, on the back porch of her house on Clay Street in Jackson Ward, Richmond's oldest African American neighborhood.

asked Claudine if he'd like to come into the kitchen and wait till we were through talking.

"Oh, I don't think so," Claudine smiled. "He's listening to the ball game on the radio. But thank you all the same."

Mother liked Claudine so much that she offered her the job on the spot, and Claudine said she could start the next day, if that was all right.

I couldn't wait for her to arrive and I ran out to greet her as she stepped from Miles Darling's shiny blue car.

"Let's roll down the hill together!" I suggested, taking her by the hand. Whenever I'd ask Rhoda to do this with me she'd always demur, saying she was too old for such things. But Claudine thought it was a fine idea. "All right, sugar," she said. "Just let me change out of my good clothes into my uniform." When my father looked out the upstairs window, there were the two of us flying down the hill with our skirts up over our heads and our wild laughter ringing out up and down Wilton Road. Daddy always feared we'd do something to arouse the contempt of our neighbors; when he came down to breakfast, he politely told Claudine that in the future she and I ought not to put on such a show.

Claudine turned around from the stove after he'd left the kitchen and gave me a saucy wink. "Looks like you got me off on the wrong foot, baby." But she was smiling all the same.

$\mathcal{Q}$

CLAUDINE TOLD ME I should call her Deanie. "That's what all my friends call me," she said. After that first morning roll down the hill, the two of us were friends. She became my ally in a way quite different from Rhoda. Rhoda was my guardian and she was strict; if I disobeyed her—which I almost never dared to do—she'd break a branch from the forsythia bushes that grew out back and threaten to switch my legs, which always terrified me into submission. And if Rhoda had men friends—which I now know from Sophia Norrell that she did—she kept it so totally hidden from me that I assumed she was past caring about such things.

Deanie was completely different; she was earthy and made no secret of the men friends she kept company with after work. (Miles Darling was not her main man; her true love was a fellow named Joe with whom she often fought but always made up.) She'd tell me about Joe as if I were much older, with an amazing combination of sly humor and ladylike composure that made me wonder if I'd ever become as worldly, as *cool*—my sister Mary's admiring word for Deanie.

In the evenings after supper, Daddy and I would drive Claudine home. She lived in a tiny black neighborhood called Westwood, a few square blocks of very old dwellings smack in the middle of our otherwise all-white West End. I was always mystified by how Westwood came to be where it was. Not till years later did I learn that it had been settled by free people right after the Civil War, former slaves from an enormous plantation that had covered all the land in the West End.

Deanie's house had once been white clapboard but now it was weathered gray; it was what we called a shotgun house because you could stand in the front hall and fire a gun through it and out the back door. Her neighbors would be sitting on their porches when we cruised by, rocking on gliders. Or, if it was full summer, tending their gardens. In winter there'd be wood smoke curling from the chimneys. Claudine had a dog she adored, a white spitz named Connie, and as soon as Connie saw us she'd start barking ecstatically and not stop till Deanie lifted her into her arms.

WHEN DEANIE WAS working, I pretty much lived in the kitchen so I could be with her. She never nagged me about my seemingly bottomless appetite the way Mother did. Mother and my sisters had started to drop dark hints about the agonies I was going to suffer in a few years, when I started caring about boys. Mother was on the verge of taking me to our family doctor and getting me a prescription for diet pills, which were all the rage at the time.

One afternoon I was sitting at the kitchen table, eating potato chips and Lance peanut-butter crackers and Oreos by the fistful. While I munched on these goodies I was counting the dimes and quarters from the soda bottles that Rudy, the deliveryman from our market, collected every Friday. Deanie was standing at the sink, plucking the soft brown and gray feathers from a bobwhite quail Daddy had shot. He said you had to pluck quail; if you skinned them, they lost their flavor.

"That's what your daddy says," Deanie scowled. "But he isn't the one has to pluck them."

The feathers made a nasty ripping sound as she tore them from the skin. Even though she was humming to herself, I could tell she wasn't happy. She looked over at me and then she muttered something that took my breath away.

"Just like we always say." Deanie shook her head. "Negro's always singin' an' workin' . . . Jew's always eatin' an' countin' his money."

Whoosh! My lungs collapsed as if I'd just fallen out of a tree or off one of those runaway horses at the stable where I took riding lessons. But even as I was struggling to suck in a little air and fight down the lump in my throat, I found myself thinking, "Well, she's right. She *is* singing and working, and I *am* eating and counting money."

I forced myself to smile because I loved Deanie and wanted her to see that I could take a joke. But I needed to get out of there, fast. Deanie's back was to me; she was plucking that bird again. I climbed down from the chair and backed out of the kitchen without a word. Knowing that I had to find someone to talk to—and that it couldn't be Mother, because if I told her I'd be sure to get Deanie into trouble, and my loyalty to her was still absolute—I went upstairs to see if Mary was in her room. She was doing homework at her desk beneath the window, and when I told her what Deanie had said, she tried to smile. But only with her mouth, and not her eyes.

"Well," Mary said, heaving a sigh, "I guess she was just showing you something about how *her* people see *our* people."

She let it go at that.

But I kept fretting over Deanie's comment for days and weeks that turned into years. I never could forget it. What she'd shown me rocked my world. I had been so certain that all black people were saints. I'd also thought they saw us Jews as different from other white people—more like kin, in fact. On the same side. Well, I'd evidently gotten that all wrong. And if what Deanie said was true, then black people thought we were every bit as bad, and maybe even worse than other whites. Greedier, with our hands sifting money and our mouths stuffed with food, while they sang and worked.

Now, every time I ate, I'd think of what Deanie had said, wonder if that was how I looked to Rhoda and to all the black people I knew.

I'd always thought the world was divided between black and white. But now I realized I'd been wrong. I didn't only live between two worlds. It was much more complicated than that. In fact, being Jewish, I lived in three.

four

I WAS AFRAID THAT if I told Deanie how hurt I had been by what she said, she'd stop liking me, so I never brought it up. I didn't exactly avoid her, but I threw myself back on Rhoda's companionship because I felt safer with her. But in some ways, this was only an illusion.

Late one October afternoon, the two of us were sitting underneath an old persimmon tree at the end of Wilton Road. Every fall it dropped a bounty of ripe fruit on the ground, and if we got there before the squirrels did it was ours for the picking. But you had to be sure each persimmon was squishy-ripe; otherwise, it would pucker your mouth up and turn it inside out.

Rhoda and I were sitting on the low brick wall surrounding Wilton House, an eighteenth-century gem built by John Randolph a good twenty miles down the James. Virginia has a breathtaking abundance of almost all-female societies consecrated to the preservation of the past and one of them is the aptly named Colonial Dames. In the nineteen-twenties, after DuPont built a pulp mill across the river, the Dames—as Daddy liked to refer to them—had Wilton dismantled and brought to Richmond brick by brick. I was biting into a ripe persimmon and wondering if the tree had been there back in the days when the Indians whose arrowheads we sometimes found in our garden walked this same land, calling it theirs. I was deep into Indians by then, reading everything about them I could lay my hands on. Rhoda must have been following my thoughts, as she had an eerie way of doing. She looked over at me and said, "I never told you this before. I'm part Cherokee."

She had a strange look in her eyes, almost as if she had revealed this secret in spite of herself. I let out a whoop, thrilled by the news that Rhoda had Indian blood. But she shot me a frown of serious disapproval.

"Hush!" she whispered, looking around the Wilton parking lot to make sure no one could have overheard us. "I don't know why I told you. It's not something I'm proud of. Being a half-breed is nothing to brag about. And don't you ever forget it, you hear?"

I sat stock-still, gnawing on my persimmon and reflecting on the fact that this was exactly what *I* felt like most of the time. Part of me was white, part was Jewish, and the part no one could even see was black. I was about as divided as any one person could be. I wondered why Rhoda was ashamed of being what she was.

I was too young to have read any of the history of Cherokee Indians and blacks, to know there were some Cherokees who owned slaves, and thus to ask myself whether some of Rhoda's own ancestors had been among them. Was there something more shameful about being the property of an Indian than of a white man? At this point in my young life, I did not think having ancestors who once were slaves was something to be ashamed of. When we celebrated Passover, we looked back upon our bondage in the land of Egypt with (it seemed to me) a certain pride, for we had made ourselves free.

I did not yet understand that black people saw things differently. Or that having slavery in your immediate past was not the same as four thousand years ago.

❧

Not long after this revelation of Rhoda's part-Indian ancestry, when I was eight or nine, she began very deliberately to make me more self-reliant. She showed me how to fold my clothes neatly, or hang them in my closet, and also how to iron, which I found especially flattering because it meant she trusted me to use a potentially dangerous appliance. She showed me how to make a bed the right way, stripping off all the blankets and the top sheet to begin with instead of just pulling them up "any which way," as she said.

I think that Rhoda intuited how great a need I had for order, given the emotional chaos of our household. She must have known how I longed to inhabit my own space as an adult would, taking loving care of it and even beginning to know something of the joy I would later take, as a woman, in creating my domestic sphere. The other thing that Rhoda may have perceived was that I did not like being waited on, by her or anyone. One of my earliest memories of Rhoda saying something to me on the subject was when I was around five and she casually remarked, "When I was your age, we used to say that a colored child was old enough to work when she could see above the table." For weeks after that, I went around our house peering over the waxed surfaces of tables and wondering when I'd start working. So I was ready when the time finally came for Rhoda to show me how to do housework.

One afternoon, she and I were in the cool, dark basement where the washing machine and the ironing board were; she was giving me a lesson in how to iron. I was always afraid down there, because of the spiders and the thousand-leggers that skittered along the damp brick walls; I'd never lost my fear of arachnids after my brother scared me so with them. I was keeping one eye on the ironing board and the other on the floor and the walls.

"Now, this shirt here," Rhoda was saying, "this is one of your daddy's. And the way you do it is, you start by wetting it like this." She sprinkled the white cotton oxford cloth with water and then balled it up, dampening it so that the wrinkles came out easier.

"And I always do the easy parts first, the back and the front, and save the cuffs for last because they're a little bit harder."

While I listened, I was thinking about a book Mother had just given me, a biography of George Washington Carver. A passage told of when George was a little boy and knew how to iron so beautifully that he was able to make the ball gowns of the rich white lady he worked for stand up all by themselves. There was a silhouette illustration of George doing this with a dress while the white lady clapped her hands in delight. I identified with this black boy for another reason, too: As a child, he'd suffered from whooping cough. I'd been sick quite a lot, with bouts of strep throat from bad tonsils, till I had them out when I was eight. I felt as if I could understand something of what he must have gone through.

"That's just fine!" Rhoda said, breaking into my thoughts as she admired how I was doing the shirtsleeve.

"Where did you go to school, Rhodie?" I asked. I was thinking of what a struggle it had been for George Washington Carver to get an education.

"School!" Rhoda chortled. "Wasn't any school for me, child. I was in the fields by the time I could walk, following along behind my daddy and picking the worms off of those tobacco plants."

"So where did you learn to read and write?" I asked.

"From our minister, mostly. From the Bible. We didn't have any other books."

No books, I thought to myself. That was all but unimaginable to me; I had my nose in one every chance I got, and half the time their stories were more real to me than my own life.

"Where were you born?" I asked Rhoda.

"A little town in South Carolina called Summerville. They called it that because it was where the rich folks from Charleston went when it turned hot. They'd come down with malaria if they stayed on the coast."

"What did Summerville look like?" I pictured white gingerbread houses and cool piney woods.

"It was beautiful. Lots of fine houses and plenty of trees. We lived a good ways out of the town, though. Off to ourselves."

"When were you born?"

"Well, I don't know exactly." She paused. "They weren't giving out birth certificates to colored babies back when I was born."

I had finished ironing the shirt and was buttoning it onto a hanger. It dropped onto the floor when Rhoda said she'd never had a birth certificate. I was stunned. No record of your birth? How could you do anything if you couldn't prove when and where you were born? Mother had to show my birth certificate all over the place: for vaccinations and at school and camp and all sorts of stuff.

"But I do know that I was four when we were fighting the war with Cuba," Rhoda went on, "because I well remember seeing the colored soldiers who came through Summerville on the train on their way down there. My sister, Lizzie, took me to the depot when the train rolled in. I'd never even seen a colored man in uniform and here were a hundred or more! And they had such beautiful horses, the brass on their saddles and bridles all shiny like gold. All of a sudden, I got scared. The sight was just too much for me. I wanted to go home. Lizzie was laughing, teasing me about what a fraidy-cat I was. One of those soldiers saw me crying and he took me in his arms and put me on his horse." Rhoda smiled at this memory. "Lizzie shut her mouth real quick then. Boy, was she jealous!"

Rhoda took the shirt from the floor where it had fallen. "We had some good times in Summerville. But then my daddy died and my mother took us with her to Charleston. There wasn't any work for her in Summerville."

"When was that?"

"I wasn't but ten. We lived in a boarding house with a whole lot of other people and my mother took in washing. I went to work in a cigar factory down the street. The smell of that leaf stank up the whole neighborhood. I swore I would never, ever smoke."

Before we left the basement for the kitchen where Rhoda would help Claudine with supper, I asked one last question. "What were their names, Rhoda? Your mother and father, I mean."

Suddenly, I needed to know her family name, not the one she always went by—which was her husband's, Willie Lloyd's. But she only told me their first names.

"Sam and Julia," she said softly, as if it were a prayer. She paused for a moment, like she was considering whether to tell me the rest of what was on her mind. We were standing at the bottom of the basement steps and I waited, all but holding my breath.

"They were born in slavery," Rhoda whispered.

She kept her eyes fixed on the floor, would not look me in the face. I felt as if I'd stuck my finger in a light socket. The air around us buzzed the way it does before a thunderstorm.

I had read about slavery. Plenty, for a child my age. But this was no book, no story of someone else's life. This was *Rhoda*. My beloved Rhoda. Telling me that her own mother and father had been slaves.

A silence descended over us, and it was not a comfortable one. Not the easy, companionable kind of quiet that she and I so often dwelled within. We climbed the stairs to the kitchen and I went up another flight alone, to my room, where I closed the door, slid into my rocking chair, and rocked.

"Sam and Julia." I said to myself. "Julia and Sam." I committed their names to memory. I knew I had to do this, and that one day I'd understand why. At the time, I didn't think about when that day would come. All I knew was that it would.

Mother and I (at six), in opposite moods. She is drinking whatever's in that cocktail shaker. I'm wearing a bride's costume from F.A.O. Schwarz—that year's long-awaited Christmas present. But I look as if I'm wondering whether this bridal business is all it's cracked up to be.

In Rhoda's arms, with my sister, Susan. And happy.

five

FTER RHODA TOLD me that her parents had been slaves, a loneliness took up residence inside me, like some great dark bird settling its wings.

I didn't feel like being around other children and I was somber much of the time, lonesome like the freight trains whose midnight whistle I woke to as I lay in bed. I'd listen for the sound of the cars crashing together as they coupled on the tracks down the hill beyond the Confederate woods, and I'd think about how my brother loved trains. Now, his sickness, his other-ness, was all the more unsettling to me—although he was in fact much better, living at a place in Maryland called Chestnut Lodge, where he was in treatment with a wonderful psychiatrist named Frieda Fromm-Reichman. From the reverent way Mother and Daddy spoke her name, I endowed Frieda with the ability to work miracles. And when Dickie came to visit us, he did seem ever so much better. Yet, he was still strange, and a stranger to me, and therefore I was unnerved whenever he came home.

Having a mentally ill brother made my awareness of the difference between me and other kids painfully acute. It cut my self-confidence to ribbons and therefore made me all the more vulnerable to being bullied and teased. It also turned me into one of those children with an extra helping of empathy—but what ten-year-old wants to be known for that?

My answer to all this was food. Now I ate even more desperately, trying in vain to fill the emptiness that had taken hold inside me. Rhoda had once gratified my hunger every night with our bedtime feasts; now Mother had ordered her to desist because she was fretting over my weight. So I started sneaking. When Mother took me to our Jewish country club to swim, I'd hang out in the locker room with Rosa, the kindhearted black woman who worked at the club. I was too ashamed to be seen buying a cool half-dozen Butterfingers at the vending machine, so I'd give Rosa my quarters and she'd bring me the candy. I'd cram one bar after another into my mouth, sitting on the toilet in one of the stalls.

Every evening when Mother and Daddy and my sisters and I gathered for supper in our dining room beneath the softly glowing chandelier, I'd go missing mentally and drift into a fantasy world. While we sat in that familial tableau—our formal replica of what my father's childhood dinners had been, in the mansion on Monument Avenue—I'd pretend I was an Indian, feasting on wild game in the woods. Or I'd imagine Rhoda's childhood home in Summerville, and try to conjure her mother and father. Julia and Sam.

I'd seen a picture in one of Mother's socially conscious photography books of a black sharecropper's family in Alabama during the Depression. The walls of their shack were covered in newspaper and their clothing was rags. They were sitting at a table, heads bowed, saying grace over two chipped enamel bowls only partly filled with food, collard greens and pigs' feet. As I studied the picture, I couldn't see how this could be enough to go around. Now, at our table, I thought about them and wondered if Rhoda's family had been like that, while Claudine went back and forth through the swinging door to the kitchen with one dish after another.

I'd come back to the present with a bang when Mary or Susan tipped her chair backward from the table, which they were always doing, and Daddy flew into a rage. The air would become a blur of flying hands as he hit Mary—it was always her and never Susan. The sound of Mary weeping made me want to die. The only thing that saved me was knowing Deanie was in the kitchen. Without her there, I would have been even more lost and scared than I was. And Mary would have been, too: She and Deanie were so close that sometimes I thought they had mental telepathy. All Daddy would have to do was to start berating Mary for something or other at the dinner table, and Claudine would quietly materialize next to her chair, hovering protectively like an angel.

"I'm not afraid of you!" Mary would yell at Daddy, as soon as Claudine moved to her side. "I'm gonna run away. With Deanie!"

Claudine would put one hand on Mary's shoulder. "Now, sugar," she'd say. "Don't go getting yourself all worked up. Your daddy didn't mean it. He's just tired."

"No, he's not," Mary would cry. "He's just mean."

Daddy would have regained some of his composure, a dignity appropriate to the Edwardian father he himself had had and that he considered himself to be as well. "And where do you think you and Claudine will be off to, Your Highness?"

"Don't call me that!" Mary would say. Her fists would be curled into tight balls and she would use them to wipe her eyes, the way a child would.

"All right, Miss Mary," Deanie would say, hugging Mary to her side. "Now, where you and me gonna go to?"

"Fort Knox!" Mary would sniff. "Where they keep all the gold."

Comic relief. We'd all exhale and start laughing. But I knew there was a pitiful truth in what Mary said: If she had her own money instead of having to depend on Daddy's, she'd be out of there—she and Deanie both.

This was a lesson I took to heart.

℘

OUR HOUSE WAS a place where black and white colluded, shared
the deepest of secrets, and comforted each other in myriad ways.
Mother spent hours of every day sitting in the kitchen with Rhoda
and Claudine, trading gossip or telling stories or listening to their
woes and sharing hers. She was forever sweet-talking Daddy into
giving her extra money for "the help": cash under the table at
Christmas and Easter and birthdays, larger sums if there was a
mortgage payment due or an unexpected illness brought doctors'
bills. These were never, ever loans.

"Don't even think about it, Claudine," Mother would say. "I'm
just glad I can help out." The way she said "can" was how she tried
to minimize their embarrassment at needing to ask for help; it was
as if she was trying to say, "I owe you this, just for doing all you do
for us."

As for my father, he had his own brand of generosity—he was
also given to offering financial help whenever he saw that it was
needed—and he had his own yearnings for the companionship and
confidence of other men. He ruled over a house full of women—
he even called us "the harem"—and he was much lonelier than any
of us knew.

I'd look out the window on some cool spring morning and
there would be my father in his garden, deep in conversation with
one or both of the two men who helped him in the yard, Theodore
Jefferson or Robert Tinsley. Theodore lived in Ashland and came
on weekends; Robert was a neighbor of Claudine's in Westwood.
Theodore was younger than Robert, a strapping, handsome man;
Robert was in his sixties and not given to saying very much—not
that he had a chance to get a word in edgewise when Daddy
started talking as they worked. Robert was a deacon at the Baptist
Church in Westwood, so Daddy called him "the Reverend" and set
great store by whatever Robert said.

I couldn't hear what they were saying in the garden from inside
the house, but I could feel the intimacy of the conversation even

from a distance. Three men, one white and two black, heads bent together as if in prayer, hands folded over the handles of their rakes. I'd turn from the window with a smile on my face, though I could not have said why.

I sensed the same unspoken affinity whenever Daddy and I went "up the country" to work his bird dogs with the black men he knew. Some were young and some were "old as dirt," as Deanie would say. But all of them were poor. They lived in tiny houses with woodstoves and old newspaper glued to the inside walls for warmth. They grew small cultivations of corn and maybe a little tobacco, just for themselves, and they had names like Roosevelt or Robert E. Lee. Daddy told me I would never meet anyone white named Robert E. Lee, and so far he'd been right.

These men lived in settlements, some of which would soon cease to exist. They'd be bought up by developers and become housing "estates"—a word Daddy bitterly mocked—with names like Fox Hollow and Quail Run, where no fox or quail would ever be seen again. But sometimes, before the tract houses came, these places had sported less picturesque names.

One of the spots where my father liked to hunt was a crossroads near Ashland, where Theodore Jefferson and his family lived. There was no marker at this meeting of the roads, just a beat-up country store with a sign on the side that said Drink Coca-Cola. The sign had once been colored the brand's signature red but now it was so faded you could hardly see it. An ancient, listing barn stood off to one side.

We'd stop at the store to get gas and some of the chicken livers the owner's wife fried up, which Daddy loved and always shared with Theodore. And invariably, at some point, as we sat in the car chewing on our tough chicken livers and swilling Cokes, with Daddy and Theodore passing my father's hammered silver flask back and forth between them, Daddy would clear his throat and say, "Well, here we are again. Back at Niggerfoot."

For that was the name of this particular crossroads, even though there was no sign. Sometimes, after he'd come out with the word,

Daddy would think better of it and say, "Sorry. I meant to say *Negrofoot.*"

Theodore Jefferson wouldn't say a word. He'd just smile to himself and take another bite of chicken liver. I sat in the backseat, beet red with shame. And wondering—Old Head that I was, and Rhoda's soul-divided child—just how this place came by such a gruesome name.

☬

IF DADDY AND I were not with Theodore or another of his bird-dog friends who knew the local landowners, we'd have to knock on a stranger's door and ask permission to work the dogs on their property. This was when I glimpsed the side of my father that always made me pity him; I saw how hesitant he was, how easily he could be made afraid.

We'd pull up in front of a farmhouse where a woman in a pinafore apron would answer the sagging screen door. My father would sweep his hat from his bald head and introduce himself and me, say that we were just hoping to let our dogs scare up a covey or two, he hadn't even brought his shotgun because his daughter here didn't want to see any birds killed, so might we just run them in that field over yonder?

The farm wife would consider it for a moment, usually saying something like, "That'd be fine, mister. We've just now got that other field seeded with winter wheat, so I'd be much obliged if you'd keep your dogs off that one. And watch out for the cow down by the barn. She's got a new calf and's apt to be ornery."

My father would put his hat back on and nod gratefully. "Much obliged," he would say. Obliged for what, I knew full well: for what he perceived as their valor, their true worth, because they *worked,* they earned their daily bread with honor, while he was nothing but a rich man's son. And therefore he perceived himself to be essentially worthless.

I knew this from the things he said, from the way he spoke of "working men and women" as if they held the keys to heaven, were sanctified by their honest toil. He taught me to see them the same way, black or white, and never, *but never* to think that people with money—people like us—had any reason whatsoever to be proud. Far from it. In truth, we ought to hang our heads in shame. For it was these folk, the salt of the earth, who alone could lay some rightful claim to pride.

If the farmer or his wife allowed us to work our dogs on their land, my father would indeed be "much obliged." But sometimes they'd be mean-tempered and order us off the place. Then I'd see my father shrink and wither before my very eyes. We would trudge back to the car where he would take two or three long pulls from his flask. "Just to steady myself, sugar," he would say, winking at me by way of an apology for his weakness.

I knew he was humiliated. A city man—and a Jew, to boot—who felt that he should have had his own land. Who'd dreamed for years of having a real farm, had a well-thumbed book on the shelf in our den titled *We Farm for a Living and Make it Pay*. The picture of the farmer on his tractor harvesting corn made me think of Daddy, but I couldn't imagine Mother collecting eggs from the broody hens while wearing one of her cashmere twin sets from Bonwit Teller.

Whenever my father spoke to Mother or to his elder brother, Edward, about his farm dream, all they did was talk it down. Edward thought it was impractical in the extreme: How would my father get in to work every morning, be at his big vice-president's desk at Sergeant's Dog Care Products promptly at nine? And Mother wondered how we'd all get to school, and where she'd shop for groceries—not that she ever bought a grocery in her life; she phoned in her order to a tiny upscale market named Park Foodland every morning and it was delivered to our house in the afternoon by Rudy, the ever-cheerful and always slightly drunk driver who flirted with Deanie while she unpacked the brown paper bags.

On those afternoons when Daddy and I were turned away by some landowner or another, I wished so hard for him to have his piece of earth one of these days. Then we wouldn't have to drive to the country; we'd be there all the time and I could finally have a horse. I wouldn't have to see my father tip his hat and humbly murmur, "Much obliged."

On our way home through the deepening blue twilight, he'd be silent. I wouldn't be able to think of anything to say either. We'd drive past one simple, lovely white frame farmhouse after another, the kind of southern dwellings that twist your heart if you're native-born. A very old elm tree out front, with a tire swing hanging from one of its branches, some good-looking hounds lounging on the peeling wooden steps. Two brick chimneys at either end of the house and that feeling of *age* to the place, of lives before yours lived here and births and deaths in the rooms behind those upstairs windows. Of secrets kept behind those shades.

Daddy would glance over at me with the ghost of a smile.

"That's our dream house, right, Laurie girl?"

"Right!" I'd answer, loyalty to him flooding my heart.

"That's the one I'm coming back to," my father would sigh. "In my next life."

One of my favorite pictures of my father, taken in an autumn field. This setter was the one he had when I was growing up, and typically this picture, from the family album, bore the dog's name as a caption: "Mack."

six

WHEN HE WAS in a playful mood, Daddy would take my chin in his hand and turn it so he could see my profile. He was checking on how my preadolescent nose was coming along, whether it might be developing a hook or a crook or a bump anywhere—a "schnozolla," as he called it, like the nose of his favorite comedian, Jimmy Durante. But I thought my father was handsome in the same big-nosed way as the English actor Leslie Howard, who played Ashley Wilkes in *Gone with the Wind*. I saw the movie for the first time when I was nine and was struck by the resemblance. Many years later, I learned that Leslie Howard was not an English aristocrat, as I had assumed: His parents were Hungarian Jews, and Howard had grown up in London's ghetto, the East End. After I found that out I could see why Howard looked tantalizingly familiar to me, like "one of our boys," as Daddy used to say about other Jews. I understood why Ashley got to me the way he did, with his dreamy despair, and moved me so much more than Clark Gable's Rhett Butler, who I thought was just too macho and slick.

Daddy would finish checking out my routine-sized nose and be pleased. Then he'd nuzzle me in the nape of my neck till I giggled helplessly and proclaim that there was "where the sugar was."

In my family, looks were of the utmost importance; we all wanted not to be too apparently Semitic, not to "look Jewish." Looking Jewish meant *me,* actually (minus the big nose): olive skin, dark eyes, and coal black kinky hair. I thanked God I didn't have the nose, because we were way too classy to ever consider getting a nose job. Nose jobs were for . . . well, *kikes,* a word I only heard used once in our household, since it was considered to be so ill-bred that it was beneath us. The one time Daddy used it was in reference to the new car we'd just bought after he and Mother yielded to my sisters' entreaties and got a fire-engine red Pontiac convertible.

They drove it home from the showroom and parked it out back on the turntable behind our garage, so none of our neighbors would see it right away. We stood in the cool shade of the tall pin oaks, staring at the new "Jew canoe," hellfire red with a tan roof that folded back like a bat's wing. Daddy had grown up with a Pierce-Arrow, his parents' touring car, and even though that certainly bespoke wealth, it was a lot quieter than this car.

"I don't know, Ev," he sighed, shaking his head. "I still say it looks like something a kike would drive."

"Richard!" Mother gasped. She threw a glance to the kitchen windows, hoping that Claudine and Rhoda weren't there to hear us. "Don't you dare use that word in this house!"

And he never did again.

But the harm was done already, and we all grew up in mortal dread of standing out too much as Jews. Mary even asked our rabbi—the genteel, bespectacled Ariel Goldburg—why it was that so many Jews had large noses. Rabbi Goldburg answered, "Well, dear, not all Jews have big noses. But most big noses belong to Jews."

Mary told me that my nostrils wouldn't be so wide if I quit

picking my nose; I resolved to try. No one had ever suggested to me that physical perfection was not possible, so I was still relentlessly striving for it. And no one (except Rhoda) implied that appearances had nothing to do with love, that you could be unconditionally accepted for who you were instead of how you looked. This would have been all but inconceivable to me and I would not have believed it for a minute.

The bane of my existence was my kinky hair. I'd stand in front of the bathroom mirror for half an hour after I got out of the tub, pulling it straight till it hurt, hoping against hope that it might stay that way even after it was dry, like the satiny tresses of those Breck girls in the magazine ads. When I discovered that I could have it straightened, I thought I'd found God. But that only worked until I left the salon and took a hot, steamy bath, or the ever-present Richmond humidity fogged its way into my curls and all the kink came back. Rhoda actually had straighter hair than mine—a gift from her Cherokee ancestor—and at one point I even started wearing a hairnet, the way she did. But this only made me look like one of the women ladling food onto plates in the cafeteria at school.

WHEN I WAS ten and Mary and Susan were already away at college, they were invited by a friend from Saint Catherine's to the Bal de Bois, the annual debutante dance at the Country Club of Virginia. The preparations for this event were momentous, almost as if they were making their own debuts. Mother took them downtown to Montaldo's, Richmond's most elegant women's store, and I went along to watch them try on ball gowns, their images endlessly reflected in mirrors edged in cream and gold. That night, I dreamt of Glenny Reynolds, the girl who'd invited my sisters to her debut. In the dream, I was standing on the lawn of the Reynoldses' white house on Cary Street, peering past the columns of its facade into the window of an upstairs bedroom. There, poised before a mirror and gowned in pure white, stood Glenny, or a girl whom I imagined to be her. The dream was so vivid that it brought back all my memories of yearning to be a debutante myself, all the sensations of being excluded from the rituals of the gentile world. I awoke with tears cooling my cheeks, and Rhoda thought I had a fever when she came to wake me up.

Oddly enough, the semi-mythic presence of Glenny Reynolds played out for me in yet another way, one very different from her debutante persona and one that—could I have known it then—was a portent of my later life. Glenny's father, Richard Reynolds, was the president of Reynolds Metals and owned a hilltop estate in Jamaica above Montego Bay. My sister Mary had flown down there with the Reynolds family the previous Christmas and had come home with snapshots that made a deep impression on me. They were of Mary and Glenny, both of them plump and shyly smiling, sitting astride two drowsing donkeys with four Jamaican children standing beside them. The light was stark; I could feel the tropical heat in the photographs, but even more stark was the contrast between my entitled sister and her friend and these rag-clad Jamaican children.

Not that Mary herself felt so entitled: Her first night home from Jamaica, at the dinner table, she asked Mother and Daddy what the expression "Jew 'em down" meant. My father was aghast. "Where'd you hear that, sugar?" he asked Mary. "Mr. Reynolds," she answered. "When Glenny and I were heading to the straw market in Montego Bay, he told us to be sure and Jew 'em down."

All these memories and impressions were swirling through my mind on the night when the Bal de Bois finally took place. I helped Rhoda get my sisters ready for the dance, hooking the backs of their snow-white Merry Widow waist cinchers and helping them into the wire hoop skirts they wore to make their gowns stick out. I tried to sit down in one of these contraptions and discovered that it turned me into an upside-down umbrella. Susan was flat-chested so she had to pin falsies into her bodice, and before she did we took turns throwing them at each other just for fun.

Once my sisters had departed in their froth of pastel tulle, Rhoda gave me a bath, and afterward I twirled around in front of the mirror, pulling my hair straight and pretending that my towel was a ball gown.

"Quit fanning around," Rhoda said sternly. "You're going to catch your death of cold. Come here and put these pajamas on, you hear?"

They were cotton with cowboys and Indians on them, and they were a hard comedown after seeing my sisters in their glorious gowns. Soon they'd be waltzing on the terrace of the country club, beneath fireworks that would start as soon as the June sky had grown dark enough.

Before the fireworks began, Rhoda went down to the kitchen and brought me my bedtime feast. We heard the fireworks start while I was finishing my ice cream. We rushed out onto the upstairs porch off my bedroom and saw the first of the shimmering explosions lighting up the sky. The display went on for what seemed like hours, and with each passing minute I grew more envious, agitated, and confused. I wanted to be a debutante no matter how I loathed them, no matter that I knew their fathers in white ties and tails were the same sort of men as Mr. Reynolds, who probably referred to black people as "nigras" (or worse) and made remarks like "Jew 'em down." How could I be such a traitor to myself, my family? How could I want to be one of the FFVs who despised us because we were Jews and hated Rhoda because she was a Negro?

By the time the fireworks were over and I had to go to bed, I was in such a state that Rhoda knew there was only one way to calm me down.

"Come on now, honey. You have to shut your eyes. Let's get you tucked in and then we'll sing to each other, like we do."

Once I was in bed, Rhoda stepped into her room next to mine. She began to sing "Swing Low, Sweet Chariot." After a while, I let myself fall asleep.

◒

AMONG MY MOTHER'S ART books was one called *Fifty Great American Paintings*. It had some of John Singer Sargent's opulent portraits of society beauties but it also had plenty of social-realism paintings from the thirties. I loved this book and would hold it on my lap while Rhoda turned the heavy, acid-smelling pages.

We had a favorite picture that was also named *Swing Low, Sweet Chariot*. In the foreground was a one-room cabin; beyond it, flat fields of cotton stretched away to the horizon. There were hound dogs flopped down in the dirt yard, a few scraggly plants potted in coffee tins on the front porch, and a thin plume of smoke curling up from the chimney.

We could see the inside of the cabin through the lit-up doorway; an old black man was lying on a narrow bed, about to die. His weeping kin were gathered around and his wife knelt beside the bed, her huge breasts drooping onto the blanket. But it was the sky above the cabin that was the focal point of the canvas: a moonlit landscape of indigo and silver in which clouds were parting for a chariot of gold. Surrounding it were the angels of the Lord, winging their way downward to fetch the dying man's soul. And all those angels were black.

Just beneath the chariot, struggling in the grip of an upside-down angel, writhed the devil himself, a snaky red monster brandishing a pitchfork and snorting fire. He was fighting to get to the cabin ahead of the chariot and it looked to me as if he was bound to win. Rhoda and I would stare at the picture, reading each other's minds. I would look up at her for reassurance.

"See that chariot?" she'd ask, smiling down at me, full of confidence. "See all those angels? You count them for me now."

There were sixteen. I could see a few more emerging from the clouds.

"That chariot's going to get there with time to spare," Rhoda would vow. "Because you and I, we know that soul is bound for glory. It's just got to make it home."

seven

ALTHOUGH I KNEW myself to be a child of the South, initiated into its particular ways by my elders, black and white, I was also aware that we had what I considered to be the saving grace of Yankee connections—because both my maternal grandmother Alice and my aunt Barbara lived in that bubbling kettle of ethnic soup, New York City.

Granny and Barbara were each forces of nature in their separate ways; my sister Mary said that Granny was "the last of the red-hot mamas," and she truly was—a vital, vibrant throwback to the Roaring Twenties and the flapper ethic of Too Much Is Never Enough. Barbara was the youngest of my mother's two sisters, twenty-four when I was born and earning her own living (the only woman in the family to do so) as an artist and graphic designer in New York. She was dark-haired and brown-eyed like Mother, terrifically handsome, and possessed of a sophisticated style that made me swear I'd dress that way, too, as soon as I grew up. She wore printed velvets and deep-hued suedes from little shops in

Greenwich Village, and all her friends were equally chic; most of them had jobs in advertising or fashion at stores like Henri Bendel or magazines like *Harper's Bazaar*. She was up for anything, and when we went to see her in the city it was always Barbara who'd take me on endless rambles through the streets of Chinatown or all the way up to the torch in the Statue of Liberty, a truly terrifying ascent up a rickety spiral staircase enveloped by black canvas that flapped wildly in the wind from the harbor.

It seemed to me that both my aunt and my grandmother breathed an air different from the stifling atmosphere of Richmond. Neither one of them was an observant Jew, but Granny lived in Yorkville on the Upper East Side and that neighborhood was filled with German Jews; when I walked up Lexington Avenue with her, no one stared at my olive skin or dark hair the way they always did in Richmond. There was just something so different about being in New York—I never felt as if I had to apologize for being who and what I was. The moment Mother and I descended from the night train amidst the thrilling gloom and bustle of Pennsylvania Station at dawn, I could feel my lungs expanding with the city's breath.

Granny would have breakfast waiting for us and Barbara would ride the Third Avenue El from her studio on East Fifty-second Street to join us. I would be sleepy but way too excited to doze, so I'd sit with the grown-ups and listen to Barbara's stories about where she worked, an avant-garde publishing house called New Directions.

"Oh, God," she'd say, throwing her coat on the low velvet settee in Granny's front hall. "I'm so hungover. Dylan Thomas is in town, and he was reading last night at the 92nd Street Y, and who does Laughlin send to pry the wild-man poet off his bar stool at the White Horse? Me! Thankless task."

Barbara was not a name-dropper by nature—she was much too self-assured to need to brag—but she knew what a passionate reader my mother was and how avid for literary gossip, listening with stars in her eyes to her "baby sister" who actually knew writers and poets like Thomas. "Who else have you seen lately?" Mother would ask eagerly.

Barbara would reward her with a sly smile and one raised eyebrow—she tried to teach me how to do this, but I couldn't seem to master it. "Well, I went to a dinner a few weeks ago at Laughlin's place." James Laughlin was the owner of New Directions. "Quite the lineup. Tennessee Williams and Carson McCullers, and both of them in absolutely awful moods—she was feeling lousy. So he decided to lighten things up by taking out his pillbox and showing everyone how much stuff he was on. Believe me, it was impressive."

By this time, Barbara would have had several bracing cups of coffee and half a dozen Camels and would be ready to hit the streets with me. We'd head downtown to shop a bit and then have lunch with my favorite of her friends, a fabulously playful artist named Elizabeth Smit. When I went away to summer camp and got homesick, Elizabeth cheered me up with illustrated letters about a horse made of stars who lived in the dunes on Fire Island and only came out at night.

At the end of the day, I'd fall asleep in Granny's bed while she reclined in her red velvet bathrobe on the chaise across the room. She'd smoke one cigarette after another, the orange glow from their tips like a lighthouse in the darkness, ebbing and flaring as she took drags. I was lulled by the steady pulse of sound from the street below. Even the wailing of distant sirens spoke to me of wild adventure, of the power of the city and its ceaseless pour of life.

☙

BARBARA ONLY CAME to Richmond a couple of times a year for short visits, but Granny stayed with us for two whole months, from just after Christmas till my birthday at the end of February. I counted the hours until the moment when it was time for us to meet her train. It always arrived after dark, so we'd drive through the streets of Richmond, quiet as a grave, down Monument Avenue past the frowning Confederate statues, the always-dark windows of the house where my father grew up. It had been turned into doctors' offices after his parents died, and now it presented the sad facade of all houses left unloved. The only sign of life on Monument was the glorious scent of yeast and vanilla that drifted over from the bakery on Broad Street, Finest Foods of Virginia, where the oven kept going through the night.

As soon as we'd parked at the station, I would race ahead of Mother and Rhoda, down the steps to the platform where the oily black locomotive hissed its clouds of steam into the cold night air. I was careful not to get in the way of the sleeping-car porters as they went about their all-important work, lords of this railroad kingdom as I believed them to be. Granny would appear out of the swirling steam, stepping down from the train in her black suede shoes with the open toes. I could smell the cloud of Tabu from way down the platform.

"There's my girl!" she would cry, in her throaty, two-packs-a-day rasp, folding me into her arms.

After we hugged and kissed, I would grab her train case to carry it myself. I knew what was in there: enough cosmetics for me to play with for days on end. Nail polish and lipstick to match with tantalizing names like Fire and Ice, Say it with Rubies, and Cherries in the Snow.

Rhoda would be waiting upstairs—she always came with us to the station to greet Granny—and both of them got misty eyed when they embraced. "Miz Alice!" Rhoda would say. "You look fine as ever. Haven't aged a day!" My grandmother would smile, acknowledging this compliment and knowing it wasn't true but not caring. "Rhoda," she would answer, returning the favor, "you know, you grow more beautiful with each passing year."

Amidst the sound of these familiar blandishments, these sweet womanly lies, I'd walk back to the car, warmed by the closeness between our three generations, our two races. Granny and Mother and me. And Rhoda, who knew us from forever.

◎

WITH HER RED velvet robe and glittering diamonds, her train case full of cosmetics, and the peach-colored satin corset she wore— which she always said was for her "bad back" but which I knew was to give her a semblance of the youthful figure she once had— Granny was one of those women who refused to grow old gracefully. Or even at all.

"You know something, sugar?" she said to me as she sat in a steaming bath one morning while I perched on the rim of the tub, soaping her bent back and stealing surreptitious glances at her huge, drooping breasts. "Losing your looks isn't the worst thing that can happen to a girl, unless you happen to have been a beauty when you were young. Well, I was. And let me tell you, getting old ain't all it's cracked up to be."

This made me oddly grateful not to be a beauty myself—I figured that I wouldn't suffer so much when I got old. Meditating on this small blessing, I followed Granny downstairs so she could get dressed for her afternoon card party at the club.

"Do me a favor, will you?" she said. "Get some ammonia and clean my ring for me." She knew how I adored this piece of jewelry, a wide platinum band set with three big diamonds and square chips of onyx in between. The ring came with a story, too, one that was ever so slightly shocking, much like my grandmother herself.

"My second husband," Granny said, frowning slightly as she twisted the ring up over her knuckle and handed it to me. It was heavy in my palm; there was a lot of platinum in this thing. "Ah, well . . . Edgar's taste left a little something to be desired," she murmured. "The engagement ring he gave me wasn't much. So I took it to a jeweler I knew on Forty-seventh Street who had better ideas about what a girl might like. He took Edgar's ring apart and made this one for me with the stones."

I didn't think this was a very nice way to treat your husband, but what did I know?

Granny wasn't sentimental about her husbands. What she relished and still lived for—even in her seventies—was the thrill of seduction. She adored pulp fiction, spicy movies, and the afternoon soap operas; every day she and Deanie watched the *The Edge of Night* and *The Secret Storm* together in the den. They sat before the flickering gray screen while the snaky organ music swelled to a crescendo every time there was a kissing scene.

"MmmMmmMmm!" they would cluck, shaking their heads in a mutual fit of disapproving delight. "Nothin' but trouble," Deanie would mutter.

"You can say that again," Granny would agree, as if the two of them were in on some dire secret I couldn't even guess at.

One morning when Granny was visiting us—I was twelve at the time—I came into the breakfast room so quietly that neither of them heard me. Claudine was sitting at the kitchen table, weeping, and Granny's arm was draped across her shoulder.

"Don't cry, Claudine," she said. "You aren't the first woman to fall in love with a married man and I promise you won't be the last."

I slid between the cabinets in the breakfast room so I could eavesdrop. I heard Deanie blow her nose. "Worst part of it is," she said, "he died in the night and I wasn't even with him. And that wife of his, she knows all about us. She called this morning before I came to work, said she'll kill me if I dare to show my face at the funeral."

This was like a soap opera, only better. This was real life.

"Well," Granny said softly, "it sounds like you just better stay away. But I know how you feel, Claudine. I fell in love with a married man myself, back when I was with my first husband. And it was a mess, believe you me."

"Really?" I heard Deanie murmur. "What happened?"

"I'll tell you what happened," Granny answered grimly. "Both of them died, one right after the other. They killed themselves."

I had to hope they didn't hear me gasp. Even though I already knew that my grandfather had committed suicide—Mother told me he did it because he'd lost all his money in the stock market crash of 1929—I'd had no idea that there'd been another man in

Granny's life. I was intrigued. But there was no way I could ask her about it. I was too young and she was too old, and I wasn't supposed to have overheard this in the first place. But now, for the first time, I suddenly understood what it was about my grandmother that had always made me just a little bit in awe of her. Just a tad afraid. Why I'd sensed a certain danger hovering in the atmosphere around her, like the air before a storm. She was the kind of woman who drove men crazy. Now, when I thought of Granny, I saw her as the femme fatale playing the piano in the ad for the perfume she wore, Tabu. This woman was so alluring that the bearded violinist in the picture was overcome by desire and grabbed her up from that piano bench into a mad embrace.

NOW THAT I knew my grandmother had been a Scarlet Woman, I wondered if this was the reason my father didn't like her very much. He called her a "gold digger" behind her back and muttered that she'd sent two husbands to their graves. He harped on her smoking and the stink of her cigarettes; every morning he came downstairs when she was still asleep in the den and flung open the door from that room to the porch, letting in the icy air.

Of all the secrets Granny held, the one that intrigued me most was the history of her family, the Wilmington, North Carolina, branch about whom I knew almost nothing. When Granny stayed with us, she and Mother would sometimes start to reminisce at the dinner table, to tell one story or another about their side of the family. Granny might mention that her father, Solomon Fishblate, had been the mayor of Wilmington at the turn of the century. My father's face would crease into a frown of disdain.

"Oh, for God's sake, Alice!" he sneered. "Your father was no more the mayor of that frog town than I am."

"Indeed he was, Richard." Granny stood her ground. "I remember when he was mayor and I was . . . oh, around the age Laurie is now, ten or eleven. Thomas Edison came to town and he stayed with us. I got to sit on his lap!"

Daddy threw Granny a look of pure scorn and shook his head. I knew not to question my grandmother further, lest he erupt into a rage. But his curt dismissal of my maternal relations made me all the more curious. Who were they, and what had they been like? What kind of man was this Solomon Fishblate, to have been elected—and not just once, Granny said, but three times—to the mayoralty of a southern town? Was there a secret about him, too? Some dark truth my grandmother wanted not to be revealed?

❦

OF ALL THE secrets and the sweet lies that surrounded me, the biggest, of course, was race—the separate peace my family had made with the true viciousness of the South. I knew it lay out there, lurking at the edges of our comfortable existence. I knew there was a word *nigger,* even though it was not one I ever heard from the people I considered decent. I knew something of the poverty, black and white, that held the South in its grip, from the books my mother had, like *Let Us Now Praise Famous Men.* I turned again and again to a photograph in *The Family of Man* of a black man sitting in a wheelchair, weeping into his hands while his gray-haired mother reached over to lay a comforting hand on his shoulder. The photographer's name was Roy DeCarava, and the picture had been in an exhibit called "The Sweet Flypaper of Life."

These were but a few of the images I carried in my heart. These and others I had more recently seen but was trying hard to forget—the skeletal remains of my own people, gassed and thrown onto a heap at Auschwitz. When I looked into these shadow places, I began to appreciate how and why my mother had come by her politics, her depth of soul. I could understand how living in the South, this proud and haunted place where the sorrow songs pursued you no matter where you lived, had made her see with eyes other than her own. How this life could have given her—and me—the capacity to feel another person's grief, and fear, and pain.

I could not say precisely when this awareness first dawned on me. Maybe it was there, in embryonic form, when I was an infant and Rhoda worked her roots on me, and then it grew stronger after she'd told me that her parents were born in slavery. But I remember the year 1960, when I turned eleven, as the time of my awakening to the hardball politics of race.

This was when the battle for school desegregation in Virginia took on all the aspects of a war. The fight had been coming for some time, ever since the 1954 Supreme Court decision that mandated an end to segregation in the schools. But Virginia, in thrall to its diehard Dixiecrat senator, Harry Flood Byrd, was determined to hold out. Byrd and his cronies had hatched a scheme they called Massive Resistance to block every federal move to integrate the state's schools. The ones in Prince Edward County had recently shut down, denying all the county's children the right to an education rather than allow them to attend school with "nigras," as Byrd and his ilk continued to refer to black people.

My parents loathed Harry Flood Byrd, especially my father. Daddy had despised the man ever since the thirties, when Byrd had done everything he could to thwart Franklin Roosevelt (Daddy's hero) and the progressive programs of the New Deal. Now, in the winter of 1960, the talk at our dinner table was of what would happen if "that sonofabitch" managed to shut down the public schools. I knew there was no way Mother and Daddy were going to cave in and send me to a private school—they had learned their lesson from my sisters' misery at Saint Catherine's—and I wouldn't have willingly gone to such a place, either. But I was worried that Mary Munford, my school, might close, like the ones in Prince Edward County, and then what would I do?

I was in the fifth grade that year, and I loved it. I had a pigeon-breasted teacher, Mrs. Smith, who looked like Eleanor Roosevelt and had a manner to match. She was genteel and cultivated and was giving our class a wonderful course in art history, for which we filled loose-leaf binders with black-and-white prints of famous paintings and buildings and sculptures. She praised me to the skies and also to Mother, at PTA meetings and such. I couldn't quite understand why Mother kept referring to Mrs. Smith as "a lady of the Old South," but this might have served me as a warning.

In the midst of the school crisis, my world was rocked by another event that touched my family every bit as deeply. On the morning of my eleventh birthday—February 22nd, 1960—Richmond's black citizens began a boycott at Thalhimer's department store downtown. The boycott was in response to the ongoing refusal of William Thalhimer, Jr., the store's president, to desegregate its facilities: the lunch counter on the main floor, the fancy dining room upstairs, and the dressing rooms storewide. In addition, the demonstrators demanded that Thalhimer's begin to hire blacks in jobs other than floor sweepers, waitresses, and maids.

The boycott hit my father hard, because he was friendly with William Thalhimer. The Thalhimers belonged to our synagogue and (even more important, in Daddy's eyes) to a family that had been part of the same migration from Germany to Richmond, in the 1840s, that included Daddy's own grandfather. The Thalhimers were a prominent family, and they had been especially courageous during the Nazi terror, when all too many other Richmond Jews of German ancestry had turned their backs on their brethren trapped in Europe. Most of the members of our congregation, Beth Ahabah, came from German families that had arrived in Richmond before the Civil War, and even as late as the early forties, they still couldn't bring themselves to believe that "their" Germany, their cultured fatherland, was now waging a war of annihilation against the Jews. But Billy Thalhimer and his father, William Sr., faced that fact head-on. They signed hundreds of affidavits, the guarantees of financial support without which Jews could not emigrate to the United States. And in 1941, when America's golden door had all but slammed shut entirely, this father and son joined forces with a German émigré professor and brought fifteen young men and women to live and work on a Virginia farm the Thalhimers had purchased for the express purpose of rescuing as many young people as they could.

For this noble act, Daddy revered the Thalhimers, all the more so because he could never expiate his own guilt for having done nothing to save a single Jewish life. He was devastated by the boycott and he took it personally, as an affront to his sense of fairness and his loyalty to the Thalhimers. My mother, on the other hand, supported the boycott with characteristic fervor. She kept secret from my father the fact that Mary and Susan—on a visit home from their colleges up North—had briefly joined the picket line. Before they left the house, Susan beckoned me into their bedroom and proudly showed me the placard she was going to carry. It said DON'T BUY WHERE YOU CAN'T EAT!

I didn't want to be around if and when Daddy found out they were picketing Thalhimer's. As it was, our fights at the dinner table were bad enough. Mother was adamant in her belief that the boycott was a necessary step in Richmond's campaign for civil rights, and I had become one of those infuriatingly precocious, self-righteous adolescents who thought they knew it all. I already saw the world largely in black and white, and now this belief had been affirmed.

I mounted a frontal assault on Daddy for what I saw as his utter stupidity about civil rights. In my eyes, his refusal to stand up for the struggle for equality *now* was no different from his having done nothing *then* to save Jews in Germany. This was the cruelest attack I could have made and I knew it, but I wanted to hurt him. I was still enough of a child to believe that he could have single-handedly staved off Hitler, and I was furious over his failure to be the hero I needed him to be.

In retaliation, Daddy goaded me to a frenzy by insisting that whatever Negroes were suffering in the South, it was nothing compared to what had been done to the Jews. Every night he ritually invoked the six million, this unimaginably overwhelming number set against what he considered to be the comparatively few martyrs of the black South who had given their lives in the struggle for freedom. I was still way too young to know enough history to argue with my father; to tell him that, in fact, the body count of those dead and maimed and tortured because of slavery and Jim Crow was significantly higher than six million. And what would it have mattered? My father and I were not really pitting one atrocity against another; we were engaged in a running battle, an undeclared guerrilla war, for supremacy in this house of women he called "the harem."

It happened that Granny was with us then, on her annual winter visit, and so my father felt well and truly ganged up on by this regiment of women. To make matters even worse—in his eyes— some of us females were black. Rhoda and Claudine were always in the kitchen, overhearing our every word as we duked it out at the dinner table. Like his straitlaced Edwardian parents before him, Daddy had a horror of the servants listening in on what the masters said; when he was a child, his father commanded his mother to *Stiegen fur die Schwartze*. Be quiet on account of the blacks. No sooner had Mother brought up the subject of the Thalhimer's boycott than Daddy would start to smolder. And then, one night, he burst into flame.

"Goddamn it, Evelyn!" He threw his napkin down on the table, his face quivering with rage. "Why in hell do they have to pick on us? Just tell me that! Why does it always have to be a Jew? Thalhimer's isn't the only department store in this city, you know. Miller and Rhoads is sitting right across the street. But I'll be damned if I've seen any pickets in front of *their* doors. Hell, no. And dear boy Webster Rhoads is more of a segregationist than Billy Thalhimer will ever be. So why don't they go after him? Hmm? Answer me that."

"Richard, I have no idea." Mother rolled her eyes to the ceiling. "As far as I'm concerned, they ought to boycott *both* stores. But you know and I know that Billy's being Jewish has nothing to do with this. Even if it did, so what? Because he, of all people, ought to do what's right. What's the point of being a Jew if you don't stand up for other oppressed people?"

"Oppressed, my ass! You think your precious Negroes would stick up for us if the tables were turned? Not on your life!"

I was squirming in my chair, waiting to dig the knife into the one wound of my father's I knew went deepest.

"That's not true, Daddy. When the temple in Atlanta was bombed, Dr. King was right there afterward, with Rabbi Rothschild. And anyway, it's not as if you're the expert on ethics, are you? I mean, what did you do when Mr. Thalhimer and his father were saving at least a few of the six million?"

My father's face began to tremble as if he had been slapped. He was drunk, and I knew he couldn't find the words to win this fight. Because there weren't any; I was right. Pure and simple. I knew he wouldn't hit me, because he never did, although he would have let Mary have it if she'd dared to insult him this way.

He rose unsteadily from his chair at the head of the table, looking down at Mother and Granny and me, we three harpies who had turned against him, who bit the hand that fed them, like faithless curs. There was no way to preserve what was left of his dignity except to stalk from the room.

Claudine took this opportunity to swing open the door from the kitchen and peer around it. "You all done, Miz Evelyn?"

Mother put her fingertips to her temples and rubbed them, managing a wry smile. "I suppose we are, Claudine. In more ways than one. Thank you for dinner. Everything was wonderful, as always."

$\mathcal{O}$

As RICHMOND'S RACIAL atmosphere heated up, there was a word I began to hear for people like us, white people who were for what was called *civil rights* and against what it seemed almost everyone else was for, which was something called *states' rights*. I knew exactly what *states' rights* meant; it was just a code phrase for segregation.

The word I was hearing—sometimes muttered, often shouted, as it was in the faces of the few righteous whites who joined the picket line at Thalhimer's—was the worst thing a white person could call another. No one had flung it in my face yet, and I did not know what I would do when that day came, because it was just a matter of time.

Nigger lover.

When I got called this, what would I do? Even though this word was a killing offense for everyone else, for me it made no sense. How could I be a *nigger lover* when the black people I loved weren't *niggers*?

But I wasn't going to have to wait very long before it was my turn to become that outlaw who loved what did not exist.

⌒

SO FAR, SIX years after the Supreme Court decision, my elementary school, Mary Munford, was still as lily-white as the portrait of Mary herself that hung in the school's front hall. She was a child in the painting, a little blonde thing wearing a white dress with a wide blue satin sash, looking smug and self-satisfied in that hateful First Family of Virginia way. I'd look up into her bland blue eyes and feel the way I used to about those Saint Catherine's girls my sisters grew up with, the debutantes I envied and hated and longed to be.

I traipsed down the hall with the rest of my classmates to our homeroom where Mrs. Smith presided, her portly, maternal body adorned by a different dress every day. I wondered if she still shopped at Thalhimer's like everyone else these days who wasn't black.

Sometimes, just before the final bell rang at ten past three, Mrs. Smith let us talk about what she called "current events." This meant the school crisis. The other kids would parrot what they heard at home from their parents, and what they said was disgusting to me.

Well, I'm not gonna sit next to one. Next thing you know, they'll want to marry us. If you think I'm gonna eat my lunch with them, you're crazy!

Hearing these things, I'd flush hotly and my skin would stick to the chair. I'd think of Rhoda and Deanie, their warm arms encircling me, their skin, their smell. *I'm not gonna sit next to one.* I'd been sitting next to "one" since the day I could climb into a chair. So what did this make me?

One day I swallowed hard and raised my hand.

"No one is talking about getting *married*," I said, with what I thought was just the right note of light humor. I'd honed my debating skills at the dinner table with my father, so I figured I could handle my peers. "This is about an equal right to a decent education. Don't you all believe everyone has that right?"

Silence. I was sitting next to a boy I had a serious crush on, one of those fierce grade-school passions where you love someone so much that you hope he'll knock you down when you're playing rough during recess, just because this would mean at least he had noticed you. That was how I felt about Jimmy Buford. I loved his little buzz-cut dirty-blond head, the tough-boy way he talked, and even his sunburned neck. His eleven-year-old whiff of sexuality. But I didn't love him enough to keep my mouth shut, even though I could just about *smell* the hostility coming off him, like the dreaded body odor we were never supposed to talk about.

"What this really comes down to," I went on, giddy with fear, "is whether you're for civil rights or states' rights. I'm for civil rights, and I think it's high time we obey what the Supreme Court says."

I felt a sharp pain in my left shin. Jimmy Buford had kicked me.

"*Nigger lover!*" he hissed.

Everyone heard him. The kids started to titter, thrilled at hearing the forbidden, fighting word. The one you punched and scratched and spat over, rolled in the dirt and ruined your clothes. Even if you were a girl. *Especially* if you were, because what the word meant for a girl was even worse. It meant you let niggers kiss you, and maybe even something else.

Jimmy's face creased into a grin of triumph. He had me now, and he knew it.

I broke out in a cold sweat like I did right before I puked.

Oh, God, I prayed silently, *please don't let me throw up in front of everyone. Please, please.*

"I'll tell you one thing," Jimmy went on, "if they let niggers into our schools, I ain't gonna let one of 'em sit next to *me!* No, sirree! Never ever in a million years."

All right, I said to myself. *Mrs. Smith isn't going to stand for any more of this. She's going to step in now, call you down but good, Jimmy Buford.*

But to my horror, she winked at him. One conspirator to another.

"I know just what you mean, Jimmy," she sighed sympathetically, shaking her head and smiling. "Some of them *do* smell to high heaven, don't they?"

The bell rang just at that moment, clanging above the din of jubilant laughter. The kids were vindicated; the teacher was on their side. I stumbled down the echoing stairwell, feeling filthy inside, as if someone had laid a dirty hand on my heart. My eyes were stinging with tears of mortification. Jimmy Buford had won. He'd gotten away with murder, soul murder. Mine. And I hadn't even known how to shut him up. I had just sat there, wordless, while everyone laughed.

There was no way I could face the woman who was carpooling that day. Mrs. Lichtenstein was a nervous wreck, she had a tic that made her blink and tremble, and I knew once she saw I'd been crying she'd drive me crazy with questions. I decided to walk home by myself. I had never done this before, it was strictly forbidden, and I knew it was going to land me in some serious trouble. But I didn't care. I would have to walk up Cary Street to Wilton Road, a distance of about a mile. Cary was always roaring with heavy traffic, trucks and buses, and it had no sidewalk or shoulder. I knew it was dangerous to walk there, but at the moment this prospect was a lot less scary than the thought of facing Mrs. Lichtenstein and a car full of laughing kids. All the ones in our car pool were Jewish, but that didn't make them different from the little gentile rednecks in my class. All of them had maids, and when I went to their houses I'd seen the way they acted with these women. The kids ordered them around like they were slaves.

Nigger lover, nigger lover, nigger lover. My feet pattered in time to the word as I lit out for Cary Street, running across the damp grass behind the school. Once I hit Cary I walked facing the oncoming traffic, so I could flatten myself against a wall or hedge when a big truck thundered my way. It took me a good hour and some to get home. By then, Mrs. Lichtenstein was so frantic that she'd been phoning our house every two minutes; Mother and Rhoda and Granny were just about hysterical. Rhoda was so upset that she threatened to switch me, right in front of Mother, who she knew disapproved of corporal punishment. But Rhoda was at her wits' end.

All three of them bent over me, talking at the same time. "What's wrong, honey?" Granny kept saying, over and over. "Why did you run away from Mrs. Lichtenstein?" Mother demanded. Rhoda just stood there, rooted to the ground, glaring at me with a mixture of incomprehension and wrath. I had never been a disobedient child, and she could not fathom what had gotten into me now. I couldn't say anything. How could I bring myself to say that word, the one Jimmy Buford had flung at me, tasting it in my mouth again like vomit and seeing the look on Rhoda's face when it came out?

"I just wanted to walk home, you all," I said. "Okay? It's not like I can't do that if I want to."

Baffled, they let me go, and I went up to my room. But just before supper, Mother came in. She made me tell her what had happened. I stammered my way through the story, crying, while she sat very still.

She was always acutely uncomfortable in the presence of strong emotion. All her children knew this, so we usually tried to hide ours, if and when it rose up. And she had never been one for touching, either, for comforting us with her body. For that, I knew to run to Rhoda or Claudine. Not since she had nursed me had Mother taken me in her arms. And she wasn't about to begin now.

"Now, let's not have any tears," she said. This was what she always said when one of us started to cry—the verbal equivalent of ice water thrown in your face. I wiped my eyes like the good little girl I was.

"I'm sorry," Mother said. "I'm sorry this had to happen. But you have to understand . . . " She sounded more like she was talking to herself than to me. "You have to forgive Mrs. Smith. She doesn't know any better. She's just a lady of the Old South."

eight

THEN, WHEN I was twelve, Rhoda retired. She left us. I was not consulted. Mother and she decided between the two of them that I did not need her any longer; I was old enough now to live without a nurse. As it turned out, Rhoda had met an elderly gentleman from Washington, Mr. Tuckson, and he wanted her to marry him and live there.

"I'll only be up the road," Rhoda told me. "And I'll come back to visit, I promise. I won't forget you. You'll be in my prayers every single day."

"But Rhodie," I said, weeping. "I can't see how things will be the same." I was trying very hard to share her happiness, to be glad that she had found a companion after so many years alone. But I wanted to believe that I had been enough for her, wanted for the love between us to have been so deep and true that she would not have needed anyone else. Now I realized that I had never filled the role in her life that she had filled so completely in mine.

"You'll be just fine, sugar," Rhoda said, her arms wrapped tight around me. "You're a big girl now and you don't need me anymore."

I cried all the harder. "I'll always need you. I won't ever get old enough not to."

But I was powerless against this greater need, this desire of an adult woman for the love of a man. I knew that Rhoda would leave me for Mr. Tuckson, no matter if I begged her to stay, and that I would not do.

She kept her house on Idlewood Avenue but rented it to people I did not know. I could not bear to gaze down Lady Street when Mother and I passed that corner as we drove downtown.

Mr. Tuckson died of a heart attack less than a year later. Rhoda came back to Richmond, to her house on Idlewood Avenue. I was overwhelmed by guilt—and relief, a combination of emotions that all but stunned me mute. Bitterly ashamed that I had let Rhoda go with anything but the purest gladness, I blamed myself for Mr. Tuckson's sudden death. But I was also secretly ecstatic that she was back in Richmond once again, and that I would not have to face life without her near. Her grief over losing her husband was painful for me to witness. I did my best to console her, and to conceal my joy that she was home.

NIGGER LOVER. INDEED, I was; my response to Rhoda's brief absence proved it. I loved her as my life, and now I knew it all too well; I could not imagine myself without her. Yet, I could not find the words for this love. Mother? Almost-Mother? More-Than-Mother? Unable to express these conflicted emotions—of loyalty to Rhoda coupled with betrayal of my "real" mother—I turned them outward, poured them into the one vessel I believed was deep enough to hold them. I took my own small, private anguish and joined it to the public sphere, to politics. This shift was reflexive, all but unconscious, and thus—like all unconscious emotions—it became all the more intense.

This was the moment when the burgeoning struggle for civil rights came to dominate the life of the South and the nation. It was a time when white people like us were finally able to "out" our passionate belief in equality; no longer did we feel like misfits, like pariahs. Now we could stand shoulder to shoulder with people of color, march alongside them, and lift our own voices in behalf of freedom.

I was still quite young so I wasn't able to join the Freedom Riders or the protesters who sat in at lunch counters across the South. But I had words, the weapon I'd always been taught could be as powerful as any, and I began writing letters to the Richmond newspapers in response to the vicious segregationist editorials they were pouring forth. My main target was James J. Kilpatrick, the editor of Richmond's evening paper, the *News Leader,* which was even more racist than the morning *Times-Dispatch.* The paper printed almost every letter I wrote, probably since I always took care to mention my age and the fact that I was white. I was hell-bent to let the world know that not all white people were devils.

Daddy said I shouldn't go sticking my neck out but Mother was proud of my letters. She saved them all, but somehow they were lost over the years, and the only one I still have is the letter I wrote just after the murders of three civil rights workers in Philadelphia, Mississippi, in the summer of 1964. Their deaths hit me with particular force because two of the young men, Michael Schwerner and Andrew Goodman, were Jews. They were driving on a lonely road with a black colleague, James Chaney, when their car was ambushed by Klansmen and they were killed. After their bodies were unearthed weeks later in a clay pit, I heard someone describe them as "two kikes and a nigger who should have known better."

The *News Leader* promptly ran a vicious editorial saying that the three young men had only gotten what they deserved, that their very presence in Mississippi was a threat to "law and order." That editorial enraged me, made me feel so helpless that when I sat down to answer it, sarcasm seemed like the only possible response.

It is heartwarming to see the South and its journalists so devoted to upholding "law and order." A fine promotion of this ideal has been shown in the past few months. We have certainly done a beautiful job of standing by complacently while law, order, freedom, democracy, and human dignity were trampled upon in Mississippi. Where was respect for law and order then? The law and order you seem to want to uphold is marked "White Only." This law and this era have gone; it is time to change and to move. The civil rights bill is a law. Let us uphold it.

Nigger lover. Jew-girl nigger lover. I knew these shoes fit, so I figured I might as well wear them. I was still a little too young to realize that singling myself out in this way was not an entirely selfless act; that maybe, just maybe, I wanted to distinguish myself for my beliefs because I had a huge chunk of my ego tied up in that. In some weird, warped way, being a pariah was deeply gratifying to me—even as I dreaded the consequences, which I knew would just be more of the loneliness and alienation I already felt.

I did not fully understand this until I was much older—in my forties—and when the awakening came, I was ashamed. Mother was then in her eighties and she and I were discussing her activism of earlier years. When I asked her why she had been willing to stand apart from the crowd, she thought for a moment and then said, "Well . . . I *wanted* to be different. I really liked being seen that way. There was a lot of ego in there, you know what I mean? It wasn't entirely about altruism."

I was shocked by this, but I admired Mother's honesty in confessing it. For the very first time, I realized that this secret egotism she and I shared was something African Americans recognized in many white people who joined the civil rights movement. And, suddenly, I could recognize it in myself as well; in the sarcastic, self-aggrandizing voice of that fourteen-year-old I had once been.

At that time, I had been feeling even more lonely for another reason: Not long before the grisly murders in Mississippi, I had lost

my grandmother. Granny died in March 1964, and Rhoda and
Claudine were with me for her passing. Once again, as always, I
turned to them for love, for comfort. They were as much a part of
me as Granny had been.

℘

GRANNY AND DEANIE had been in Richmond with me while
Mother and Daddy went to Cozumel. It hadn't become a tourist
destination yet and was still so undeveloped that there was only
one phone on the island.

Granny and Deanie and I had been having a nonstop party
since Mother and Daddy left. They were letting me eat whatever I
wanted; Granny pretty much dispensed with the idea of regular
meals and was subsisting on her favorite diet: Her drink was
Coca-Cola and her food—breakfast, lunch, or dinner—was two
slices of Wonder Bread with a dollop of ketchup squished in
between.

I was staying up way past my bedtime to watch the really frightening shows on television, *Alfred Hitchcock Presents* and *Boris
Karloff's Thriller,* both of which scared me so much that I couldn't
fall asleep unless Granny *and* Deanie were both in my room.

One gray afternoon, Granny was walking from the den out to
the porch when she slipped on the slate floor that Deanie had just
waxed. When she fell I heard a bone crack and I knew that this was
it, she wasn't going to be able to get up. I sat beside her on the
freezing stone floor, holding her bony, blue-veined hand while
Deanie phoned for the ambulance.

Granny was wearing the little wiglet she'd recently bought to
plump out her thinning hair, and it had slid askew when she fell.
Even in her pain, she let go of my hand long enough to try to get
it back in place.

"Sugar," she grimaced, "do me a favor, will you? Get this thing
on right for me." God bless the Last of the Red-Hot Mamas: I
knew she wanted to look her best when the men from the ambulance squad came.

Sometime between when they arrived and when they carried her on the stretcher from the house, she tugged that diamond and onyx ring I adored from her finger and pressed it into my hand.

"I want you to have this," she said. The pain was making it hard for her to talk. "You're the only girl in the family with hands pretty enough to carry it off."

And then we kissed each other goodbye.

She died two days later from pneumonia. She never regained consciousness after having lapsed into a coma in the hospital. She died before Mother and Daddy made it home. Deanie had been trying to reach them on Cozumel but couldn't get through in time. Mother was beside herself and she took it out on Mr. Bliley from the funeral home, who tried to get her to buy a fancy, expensive casket for Granny. Joseph Bliley, undertaker to the First Families of Virginia, was not accustomed to requests for plain pine boxes. Mother blew up at him—the first time I had ever seen her yell at someone and also cry.

"No, damn it!" she swore into the phone. "*You* listen to *me*, Joseph Bliley. I don't care what you think. My mother always said that what she wanted was a plain pine box, and by God, that's what I'm going to give her. So don't argue with me. If I had my way, I wouldn't have anything to do with you at all. I'd bury her right here in our garden."

My sister Mary came home for the funeral. She had gotten married two years before and was very pregnant with her first baby, the great-grandchild she had dreamed that Granny would live to see. But now, instead of placing a baby in Granny's arms, Mary would be the one to take Granny's favorite red velvet robe down to Bliley's for her to be buried in. She had donated her eyes to the blind and so the coffin would be closed. But Mary knew that Granny wouldn't want to go anywhere with her gorgeous hands looking less than perfect, so she took a bottle of *Cherries in the Snow* to Bliley's and did Granny's nails for the last time.

"She was so proud of her hands," Mary said to Mother, wiping her eyes.

"But none of that matters now," Mother answered.

"I know. But I want to go to Bliley's anyway just to make sure they don't put makeup on her, that awful crap they always do."

"Can I come with you?" I asked.

"Oh, sweetie." Mary shook her head. "I don't think you really want to."

The funeral was in our living room, with Granny's plain pine box resting on a couple of wooden sawhorses in front of the fireplace and chairs set up all around. I wandered through the house before the service, feeling useless, not knowing what to do. This was my first funeral and I could not fathom how all these people could be eating and drinking and even laughing when I thought they should be grieving quietly. Rhoda was crying, sitting in the kitchen with Claudine.

"Honey, why don't you go outside?" Rhoda said. "The camellias are blooming. Go around the back and pick some for your grandmother." Rhoda tried to smile. "She loved them so. They always were the first flowers to bloom in Wilmington, before anything else was out."

I wandered around out back for a while, waiting for Rabbi Goldburg to arrive. I stood under the holly tree where Daddy's dogs were buried, then picked my way through the azalea bushes to the hill behind the toolshed where he threw his empty whiskey bottles.

I heard cars pulling into our driveway, so I went to pick a handful of the pink and red camellias and returned to the house with my flowers, laying them gently on Granny's coffin. Jews don't have flowers at funerals, and the hot-pink blossoms stood out all the more against the dull black of everyone's clothes. I told myself that Granny would have loved this flash of bright color. I hoped her hands looked beautiful and so did she, in her red velvet robe inside that plain pine box.

Claudine sat through the funeral with tears streaming down her cheeks, sobbing unrestrainedly in her seat directly behind Mother, who kept turning around with an aggravated expression, making faces to get Deanie to hush. But Deanie wasn't about to stop crying. She'd come to say goodbye to a lady she had loved and she was going to weep and weep plenty.

I was sitting between her and Rhoda, who was crying quietly. I knew she was diving deep into her memories, forty years' worth of them. She and Granny, threading in and out of each other's lives, from Wilmington to Richmond, then to New York City. All of that gone forever now. Deanie dried her eyes and began to pray in a low, soft voice, so Rabbi Goldburg did not hear. "Oh, Lord," she whispered. "Take Miz Alice home now, please. Make a place for her, and tell her we'll be comin', too, one of these days."

"Amen," I whispered back, squeezing Deanie's hand.

She and I and Rhoda and Mary rode together in one of Bliley's black sedans to the cemetery downtown. We drove down Broad Street, past the railroad station; I thought about how my feet would never again race ahead of Mother and Rhoda to the platform where Granny's train was rolling in. We turned left onto Second Street, the heart of Richmond's oldest black neighborhood, Jackson Ward. Most of the stores and hotels and the old movie theater were boarded up now that integration had made them unnecessary. Three winos sat on a stoop in the pale March sun, drinking out of bottles inside paper bags.

Deanie looked out the car window at the green of the Hebrew Cemetery as we drew up alongside its wrought-iron fence. I could see Granny's open grave and the mounded-up earth beside it.

"There ain't ever gonna be anyone like your grandmother," Deanie said. "After God made her, he broke the mold. The thing was, she didn't care what color you were. She knew we're all the same, underneath our skins."

the *poison~flea~collar heiress*
and the *rastas on tory row*

nine

RHODA WAS NOW a widow for the second time. She had lost her first husband, Willie Lloyd, the love of her life, long ago. Now the man she had hoped to grow old with had died on her as well. Fortunately, however, she was able to live comfortably on her Social Security and Mother kept helping to support her as well. Rhoda continued to come to our house to visit, although these occasions were painful for me, on account of her refusal to relinquish what she perceived as her "place" with respect to our family. Despite the changes sweeping across the South, Rhoda clung steadfastly to the old ways.

As soon as she arrived at our house, she went up to the maid's room and changed her clothes. Her white uniform was still hanging in the closet and she donned it along with the pinafore apron with safety pins stuck into the bosom. Then she came down to the kitchen to help Claudine. When supper time rolled around, I'd always ask her to sit at the table with Mother and Daddy and me. She'd politely decline.

"Thank you all the same," she would say. "But I think I'll just stay in here, with Deanie." She never added "where I belong," but she didn't have to. I understood.

Sometimes I wished that I was as sure of *my* place as Rhoda seemed to be of hers. Or Mother—she was comfortable switching from one role to another. One side of her was Lady Bountiful, a liberal with the best political instincts who gave of her time (and of my father's money) to one good cause after another. But her other side was treacherous and thoroughly unpredictable: She could morph in the twinkling of an eye into a petulant, spoiled woman, the wife of a wealthy man who essentially "kept" her as if she were his mistress.

This was the side of my mother against which I had no defense. As a child, with Rhoda as my buffer, I had been able to dodge it, most of the time. I'd seek and find my strength in Rhoda's love. But now that I was emerging from the chrysalis of childhood, my mother's competitiveness with me, her youngest daughter, came out in the open. To her—dissatisfied as she was with her life and grievously disappointed in her marriage—my budding sexuality and dreams for the future only served to remind her of the dreams she herself had given up.

The ground began to tremble beneath our feet, or so it seemed to me. She tried to enlist me in her undeclared war against my father, a conspiracy that for a while I tried to join. But in the end, I couldn't; I loved him too much, even though I could see his weaknesses. And I'd begun to recognize how like him I was. He wasn't as quick with words or as in love with books as I, but we were cut from the same emotional cloth. Both of us were as sentimental and undefended as Mother was devious, thwarted, and given to sudden betrayals that could stun me like a slap.

The one that sent me reeling, laid bare the unspoken resentment between us, came the year after Granny died and Rhoda had retired—a time when I was all the more vulnerable. I think Mother knew this, and that was why she chose that moment to strike.

IT IS APRIL. Mother and Daddy have been invited to a fancy wedding, an evening affair at an Episcopal church. The reception afterward will be at that citadel of the gentile aristocracy, the Country Club of Virginia.

"Why don't you come with me to Montaldo's?" Mother offers, thinking this will make me feel included. "Help me pick out an evening dress."

Mother has her own favorite saleslady there, Miss Sandy, whom all her best clients affectionately call by her last name. Sandy is waiting for us, in the little atelier where the evening gowns are. Mother is already dressed beautifully in a tweed skirt and cashmere sweater, a bright silk scarf knotted around her throat. There is no way I can even hope to compete with her chic good looks. I'm a good twenty pounds overweight now and loathe my body. Mother is forcing me to acquire the social graces by attending a Jewish cotillion that meets every Saturday night at the tackiest possible location, the Executive Motor Hotel on West Broad. I spend as much of the evening as I dare holed up in the ladies' room, in a stall with my feet pulled up onto the toilet so that the chaperone can't see me if she comes in. Hiding, just as I used to do when I'd secretly devour those candy bars Rosa brought me at our club. I am mindful of my weekly ordeal at the "motor hotel" as I imagine my mother buying a splendid ball gown and wearing it to a glittering reception at the Country Club of Virginia. This is not a happy comparison.

Today I am wearing a hand-me-down that belonged to Mary, a wool kilt she had when she and Susan were at Saint Catherine's. I have to pin the waistband because I can't button it. The mirrors at Montaldo's throw my reflection back at me, an endless series of retreating images. Not one of them is pleasing to my eyes.

"My!" Sandy exclaims. "Isn't Laurie growing up to be a beauty, just like Mama!" Hers is the patented insincerity of southern women. She pronounces it "Ma*Mah,*" with the accent on the last syllable. I grimace, trying to smile. Miss Sandy produces a tiny gold-painted bamboo chair for me to perch on while she starts opening one mirrored case after another and taking out exquisite gowns of silk and chiffon for Mother to try on.

In an agony of jealousy, I watch while Mother undresses, down to the Merry Widow waist cincher she has worn for the occasion. Her figure is all but perfect—she has kept it even after four children—and only her slightly flabby upper arms betray her fifty-three years. She tries on one gown after another, each more beautiful than the one before, and asks me what I think. I sit in sullen silence while Miss Sandy prattles on, announcing the advantages of this gown or that.

Finally, when I can't stand it anymore, I mutter something under my breath.

"What did you say?" Mother asks.

I have never dared to confront her about anything. But now, I summon all my nerve. "I said, 'This is disgusting.' This whole thing. It's just *disgusting.*"

Luckily, Miss Sandy is momentarily out of earshot. "What on earth are you talking about?" Mother demands.

"*You,*" I say. "Buying this outrageously expensive dress that you're going to wear all of once! Spending all this money, just to go to some stupid society wedding."

Mother's face darkens to a plum red. And then she says the one thing that no one, but no one, in our family ever does. It's one of those coarse, ill-bred expressions that we simply do not use.

"*Shut up,*" she hisses in a stage whisper, so Miss Sandy will not hear. "I've had just about enough from you."

Miss Sandy reappears, trailing a gown of hyacinth blue chiffon and a silk peau de soie stole in a lush shade of cerise. Mother's eyes light up.

"Oh, Sandy!" she breathes. "This is the one. It's simply *divine.*"

Miss Sandy beams. "Isn't it just? And I brought the stole because

I know even though it's April, it'll be chilly out there on the terrace at the club."

The dress needs to be shortened an inch or two, so we leave Montaldo's with only the stole, wrapped in many leaves of snowy white tissue paper and folded lovingly—by one of the store's black women, who only work behind the wrap desk or as maids—in a pale gray-and-white-striped bag. Mother and I drive home in silence.

She asks Rhoda to come to our house and stay with me on the night of the wedding. Mother does not think I am old enough to stay home by myself. A few months ago when my brother, Dickie, was home from the special school he attends now, she asked him to babysit me, and the minute Mother and Daddy drove off up Wilton Road, Dickie took a flashlight and started in on one of his sadistic games. He sneaked from one window to another outside, his face suddenly springing from the darkness lit up like a monster by the flashlight, while he moaned and shrieked like a ghoul. After I'd screamed in vain for him to stop, I gave up and fled from the house. I hid behind a low stone wall halfway up Wilton Road and didn't come out till I saw Mother and Daddy come home. It was way after midnight by then and I was freezing cold.

That was the end of Dickie's babysitting career.

On the night of this wedding, Rhoda's presence has catapulted me back to my childhood, and so I am both grateful and furious; part of me wishes I was Rhoda's "baby" again, could slip into my bed and wait for her to bring me "our party," the love feast she used to indulge me in. Yet the prison of fat I'm caged in these days is a direct legacy of those bedtime orgies, and I know it.

Mother wants Rhoda to take pictures of her and Daddy in the living room before they leave. He's wearing white tie and tails, a rare occasion. I try to hide in my room but Rhoda won't have it.

"What on earth is ailing you, child? You come downstairs this minute!" she commands. "You have to see how fine your mother and daddy look."

They're in the living room, having their first drink of the night. There's a Marlboro of Mother's burning in the ashtray on the coffee table next to a full tumbler of Scotch. Daddy is standing beside her, looking sort of baffled in his finery, as if he doesn't quite know what to do. Mother ignores him as she pulls on her long white kid gloves. When she gets to the second one, she can't do up the pearl buttons with her already gloved hand, so I step forward to help her.

We are standing close as lovers, our faces only a few inches apart. But somehow we manage not to look at one another. I am staring down in the vicinity of her shoulder and she is looking at her glove, smoothing out the soft white kid. Her face is heavily powdered, a mask. She doesn't seem happy with herself.

Rhoda snaps the picture at just this instant. There I am with Mother, the two us of frozen in our tableau. The fat, sad-eyed, docile daughter, playing lady-in-waiting to her mother, the queen.

☙

NOT LONG AFTER that fancy wedding, Mother and Daddy and I took a trip to New England, to visit Mary and her new husband. They were living in Concord, New Hampshire, in a tiny, romantic *La Bohème*-like garret of a flat, above a bookstore called the Apple Tree. The five of us piled into the car one morning and drove down to Cambridge, to see Harvard.

It was one of those fiery, lambent autumn days, the golden New England light filtering down through the turning trees. We entered Harvard Yard through one of its wrought-iron gates and I was hit with a pang of longing so intense that it felt like hunger. I saw these young people, not much older than me, walking around in what looked to me like splendor, carrying bulging notebooks and green canvas book bags, whispering and laughing and calling out to one another. The boys wore faded blue jeans and well-worn tweeds; the girls all looked to me like Mary's record-album pictures of Joan Baez, severe beauties with pale faces and long, straight hair. The way they walked made me think of giraffes; they stalked and ambled and still managed to appear so wonderfully serious, purposeful, intent.

I wanted to be one of them, to dwell in this little kingdom consecrated to the life of the mind.

My brother-in-law mentioned that Harvard had a college for women that was called Radcliffe. I thought I had never before heard such a lovely name.

"I'm going to come here!" I announced. "I'm going to be a Radcliffe girl." Mother didn't say a word. Not then.

When we returned to Richmond, I sent away for a catalogue and an application, even though I was only a sophomore. My grades were excellent in everything but math, but who cared about that when I was soaring through advanced-placement classes in English and history and French? Strangely, though, Mother kept talking me down, saying I should only aim for second-string schools like Boston University and Colby and Clark, places I had no interest in whatsoever. When I asked her why, she let me have it.

"Darling," she said, in her all-too-familiar "Now-let's-not-have-any-tears" voice. "I'm sorry to have to say this. But I just don't think you're Radcliffe material."

All the breath left my lungs, like it had on that day years before when Deanie socked it to me about Negroes and Jews. I was so shocked that I could not even feel the rage that should have risen in my throat. I was stunned into silence. What was there to say? Not only was she my mother, she was only a couple of courses shy of earning her master's degree in clinical psychology and her specialty was guidance counseling; she had read every issue of *Lovejoy's College Guide* for the past ten years. She could recite statistics about student bodies and admissions at the drop of a hat. So when she told me I simply wasn't Radcliffe material, I figured she had to know whereof she spoke.

The word that really nailed me was the last one: *material*. Like I was just an inferior scrap of cloth.

℘

CLAUDINE WAS STILL working for us but her health was getting steadily worse. She had diabetes and high blood pressure—"the

sugar" and "the pressure," as she called them—twin afflictions that
brought her low. I would go into the kitchen to find her scrunched
down at the table, rubbing her eyes with their deep, dark circles
underneath, trying to ease the throbbing in her head.

She said the pressure got worse if she'd had a fight with her
boyfriend. They were always having spats. "I know I'm not easy to
live with," Deanie said to me one scalding summer afternoon. "The
only man I ever really and truly loved, I ran him off. Just by bein'
mean."

"Who was he?"

"Oh, someone I married when I wasn't much more than a girl.
I was living in New York City then, kickin' up my heels."

Deanie meant this literally: She'd danced—"for about a
minute," as she put it—in a Harlem chorus line behind the legendary Richmond-born jazzman, Bill "Bojangles" Robinson. She
called him by his first name and said how nice to her he was, a perfect gentleman, even though it was evident that Deanie wasn't
going to make it as a dancer. "I just didn't have the legs for it," she
said. "Those chorus girls were nothin' *but* legs, and bosoms. I was
way too short and stubby. Just loved to dance, was all."

"What was your husband like?" I asked her now.

"He was a West Indian, name of Jack Dawkins. Big, strapping
guy, worked on the docks. He was so crazy about me I thought
there wasn't anything I couldn't get by with. So I teased him. I
made him jealous, went out with other men. I jes' pushed him and
pushed him till one night he went crazy. Took his things and left
me and never came back."

"That's so sad, Deanie. Didn't you ever see him again?"

"Oh, yeah! He took up with my best friend, June. And they got
along so good together that they married after a while."

"I think I'd go insane if someone I loved married my best
friend," I said.

"Funny enough, though, I didn't mind. I was glad the two of
them had each other, 'cause I loved them both. They had a baby
girl and they made me godmother to that child."

As it turned out, this was to be our last heart-to-heart at the kitchen table. Because Deanie's health had gotten so bad, Mother "let her go" soon after. But she stayed in our lives because Rhoda invited Deanie to share her house on Idlewood Avenue; Rhoda's sister had died by then and so she had an empty room upstairs. No two women could have been less alike—Rhoda with her churchgoing religiosity and Deanie with her freewheeling spirit—but they got on well together.

"I'm over to my boyfriend's place as much as I can be anyway," Deanie told me. "And when I'm at Rhoda's, we just stay out of each other's hair."

$$\backsim$$

I COULD NOT have predicted the train of events that Claudine's departure set in motion. Her leaving seemed to be just one of those routine happenings in the black-and-white domestic arrangements of the South: A cook has to retire because of old age or ill health and someone takes her place.

But we were not your average white family and the woman who took Claudine's place was not a "someone." Her name was Elizabeth Harris, and she was the sister of Theodore Jefferson, my father's yardman and (by this time) as close to being his friend as was possible, given the Jim Crow rules by which we lived.

Elizabeth Harris—she called herself "Lizzie," so we did, too—lived about an hour away in Ashland, as did her brother. She was built like a small barrel, with a wide torso perched on skinny legs. Her laugh was infectious, a slightly manic cackle, and she laughed often because she was almost always at least a little bit drunk. When she was cooking she'd often forget to use a pot holder and just grab things straight from the oven or the stove. So her hands and arms were covered with scars from hot pans and popping grease. She'd rub butter into the burns.

"Lizzie, let me put some ice on it," I'd say. "It'll take the heat out faster."

"Nope. Thank you all the same, honey. I likes to use butter."

◯

SHE DRANK DESPITE her diabetes and gave herself a shot of insulin every day, sitting at the kitchen table. She'd hike up the skirt of her white uniform to reveal legs that were as badly scarred as her arms, then plunge the needle in anywhere. I would watch in horrified fascination.

"Doesn't it hurt?" I would ask her.

"Oh, not too bad." Then she'd duck into the pantry for a nip.

Mother begged Lizzie to stop drinking, fearing that the combination of alcohol and diabetes would send her into a coma.

"I knows it, Miz Gun," Lizzie would answer, solemnly—she never bothered with the last two letters of our name—"I do. But I only takes a little every now and then."

One afternoon, Mother came into the living room to find Lizzie sunk deep in the cushions of the couch, her feet propped up on the seventeenth-century French dough-warming trough that Mother had recently bought as a coffee table. Lizzie had a bottle in her lap.

"Lizzie!" Mother exclaimed—somewhat disingenuously, since it was pretty clear—"What *are* you doing?"

Lizzie looked up at Mother with her wonderful, cheek-dimpling smile and said, "I was just takin' a little break, Miz Gun. Matter of fact, I was sort of pretending I was *you!*"

◯

LIZZIE'S BROTHER THEODORE was a heavy drinker, too, and soon he and Daddy were becoming confidants around the whole issue of alcohol and the mess it made in both their lives. You might think that because my father was rich and Theodore was poor, the similarity in their alcoholism ended there. But you'd be wrong. Both of them had a tribe of female enablers—wives and daughters—and both of them wrought havoc in their women's lives with the grief that alcohol engendered.

My father had begun to cut back on his own drinking by then, forgoing the hard stuff he used to nip at throughout the day in favor of a few glasses of champagne in the late afternoon. He therefore felt himself to be in a position to offer Theodore some help. Together in the garden, raking and hoeing or scooping the poop from the sandy soil in the dog run, Daddy and Theodore struck up their own version of an Alcoholics Anonymous sponsor relationship, even though the two of them never exactly found complete sobriety.

One afternoon, Theodore told my father about his youngest daughter, of whom he was very proud. Her name was Carrie. She was only eight but already reading books way beyond her age. Lizzie had suggested that maybe my mother would like to meet Carrie; might Theodore bring her by some evening, after work?

℘

THE SUMMER NIGHT when Carrie came to visit us for the first time was so hot that Mother asked Lizzie not to cook; we'd all get takeout from Bill's Barbecue instead. My sister Mary was home with her three-year-old daughter, Caerthan, who was splashing in the pool while Rhoda watched over her. Rhoda was sixty-eight. Caerthan was the fifth generation of my family she had lived to see.

Mary and I drove to Bill's and brought the barbecue home, greasy paper bags with sweet-smelling shredded pork and hot sauce. We grown-ups sat in the dining room; Caerthan refused to leave Lizzie and Rhoda even for a moment, so she ate in the kitchen with them.

Waiting for Carrie, I was nervous as a cat. I had a feeling that she was going to be different from the other black children I played with when I was young. From what Lizzie had said about her niece, I knew she was whip-smart and I had a feeling it would be love at first sight between her and Mother. Carrie was still young enough not to be a threat, like I was becoming, and she was black, which meant that all my mother's best liberal instincts were going to be out in full force.

There was also the fact that I was never at ease with children. I'd always been the baby of the family and had spent most of my life around adults. I didn't know how to talk to kids, how to *be* with them. They'd chatter away, expecting me to join in, but I'd quickly become flustered, embarrassed by their silly-sounding patter, and not know what to say. I was sure the same thing would happen tonight.

After we'd finished the barbecue sandwiches, Mary tilted her chair backward like she always used to do, except that now she was too grownup and my father was too mellow for the two of them to get into a fight. She was just lighting up her after-dinner Marlboro when we heard the soft hydraulic *whoosh* of the door opening from the garage.

"Come on in, Theodore," Mother called out. "We're in the dining room." She knew he would not venture beyond the kitchen unless asked. I glanced through the open door and saw Lizzie hugging her niece, whispering what I knew were words of encouragement, plumping up the big pink bow on what I knew had to be Carrie's very best dress. My heart gave a sudden lurch. If I was nervous, I could only imagine the way she must be feeling, entering this unfamiliar house with all these white people waiting.

Theodore stepped haltingly into the dining room, gently propelling his daughter ahead of him, his big, work-roughened hands resting on her small shoulders. Carrie was a dead ringer for her aunt, except that her skin was a darker brown. But she had Lizzie's turned-up nose and apple cheeks. When she smiled at us, I noticed the little gap between her two front teeth.

"Evenin', everyone," Theodore murmured. "Mister and Miz Gunst, this here's my daughter, Carrie. Carrie, that's Mary and Laurie over there."

"Would you like some ice cream, sweetheart?" Mother asked.

Carrie glanced up at her father.

"That would be fine, Miz Gunst," Theodore said. "Thank you kindly."

Carrie was so poised that she didn't have to be prompted. "Thank you," she said.

"You're welcome!" Mother beamed, already besotted. I could tell.

Lizzie brought the ice cream in a crystal dish with a silver spoon. Carrie sat next to Mother, who began asking her about school, did she like Ashland, what were her favorite things to do? Carrie did not duck her head or cast her eyes down; she answered all these questions with the composure of a girl twice her age. But every now and then, her glance would wander from the table to the hall with its carpeted steps disappearing up into the shadowed upstairs, then out through the living-room windows to the pool where Caerthan was splashing in the glittering turquoise water while Rhoda stood guard. Her eyes did not widen in wonder, and neither did her expression betray what she was thinking. She just smiled secretly to herself.

◎

CARRIE SOON BECAME a regular visitor to our house; she came with Lizzie or Theodore on the weekends and spent the day with Mother. They went to Bill's Barbecue for lunch and then to a movie or to the Virginia Museum, which had just installed a new Egyptian exhibit with a mummy. It lay swathed in linen in a replica of a grave, surrounded by shards of pottery, and you looked down into this pit from above. The lighting in the grave was an eerie blue-green, and if you stared long enough, you could scare yourself silly imagining that the mummy was about to revive.

The Egyptian room was one of Carrie's favorite spots. The other was the downtown branch of the Richmond library, where Mother took her to get a card of her own. One rainy Saturday morning, Mother suggested that I sort through my own children's books and put them in a box for Carrie. I was happy doing this, thinking of the worlds these books would open to her. I piled up the ones about distant countries and famous people. I put in the Nancy Drew mysteries, even though I knew they were a bit "old" for Carrie to read just yet, but she'd get around to them pretty soon.

I came to the biography that had been my favorite book when I was a child, the one Mother had given me about George Washington Carver. I had not glanced at it for years, but now I opened it to the page with the picture of George and his mother being kidnapped by night riders from their cabin in the pines. I stared at it, long and hard: George's mother on a rearing horse with her hands thrown up in supplication, asking for mercy from those who had none. And the tiny baby being hoisted into the arms of a waiting Klansman.

I knew the picture would frighten Carrie, would haunt her worse than it had me. "She's still a little young for this," I said to myself, and decided not to give her the book. But that was not the only reason why. I couldn't part with it. At this time when the cord between Mother and me was unraveling, this book she had given me half my life ago had become a treasure to me.

I slid the book back onto the shelf.

As I WATCHED Mother adopt Carrie as a daughter in all but name, I tried not to feel jealous. Perhaps this was because I would have been ashamed to acknowledge such selfishness in myself toward a child of color who was so very gifted. But it was also because I had learned all too well to quash my unacceptable emotions; if I revealed them, I knew my mother would love me less.

I watched the unfolding relationship between Mother and Carrie from a distance. I knew that I did not belong here; there was something between these two that excluded me. I felt an odd empathy with Carrie's own mother, Dorothy, who came to our house every now and then to see my mother and to talk. Everyone in her family called her Dot. She was a Gypsy-beautiful woman with straight inky hair and brilliant eyes; she was half-white and could easily have passed. Dot would sit with Mother by the pool while Carrie and Caerthan played together in the shallows and the two women talked across the divide of race and class. Mother was full of herself, having earned a degree in clinical psychology, and she threw fancy words around like a professor. Dot would listen politely and not say much in return. She worked the night shift at a shirt factory in Ashland, and was exhausted by that and by the strain of living with an alcoholic husband who was often violent.

When Carrie came in from the pool, I'd offer her a choice of bathrooms where she could change out of her wet suit. I knew from Lizzie that Carrie often spent the night at her grandmother's house, down the road from Dot's, and that Grandma Carrie had no running water. She had an outhouse in her yard.

In response to my offer of bathrooms, Carrie would smile, revealing that little gap between her two front teeth. Then she'd give my arm a small pat. "Don't worry," she would say. "I'll just use the one off the den."

◎

SEVERAL YEARS LATER, when I was about to graduate from high school, I was accepted at Boston University and decided to go there. Since Mother had told me I wasn't Radcliffe material, I hadn't even bothered to apply. But I still wanted to be in Boston; I thought that just being across the river from Harvard would allow me to bask in its reflected glory.

Carrie was twelve and had never been off the honor roll at school. One night, when Mary was visiting, she and Carrie were sitting in the bedroom Mary used when she came home. They were close in a way that Carrie and I were not; Carrie was old enough to help take care of Mary's children—her second daughter, Maia, was born in 1968—and on the weekends Carrie came to our house with Lizzie to earn extra money babysitting. She and Mary had a bond that was almost physical, an ease with each other that I could only envy.

That night, the two of them were in the bedroom talking while Carrie brushed Mary's hair. As Carrie described the scene years later, when she and I had become friends and were beginning to be able to laugh about such moments, "Girlfriend, it was like *befo' the war,* as we say. There I was, the little black girl, brushing the white lady's long, silky hair. I was standing by the bed, behind her, and she started telling me about how she dropped out of college in her second year, I think it was, to run away and get married. Well, I got so mad I thought I was going to hit her upside the head with that hairbrush!"

Carrie shook her head and the two of us laughed. "I mean, here she was, talking about how she'd had this unbelievable chance and just thrown it away. *College!* Lord have mercy! No one in my family had been able to stay in school past the eighth grade. They all had to go to work. I knew I wasn't supposed to let my anger show, but Mary must have sensed it, because she turned around and gave me a good, long look. And what she said then just about blew me away."

My sister told Carrie that if she wanted to go to college, Mary thought that Mother and Daddy would pay her way. That remark was the turning point of Carrie's life. Later that night, my sister spoke to Mother. Several weeks later, as Carrie stood by the stove poaching an egg for Mother's breakfast, Mother said, "Carrie, I've talked with Mr. Gunst. And he and I would be thrilled to pay your tuition and all expenses at whatever college you decide to attend."

When Carrie told me her remembrance of this moment, she still could not speak of it without tears springing to her eyes. She spread her arms wide, like a black preacher might, and intoned, "*De Lawd* done sent me to college!"

Both of us were crying and laughing at once. "Thrilled!" Carrie grinned, dabbing at her eyes. "Can't you just hear her? That was Evelyn, for sure."

@

AT THE TIME this wonderful event took place, however, I could scarcely bring myself to share Carrie's joy, her anticipation of a bright career. At eighteen, about to graduate and go off to a college I did not even want to attend, all I could think about was the abandonment of my own Radcliffe dreams, set against my mother's extravagant offer to Carrie of any college she desired.

One afternoon just before I left for Boston, Carrie and I were sitting in the kitchen, shelling black-eyed peas while Lizzie stewed tomatoes at the stove.

"Have you thought about schools?" I ventured. "Where you'll go?"

"I don't know just yet," Carrie answered. "I'm considering Hampton." Hampton is one of Virginia's oldest historically black colleges, founded in 1869.

"How come?" I asked. "Is there something you especially like about it?"

"Well," Carrie answered, "it's just an excellent school. And I've always heard people speak so highly of Hampton. We call it 'the Harvard for black folks.'"

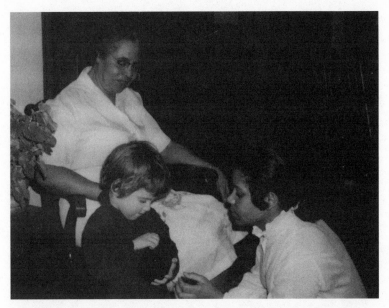

Carrie Jefferson, at eighteen, with Rhoda and my sister Mary's daughter, Maia.

Carrie, wearing her senior prom gown.

ten

M Y MOTHER'S OFFER of college to Carrie brought her into the circle of our family, engendering a closeness between her and Mother that would endure till Mother's death, and beyond. But it would take many years for Carrie and me to become the friends we were destined to be.

Mother's gesture sprang from her soul, her individual being. But over the years I've also come to perceive it as a part of the tradition Jews call *tikkun olam,* meaning "to rebuild the world"—one life at a time. I know that Mother's gift to Carrie was a way that she could make something good happen where so much evil had thrived for so very long. Even though my father had generous instincts, he did not feel the South's racial injustice as deeply as Mother did; neither did he believe that it was his responsibility to do whatever he could to alleviate it. Yet, he was the one who provided the money for Carrie's education, and this was made possible by a windfall from the family business he and his elder brother,

Edward, owned. Carrie Jefferson's was not the only life that would be transformed by it.

I can trace the beginnings of this rise in our family fortunes back to 1916, when Prohibition forced my grandfather, Emmanuel Gunst, to shut down his very profitable whiskey distillery in Richmond. Straus, Gunst & Company had been making whiskey since 1879, when Emmanuel's father, Henry Gunst, founded the firm, and it broke Emmanuel's heart to close it down. But of course he had no choice. A few years later, he bought from a friend of his, a drugstore owner named Polk Miller, a sideline in dog-care products that Miller had just started developing. Miller had named it after his favorite bird dog, a black-and-white English setter named Sergeant, and when Emmanuel purchased it, he kept the name and the logo of the setter's elegant head superimposed on a sergeant's chevron. At first, Sergeant's only manufactured a few items—cough syrup, mange medicine, a powder to rid dogs of fleas and lice. But it also made dog biscuits, and in 1928 Virginia's own Admiral Evelyn Byrd provisioned the sled dogs he took with him to the South Pole with Sergeant's biscuits. Emmanuel and Daddy and Edward posed for publicity photographs with Admiral Byrd, and for the first time Sergeant's began to acquire what advertisers nowadays call "name-brand recognition."

Daddy and Edward took over the company after Emmanuel died in 1939 and built it up from there. Daddy got his first bird dog around that time, from a young University of Virginia friend of his who'd been in the parlor of a popular Charlottesville whorehouse run by a madam named Miss Mattie when a client came in and mentioned, in passing, that he had a very fine bird dog he was going to have to put down. Reason being, times were just too hard and he couldn't afford to feed the dog. Daddy's friend thought to himself that times couldn't be that hard, if this man could afford Miss Mattie's, but what he ended up saying was, "I'll take your dog." He knew he couldn't keep the dog in his room on the Lawn, the historic row of dwellings that Thomas Jefferson had designed for the university's first students. My father adopted the dog and named him Major.

Major was the first in a line of English setters that continued until my father's death, sixty-odd years later. Once you have a setter, you have to start to hunt—that is, if you have the proper respect for what these dogs are bred to do. It wasn't long before my father's delight in the outdoors and the beauty of open land, the pleasure he found in being with country people, led him into the field.

❧

AFTER HE TURNED into a "bird-dog man," as my father's hunting cronies called him, Sergeant's became infinitely more to him than a mere place of work. It was his identity, his link to all the things about the South and about his own character that he cherished.

It was almost the same for me, as a child growing up. I used to go with him all the time to "the plant," as we called the building where Sergeant's was housed. I loved visiting the women who worked on the assembly line, watching them operate the shining steel machinery as it filled brown bottles with one medicine or another, dropped transparent capsules into cellophane packets that in turn went into boxes with the Sergeant's logo on them. I glowed with pride when I went into a drugstore and saw these products on the shelves, knowing that my father and my uncle made them.

❧

THE WINDFALL THAT changed our lives came in 1964, when I was fifteen. Sergeant's invented the first collar for ridding a dog of ticks and fleas. This little strip of insecticide-laced plastic was christened the Sentry Flea Collar, and it turned Sergeant's—almost overnight—from a good but small family-run business into a front-runner. The profits from that collar catapulted us from being "comfortable" (the modest word my parents had taught us to use) to being millionaires.

I was slow in waking up to what the flea collar meant for us; I don't think I really wanted to go there. I just wanted to be normal— whatever that was—a teenage girl in my second year of high school, not some rich kid everyone secretly envied and loathed. Outwardly, not much changed; we didn't go on an orgy of acquisition. But nevertheless, tectonic plates were shifting somewhere down there in our underground lives.

My elder sister, Susan, had a crack-up in the winter of her first year at the Cranbrook Academy of Fine Arts. Not that this was in any way related to the advent of the flea collar, but the two events occurred at about the same time and thus are bound together in my memory. Susan blamed Daddy for her breakdown.

"He's *dumb*," Susan muttered to me, when Mother took me to visit her in the mental wing of the University of Virginia hospital, where Susan was taken when she became suicidal. "He's got weak genes, and I inherited them. That's why I'm in this mess. You probably have them, too."

Susan pretty much quit speaking to Mother and Daddy; the only ones in the family she didn't turn against were me and my brother. Dickie was living in Richmond by then and doing really well, studying photography and painting and living on his own, and he was wonderful with Susan, kind and empathetic. But when she came out of the hospital, it was me she turned to for companionship—she had no friends in Richmond—and so I became my sister's keeper. Oddly, I began to dress the part. I took to wearing a navy blue nurse's cape I'd found in a thrift shop and to pulling my long dark hair into a tight chignon at the back of my neck. At fifteen, I grew much too fast into the role scripted for me by fate. The youngest child, rescuer of my shipwrecked elder sibling.

Mother responded to Susan's collapse by going into analysis with a pudgy, pink-cheeked, gray-eyed psychiatrist in Charlottesville. Soon, she was infatuated. Dr. Congdon and his German wife started coming to our house for supper now and then; he would regale us with stories about running into William Faulkner at the university—Faulkner was writer-in-residence at the time—and Rue, the German wife, would play a little Mozart on Mother's Steinway baby grand. So cultivated, so cultured. Daddy called her "Rue the day" and couldn't abide Dr. Congdon, whom he thought was nothing but a charlatan. This turned out to be true; years later, Congdon was disbarred for sleeping with his female patients.

Despite these black-comedy interludes, Mother's unhappiness with Daddy was no joke. She took to jibing at him all the time, mocking him for his dull-witted hunting friends and his lack of interest in the life of the mind. She read constantly, as always, and her book of the moment was Rachel Carson's *Silent Spring,* a passionate screed against the use of pesticides that all but launched the environmental movement. Mother knew that the main ingredient of the Sentry flea collar was a deadly insecticide named Vapona, invented by Shell Chemical. When Daddy's brother, Edward, and Edward's frosty wife, Virginia, came to our house for dinner, Mother and Edward got into heated arguments about Vapona, *Silent Spring,* and what insecticides were doing to poison the earth.

"Never mind, Evelyn," Edward would say witheringly. "Just keep nibbling on that filet mignon, and Richard and I will forgive your pinko tendency to bite the hand that feeds you."

℘

WITHIN A COUPLE of years after the advent of the poison flea collar, the big pharmaceutical firms—Squibb and Upjohn, Eli Lilly and A. H. Robins—came knocking with offers to buy Sergeant's. In the end, Richmond-based Robins was the one to whom it was sold. The price was a little over sixteen million dollars, which may not sound like such a lot nowadays but was a fortune then.

And so, we went to live in another country: the exhilarating, guilt-engendering kingdom of the trust-fund rich. As anyone who's got it without working for it knows, unearned money is a shameful thing. You're better off admitting to having sex with your poodle than confessing to the sin of living off a trust fund. We had never talked about money in our house before; there had always been enough to go around, and that was that. Not that I hadn't ever confronted the stark contradictions between the way we lived and the lives of Rhoda and Claudine. Not that I hadn't felt a certain guilt over our good fortune. But this new situation we were in threw everything into much sharper relief.

"Just think!" Mother glowed, despite her dismay over the poison flea collar. "You'll never have to work a day in your life!"

But what if working was a thing I'd always dreamed of? What if it was my ticket to normalcy, to being at least a little bit like everyone else in the universe? I was the girl child Rhoda had taught, the one to whom she said, "A colored child's old enough to work when she can see above the table," prompting me to ponder what my own task in life would be. And I was my father's daughter, watching closely on those autumn days "up the country," when the two of us walked across the fields together with his friends, men he taught me to respect because they worked, long and hard.

"But, sweetheart," Mother said, when I told her I wanted to get a summer job before I went to college, "you don't *need* a job. You'd just be depriving someone who really does need one."

Not wanting to deprive anyone of an income, I volunteered for the summer at a Quaker work camp in a poor white suburb of Indianapolis. I was the only southerner. The first night there, our little posse of preppies—which was what we were, except for me and two token black teenagers from inner-city Philadelphia—went across the street from the Catholic monastery where we'd be living to a stomped-dirt patch of a park. One of the two kids from Philadelphia had a joint, the first I'd ever seen, and when I turned it down—too much of a sissy to take a toke—the other one quietly dropped his lit cigarette down my back.

I knew they were waiting for me to yell the fatal word, the one they were so sure was right on the tip of my tongue. But I fooled them. I didn't shriek, even though it hurt like hell. I reached behind me and put the butt out with one fist. Then I walked back through the twilight to the dormitory, thinking, Maybe that was only a joke. Or maybe it was a warning. But one thing I was sure of: Giving the Southern white chick a little righteous grief was impossible to resist.

❦

I WENT OFF to Boston that fall. Whatever remained of my shining Radcliffe dream dissolved as I milled around at BU mixers like a cow in a feed lot, listening to the Long Guyland accents of the other Jewish girls who'd come to snag a boyfriend from Harvard or MIT.

This was my first exposure to what I came to think of as "real" Jews—the "pushy," "clannish," in-your-face New York kind that we polite southern Members of the Hebrew Persuasion were instructed *never* to be like. I made friends with one of them anyway, a petite, redheaded fireball from rural New Jersey whose Polish parents had survived Auschwitz and now ran a poultry farm. Edie's grandmother lived with them; she was the only older member of the family who had not perished in the camps.

Edie invited me to come home with her that Thanksgiving. I had never before met a Holocaust survivor, and I found myself mysteriously drawn to her grandmother. While Edie went off to reunite with her high school chums, I hung out with the old woman in the kitchen, helping her make strudel and warming to her fussy, maternal energy. She and I sat at the kitchen table and traded stories of her Poland and my Virginia.

"*Nu?*" she said, a Yiddish word that I had never heard before, meaning something akin to "Well?" "Edie tells me you have a boyfriend, *nu?* And he's Jewish, *nu?*"

Actually, he wasn't. Frank, my high school sweetheart—to whom I'd given my virginity as soon as the Quaker work camp ended—was a Christian Scientist from a fearsome family of blue-blooded FFVs, all of whom seemed to be female; they managed to kill off or emasculate every one of their men. Frank was the only son, and by the time he finished high school, his driving passion was to put as much distance between himself and Richmond as he could. At the moment, he was in Philadelphia, at Penn, and the two of us were suffering through this separation.

"No," I said, to Edie's grandma. "He's a Christian Scientist, actually."

The old lady's eyes narrowed into slits. "Vell," she hissed. "You sink he luffs you. But vun day he vill spit on you, call you a *dirty Jew!*"

❧

BACK AT BU, my classes were so huge that I'd pass one of my professors in a hallway and say hello, only to realize—as he walked blithely by—that he had absolutely no idea who I was. Soon I quit going to classes at all. To pass the days, I'd don my thrift-shop hippie velvets and ride the Red Line train to Harvard Square. I walked the enchanted streets, turning my ankles on the rippling brick sidewalks and pretending I was a Radcliffe girl. I browsed in all the bookstores, my favorite one being the tiny Grolier, where the poets hung out. I eavesdropped on their book-rich conversations and then traipsed behind them to one coffeehouse or another, too shy and overawed to insinuate myself into their bantering male talk.

When dusk fell and I had nowhere left to go—for I was way too genteel and insecure to even consider picking someone up—I rode the subway back to my grim Victorian dormitory near Kenmore Square. Only in a place as strange as Boston could this concrete forest of buildings, in the shadow of a thundering overpass, be described as a "square."

One night shortly before I went home for Christmas, I was in my room listening to the radio when I heard the news that Otis Redding had just died in a plane crash. I burst into tears.

My feelings for Otis Redding ran deep. What drew me to him was his gospel soul, the mystifying joy amidst sorrow, hope in the face of despair that brought me to my knees. And to my feet, dancing and not caring how white girl, white bread I was. Otis was a frequent star at college dances around the South, and when I was in my early teens, fat and very much a wallflower, I hoped and prayed that a boy I had fallen hopelessly in love with—who went off to the University of Virginia before Mother put me on amphetamines and I slimmed down and met my sweetheart, Frank—would invite me to one of the fraternity dances where Otis played. The boy I was smitten with was the epitome of hip; he spent the midnight hours hanging out with the deejays at Richmond's black radio station, fittingly named WANT, and all I wanted was for him to invite me to come along. But he never did, and he didn't ask me to any of those dances at the University of Virginia, either. I never did get to see Otis Redding perform, and now I never would.

I knocked on the door of Edie's room, hoping she would share my sorrow. "Who is Otis Redding?" she asked.

◠

I WENT HOME for Christmas. Rhoda took me to Bethel AME for Christmas Eve, just like she used to, but it wasn't the same. I was too old now to ever be Rhoda's "baby" again, and too self-conscious to fool myself into believing that I belonged at Bethel, among the rows of black faces turned eagerly to Reverend Judge's sermon. Deanie came to visit us on Christmas Day and the two of us had a good cry over Otis Redding while we listened to his last song, "Dock of the Bay," which had crossed over, musically speaking and was now being played on Richmond's white radio station, WLEE. (The black people had WANT, and we had the Civil War general who many whites thought was right up there with Jesus.)

Carrie Jefferson dropped by with her father and her aunt, and Daddy got pie-eyed with Theodore on some crystal clear moonshine that one of his hunting buddies had given him. After he went upstairs to pass out, I asked Carrie how her freshman year in her newly integrated Ashland high school was going.

"Oh, it's okay," she said. "My sister got into a fight with a white girl in the cafeteria. You know, the usual. She got sent home and Mother grounded her for two weeks."

"Damn," I answered, embarrassed. "I'm sorry to hear that."

"Well, nothing to be surprised about. I've got a new boyfriend, by the way."

"Have you told him about your college plans?"

"I don't think he quite believes me," Carrie said. "When I told him, you know what he said? He told me I'd better watch out.

'Maybe that Mrs. Gunst just wants you to be her first college-edu-
cated maid.' "

&

TWO YEARS LATER, in the summer after I had flunked out of Boston
University, I came home for a visit, dragging my failure behind me
like an invisible tail. Instead of sleeping in my former bedroom in the
main part of the house, I had taken to staying in what we still called
"the maid's room" over the garage—even though no "maid" had
occupied it since Rhoda left, eight years before. Mother had turned
it into a guest room now and though it was a dark little garret, with
only two small windows, they looked out into the trees behind the
house and the sound of birdsong fluted in all day. This was the one
room in the house where no one would barge in on me, and at the
time, privacy was what I needed most.

One night, before I went to bed, I turned my radio to WANT
and caught a soul song that took my breath away. It was one of
those sixties-spectacular productions, with a solo singer backed up
by a full orchestra and a gospel choir. The lyrics were about a girl
the singer called "Black Pearl," and it seemed to me that she was
lifted straight out of Eldridge Cleaver's autobiography, *Soul on Ice*—
which I had just read, and which was in part a praise song to black
women. (The author also managed to justify the rape of white
ones, but never mind; that was well within the acceptable parame-
ters of liberal politics at the time. White males were shouting, "Take
her down off the stage and give her a good fuck!" when women
tried to speak.)

Anyway . . . this song was about a young black woman who had
been working all her life for white people, cleaning their houses and
raising their children. But now the singer was going to put her where
she belonged, in his loving arms where she would reign supreme, as
his "queen" even though, as the singer put it, she would never win a
beauty show and was no Miss America; his love for her was deep and
true. The song was beautiful. It was about Rhoda. It was about
Claudine. It was to and for and about every black woman who had

ever been a bending, stooping, fetching servant in a white man's house. Right? Definitely. So why did I feel that this song was also about . . . *me?*

"That was Mister Sonny Charles and the Checkmates!" the dee-jay announced. "Tellin' us all about his 'Black Pearl.' "

The next morning, I tore downtown to the black record store on what whites called the "wrong" side of Broad Street and bought the forty-five. I came home, shut myself in the maid's room with the portable record player Susan and Mary used to take to high school sock hops, and played "Black Pearl" in intervals, lifting the needle every five seconds so I could write the lyrics down.

When the last strains of music died away, I looked up into my reflection in the mirror above the old dresser. How many times had I stared at myself in this oval of glass? Countless rainy afternoons when I played dress-up in this room, with Rhoda, or sat here with her while she rocked in the chair that was still on the other side of the room. Now my reflection looked strange to me, as if I had been transformed.

I remembered Rhoda saying to me, "*You* are my Miss America!" on those days so long ago, as if she could read my thoughts and knew how unlovely and unloved I truly felt. Now, as if I were in a trance, I understood what it was about this song that made me want to cry: It was about Black Pearl's longing for love, and how her dreams came true. But suddenly I knew that mine never would. Because unlike Black Pearl, it wasn't a man's love I pined for. It was for the mother I had never had: my own. For no matter how much I adored Rhoda, she had been paid to love me. *Paid.* My real mother didn't want to raise me, so she hired someone else. Rhoda wasn't my mother, any more than Black Pearl was to the white children she was paid to care for.

Maybe the other white kids I knew only wanted a smattering of acceptance from black people: To be welcomed into a dance or a nightclub and teased good-naturedly about being a "blue-eyed soul brother" or "sister" would have been enough. Not for me. I wanted to be loved, like a child by her mother. And this wasn't in the cards.

Not for me, Rhoda's part-time, off-white stepchild, misbegotten daughter of the black and Jewish South.

❧

THIS WAS THE moment when someone who had known me from the cradle reappeared. Maybe it was meant to be. Sophia Norrell— the high-spirited, take-no-prisoners girl-woman who'd worked for us when I was born and then had been so tormented by Rhoda that she left—returned to Richmond and began to work for us again. Sophia was a powerhouse of a woman, now in her late forties; she had grown to fill the role her mother predicted when she nicknamed Sophia "Mouth Almighty."

I had been little more than a year old when Sophia left, in 1950, and now I was grown. It would be glossing over too many differences between us to say that we became friends—at least, not yet— but we definitely did become allies in a joint effort to stay sane amidst the craziness that was descending on our lives in the house on Wilton Road.

Sophia came back to Richmond because her mother and father, Blanche and Elmo Norrell, were old now and ailing. Mr. Norrell had been a railroad man and he used to be as strong as the folkloric John Henry, but now he was beginning to lose his bearings, wandering from the Norrells' home in Zion Town and winding up miles away, disoriented and confused. Mrs. Norrell was suffering from heart trouble and she was relieved that her Sophia, her capable, bold-speaking daughter, was back in Richmond again at last.

Sophia settled into a house in Westwood, the black neighborhood in the West End where Claudine had lived years ago. My mother found out through the grapevine that she was back. They got in touch and the next thing I knew, Sophia was working for us again.

We fell so easily then into the age-old southern custom: Two women, one black and the other white, sit together at a kitchen table and tell each other stories from their lives. Like Granny and Rhoda, like Mother and Claudine, and Mother and Sophia, too, years ago when Mother wasn't that much older—at least in spirit—than the teenage Sophia herself. Past and present; black and white; men loved and men despised, despaired of. The words, the stories weave the women's lives together, despite Jim Crow. You can't call it friendship, can you, when there is such a gulf between two people? And yet, you wonder . . . it's a strange and singular thing, this sharing and this womanly warmth.

Sophia brought me up to speed on her life after she'd left Richmond at the age of twenty-one. Her base had been Washington, D.C., where she'd gone to live with her sister, June.

"I figured I'd find work with some Jewish folks, like you all," Sophia recalled. "Seemed to me like Jews were better to work for."

"How come?" I asked.

"Well, your mother had been like a sister to me. She and I were *tight*. And my mother always told us girls that there wasn't gonna be any college for us, so the best thing we could do was to find some really classy white folks and go to work for them. Your mama and daddy were about as classy as they come. You know what I'm talking about. They just treat people right. Don't matter what color you are.

"Your mama and me, we'd sit here at this same table where you and I are now, and we'd talk about anything and everything. Man trouble, all the botheration you kids used to give her. We shared all that stuff. And she'd give me these fabulous clothes. I don't mean raggedy ole things, either. I'm talking about dresses and skirts and sweaters, coats with fur collars that she'd buy in New York when she went to see your grandma. Girl, I can still see the way I looked in those things! They were gorgeous, and so was your mama. Not that she isn't still.

"She was a regular fireball back then. Went out almost every night to some political meeting or another. She got involved in the fight to save Westwood, when the city council wanted to kick us out and build some kind of whites-only park. She'd go downtown to First African Baptist for those meetings, and some of the people there even thought she was colored!"

"You're kidding! Really?"

"Oh, yeah. She had that jet-black hair and those dark eyes, that olive complexion. Some folks thought she might be a light-skinned colored woman who was passing. Believe you me, she and I had a laugh when she came home and told me that. Wasn't till someone asked her which church she belonged to and she told them she was Jewish that they figured out she had to be white."

Mother had never told me this story. I was—as she would say—"thrilled."

"Anyway . . . ," Sophia went on. "I never would have left you all if it hadn't been for Rhoda, the way she made my life miserable over you. I just couldn't take it anymore. Well, June was up in Washington and she called one night to tell me she knew some white folks who were looking for someone to do day work. I asked her what they did businesswise, because I knew that Jews were into stuff like liquor stores and clothing shops and so forth.

" 'They're in the liquor business,' " June says. " 'Hold on!' " I say. " 'I'm on my way.' "

After we'd stopped laughing, I asked Sophia what else she'd done in Washington.

"Oh, what didn't I do? I worked for a while at a lunch place called The Yellow Tulip on Capitol Hill. All the senators used to eat there. I met a lot of politicians, diplomats, and foreign-service types. Washington is such a southern town, you know that, and everything back then was still segregated. But some of the girls who worked with me were white, and they'd make me take them along when we went out to the black clubs at night. That was real iffy back then, but if I told them no, they'd show up anyway. So I'd just say, 'All right then. We'll make this nigger night.' "

"Sophia!" I shrieked.

"Oh, come on. Don't be so uptight. That's the way we talk, you know that."

"Maybe you all. But not me."

"There've been a lot of changes, honey, since you were born. Since I left outta here. I was up in D.C. for the big march in '63, and I wanted to go so bad. But Mama was scared I'd get arrested.

You know, me with my big mouth and all. So I promised her I wouldn't go, and I kept my word. But the week after, the cover of *Ebony* had a picture of the crowd and Mama swore she saw me in it. I don't think she ever believed I wasn't there.

"I did little things, though. Like once I sort of did a Rosa Parks on a bus to Norfolk. I was on my way to see a guy who was in the navy down there, and of course I was supposed to sit in the back. But I just wasn't in the mood that day. So I plunked my fanny down in one of the front seats, by a window, and when the bus driver came up and told me to move, I said, 'Mister, I'm staying right where I am. And everyone on this bus wants to get to Norfolk, just like you and I do. You know what I mean?' He walked back to the driver's seat and started the engine, and that was that."

WHEN SOPHIA SAID that Mother and Daddy were about as classy as they come, she'd been thinking of the old days, when they were still in love. When neither of them had betrayed the other yet. Not openly, anyway.

But by the time Sophia came back to us, those days were gone. In the same year I left for college, Daddy embarked on an affair with a woman half his age. Her name was Glenda. She was a strawberry blonde Englishwoman with a beautiful face and figure, a merry chime of a laugh, and she thought my father was the most charming man she had ever met. She was trapped in a miserable marriage to a lawyer who looked like a ferret, and they had two very unhappy kids.

Daddy was miserable, too. Sergeant's had just been sold; his beloved brother, Edward, was slowly dying of emphysema; Mother was making it abundantly clear that she was bored to tears with their marriage, and—as if this was not enough to set the ground quaking beneath their feet—my sister Susan had just suffered a new nervous breakdown and was trying to commit suicide. With time on his hands and all the supports of his life falling away one by one, Daddy decided he would do something he'd always longed to do: learn a foreign language—namely French.

Some friends of ours said they knew a marvelous tutor. This was Glenda.

Daddy started taking lessons from her in the basement office Mother had set up for him after Sergeant's was sold. Soon we were all hearing Glenda's laughter floating up the steps as my father tried hopelessly to master idiomatic expressions and conjugate irregular verbs.

The two of them were obviously besotted with each other, but their affair didn't flower into the open for a couple of years. When it did, I was nineteen. I don't know who I would have turned to were it not for Sophia, because she soon became the only person who looked at this mess and called it what it was: god-awful.

Not that Mother herself had taken Daddy's transgression lying down; not at first, when she still thought she had a chance of winning. But after a couple of years, when it was obvious that he had no intention of giving Glenda up, and the two of them were sneaking around Richmond like a couple of teenagers in the grip of raging hormones, Mother lost her will to fight. Prompted by her charlatan of a psychoanalyst in Charlottesville, she came to a decision: She could and would coexist with Glenda. Leaving my father was unthinkable to her.

"I've made my peace with it," she would intone—fooling none of us except perhaps herself, and that only for a moment. "I've *dealt* with it," she said to Mary and me—as well as to her younger sisters, Alice and Barbara, and to all the mystified, horrified friends she and Daddy had known for years. "I've made my peace with the situation. And you all have to, too. That's just the way it is."

This effectively meant that if I wanted to keep coming home, wanted to maintain a relationship with my parents, I had to swallow my true feelings about his mistress. Which were, simply put, that I wished her dead. Sophia was right there with me.

"I just can't believe this thing!" she said to me as we sat in the kitchen one afternoon with the door to the hall shut tight because Mother and Daddy and Glenda were in the den, having drinks and chatting away as if things were *tout à fait normale*. As if there was nothing unusual in the way my mother had betrayed herself and all of us into this devil's bargain of a lie.

"Will you tell me what on earth your daddy thinks he's doing?" Sophia said, trying to keep her voice down.

"Like I know, Sophia? Jesus. Don't ask me."

Her new name for Glenda was "Ole Dead Chicken," which signified Sophia's utter disgust. I couldn't quite figure out how she had come up with that one, except that farmers hang a dead chicken around the neck of a dog who raids the henhouse, and maybe Sophia thought my father was just as bad as that kind of nasty chicken-killing dog.

"Ole Dead Chicken," she muttered, sucking her teeth. "What's he want with that *thing*, huh? You tell me, 'cause I sure don't get it. What in hell does he see in that woman when he's got a wife as fine as your mama? Listen, I know men. I know they like to kick up their heels when they go on the road, whatever. But to bring that thing here, right into this house, rub your mama's face in it? Uh-uh." Sophia shook her head. "And you don't know the half of it. You don't be here to see what goes on every time your mama takes a trip somewhere. That thing moves right in! Sleeps in your daddy's bed, leaves her dirty underwear on the bathroom floor, like I'm supposed to pick it up and wash it? Lord have mercy."

"Oh, God, Sophia," I groaned. "Don't tell me."

"Well, I have to tell someone! This mess is 'bout to drive me crazy. I don't know how long I can stay here in this house without telling your mama straight to her face how I feel."

"If you do, she's going to fire you. I just know it. Because she can't stand for any of us, even Mary or me or Barbara or Alice, to tell her how much we hate what's going on."

Sophia got up and put the kettle on to make herself a cup of tea. "Let me tell you something," she said. "If your mama was black instead of white, that thing would be *gone* outta here. You know what I'm saying? No black woman would put up with this! We don't mess around with this stuff."

"Sophia, I've got news for you. I don't know any other white woman who'd put up with it, either."

"Then will you please tell me why your mama does? She crazy or what?"

"I'll tell you what I think it is. I think she's just scared to death at the thought of being alone. She's absolutely terrified of living without Daddy. They've been together since she was a teenager, Sophia. And you know as well as I do that money has a lot to do with it. She's gotten used to a very nice life with Daddy and she doesn't want to give it up."

Sophia shook her head sadly. "There's worse things than bein' by yourself, sugar. But let me tell you this. There ain't nothin' worse than lettin' some man humiliate you. And don't you ever forget that, you hear me? Don't you ever let any man do to you what you see your daddy doing to your mama right here and now. Promise?"

"I promise. But you don't have to worry, Sophia. There's not even a chance." She made our tea and we sat sipping it in silence. Then Sophia gave me one of her foxy smiles. "I think I'll just take a little drive out to Lynchburg one of these Saturdays. Go see this woman I know. She isn't young and she isn't old, either. But she's rootified, I'll tell you that. And I'm gonna come back here with enough candles and powders and what-all-else to fix Ole Dead Chicken's business once and for all!"

I smiled back, knowing Sophia was just trying to make us both feel better.

"Good luck" was all I said.

❧

As the ground opened up beneath my father and me, as he humiliated my mother and all the rest of us females in his "harem," there was still one tie that bound me to him. It was his love for the past, for the South and the ways his family had belonged to it. His love of storytelling was the glue that held us together through this awful time, and these stories of his turned out to be the greatest gift he ever gave me. They were my true inheritance, the legacy to which I clung.

Because I loved my parents and because, against all the evidence, I still was hoping for them to acknowledge me, I kept returning home, again and again. I was seeking their long-withheld acceptance, but also something more: In my grief over what had become of us as a family, I understood that my father was trying to fill the empty chasm that yawned between us with stories. At the dinner table, he served up a feast of memory that filled me as nothing else could. The past of *us,* of my people—this long ago and far away—became our shared refuge from the bitter present. Though there was every bit as much danger and sorrow in the past he laid out for me—the delicately woven strands of southern and Jewish, of poverty and fortune—this past was far away enough to seem manageable to me. I thought I could touch it without getting scorched.

"You're the only one in the family who gives a damn," Daddy would say, with his usual baffling mixture of praise and condemnation. He'd always taint a compliment to me with a judgment on one of my siblings, so that I'd end up feeling both flattered and disloyal at the same time. "You're the only one who ever listens," he said.

What I heard in these stories—and for many of them there was no proof that the events they described ever even occurred—was the echo of my own aloneness, the off-white sensibility I was beginning to own. I had a feeling that I would never belong anywhere, would be forever torn between the sides of myself. I began to think that this eternal interior wandering, this culture straddling, was what it meant to be a southern Jew.

Daddy's apocrypha began with a handful of tales about his grandfather, Henry Gunst, the first member of his family to emigrate from Germany. But Daddy did not even know precisely when Henry had arrived. He thought it was sometime around 1850, when Henry was a boy, and that he had sailed from Hamburg without his parents, accompanied only by his elder brother, Michael. My father did not know his grandfather—Henry died in 1907, when

Daddy was only two years old—and so he had heard no stories of Henry's coming to New York from the man himself. The only one that seemed to have been handed down to Daddy from his father, Emmanuel, Henry's son, was another snippet of Gunst apocrypha—identifiable as such because it had the two brothers, Henry and Michael, swimming across the East River from Brooklyn, where they lived, to sell straw baskets in the Fulton Fish Market. Not very likely; the currents in the East River are deadly.

But my father had met Michael, and he told me a story about his great-uncle that moved me deeply. When Daddy was a little boy, he went with his father to New York City to visit this man his father referred to as "Uncle Mike." They found him living in a tenement on the Lower East Side—one of the "Jews Without Money" about whom that book of my mother's had been written, those who had not gone to the South or made a great deal of money, who lived in New York City crowded together in tenements and sweatshops.

"Michael was ill," Daddy told me. "He had a terrible cough. And he was hungry. So my father and I took him to eat at Child's Cafeteria, which I thought was a palace. There was nothing like it in Richmond. Michael must have been starving, poor fella, and he ate everything in sight. When we said goodbye, my father pressed an envelope into Mike's hand, and I knew it was money. He stood on the steps of his tenement and waved to us till I couldn't see him anymore. I looked up at my father and saw that he had tears in his eyes."

Fledgling historian that I was, I begged Daddy to tell me more about this man, anything he could remember. But there were no more stories. It was already becoming a mystery to me why my father knew so few facts. Instead, what he possessed were mainly mystic, semimythic tales, anecdotes that might or might not have held a grain of truth. I treasured them all the more: the fleeting images that came to me of Emmanuel, for instance, such as the one from when he took his elegant wife, Hattie, and their two high-spirited sons, my father and his elder brother, Edward, to Europe on a grand tour in 1926. One warm afternoon, they were strolling on the Lido, the beach near Venice, when they ran into a wellborn friend from Richmond, Regina Milheiser. She was having a love affair with the opera singer Beniamino Gigli; in the wake of Enrico Caruso's untimely death in 1921, Gigli had become the most famous Italian tenor in the world. Regina, a woman who did as she pleased, was traveling with him from one European capital to another.

Emmanuel looked down at Regina's bare feet and noticed that her toenails were painted bright red. "Regina," he intoned, mournfully shaking his head. "No lady paints her fingernails, let alone her toes."

This was a man who was quick to judge others for their lapses, perhaps because he secretly knew that there had been a few in his own family's past. Daddy told me that when he was a little boy, a genealogist came to Richmond and offered to do a family tree of the Gunsts for Emmanuel; his fee was twenty-five dollars. My grandfather retorted, "I'll give you a hundred not to."

But the story of Michael Gunst also explained why this grand-father of mine, a whiskey baron who glided through the streets of Richmond in his chauffeur-driven Pierce-Arrow and dressed his Dresden doll of a wife in gowns from the House of Worth, never-theless revered the working man. Why, when all his well-heeled friends were supporting Herbert Hoover and his ilk, that tribe of big-money Republicans for whom Emmanuel had nothing but contempt, he never forgot how lucky he had been. He did not believe for an instant that he deserved his wealth; he knew for a fact that others were just as hardworking, but fate had not dealt them as good a hand.

My grandfather so disliked the Republicans and everything they stood for that he urged Franklin Roosevelt to run for the presi-dency when Roosevelt was still governor of New York and the stock market was giving no indication of the disastrous crash to come. Emmanuel wrote fan letters to Franklin, and he wrote back. The one my father saved, from October 1928, is a document I cherish for its unashamed idealism; it's impossible to imagine an American politician replying personally in this vein today. In the letter, Roosevelt attacked Herbert Hoover and "the materialistic and self-seeking advisors who surround him" and then went on to lambaste the Republicans for their "contemptuous casting aside of all of President Wilson's wonderful dreams of a better world."

Emmanuel Gunst's heart beat faster when he read words like those. He didn't care what his well-heeled friends thought of his liberal politics, or try to deny that he saw something of himself in the luckless souls standing on breadlines around the country. Perhaps it was the buried immigrant past of his own father that made him see life this way; maybe it was because he was a Jew. All I know is the story Daddy loved—for he, like his father, revered Roosevelt—about a day in the early thirties when Emmanuel was walking up Richmond's Broad Street with his banker friend, John Miller, and Miller was berating him, demanding to know how Emmanuel could even consider supporting Franklin Roosevelt, "this traitor to his class."

My grandfather thought this over for a minute and then answered, "That's easy, John. I'm just fair."

℘

THE SAME SPLENDID contradictions—humility amidst privilege, openhandedness in a world of tight fists—were woven through the stories Daddy told me about his grandfather, Henry Gunst. He called him "the Old Man," because Henry was the patriarch who founded the family whiskey business in 1879. Before the Civil War came, he had been living in the little Virginia town of Bowling Green, halfway between Fredericksburg and Washington. He was a German-speaking immigrant with a German-born wife and two small children, running a tannery and trying his best to stay out of the fight. This was not his war: He owned no slaves and worked the tannery with the help of another Jewish immigrant.

"But the feeling against Jews ran very high at the beginning of the war," Daddy told me. "You know, the same old stuff—accusations that Jews were hoarding food and speculating. As if no one else was. Anyway, I think the Old Man must have felt tremendous pressure to enlist."

At this point in the story, Daddy asked me to run upstairs and fetch Henry's obituary; Henry died in the spring of 1907. My father kept the tattered scrap of newsprint in his dresser drawer, tucked away in his father's ancient leather billfold, along with the stub of a ticket for a performance of *Rigoletto* at the Met.

I brought the wallet back to the dinner table and Daddy unfolded the yellowed clipping like it was a page of Holy Writ.

"In the spring of 1861," he intoned, fighting back tears, "Henry Gunst shouldered his musket and joined the Thirtieth Virginia Infantry. He was a good soldier."

"Is that all?" I asked.

"What do you mean, 'Is that all?' " Daddy shot back. "Isn't that enough? Your great-grandfather fought for the Confederacy. For the most noble cause of all. What else do you need to know?"

Mother rolled her eyes in the direction of the chandelier.

Daddy had no idea what Henry had done in the war; his name was on the official rolls of the Thirtieth Virginia, but he was not mustered out with the rest of the regiment when it surrendered at Appomattox. I wondered if he might have deserted. If he had, I would not have blamed him. But I had more sense than to say this to my father.

"When the war was over," Daddy went on, "the Yankees occupied Bowling Green. The commanding officer told my grandfather he could only get his tannery back if he signed the oath of loyalty, which involved saying that he'd been drafted into the Confederate armed forces against his will." Daddy's face darkened. "Well, the last anyone saw of that Yankee, The Old Man was chasing him down the main street with a pitchfork."

"Daddy," I said, as gently as I could. "There was no way that Henry could have run the Yankees out of town. Because after 1865, they *were* the town."

"I'll be damned if that's so!" he thundered. I knew there was no use arguing with him. This was my father's equivalent of a foundation myth. I did not share it; mine—if I had one—was Rhoda's story of her parents being born in slavery. It was a contradiction, to be sure: a Confederate great-grandfather and two formerly enslaved African Americans whose names were Julia and Sam.

℘

ALONG WITH THE legacy of the Old Man's service to the Lost Cause went the whiskey business, of course. Being a lifelong addict of alcohol, my father was inordinately proud that his family had once manufactured it. But he also told me something I already knew: that it was always a dicey business, slightly shady and disreputable, and that this was all the more true in the South because of Henry's suspect status as a Member of the Hebrew Persuasion.

"He always carried a gun," Daddy said. "So did my father. Emmanuel traveled for the company, and when he went out to the coal fields of West Virginia or the turpentine camps in the Carolinas, he'd run across some rough characters. One of them was a saloon keeper who tried to weasel out of a debt he owed the firm. He wrote my grandfather a letter. Well, I suppose you might say it was funny. But only after the fact."

"Do you still have the letter?" I asked, knowing what the answer would be. For a family so absorbed with its past, Emmanuel Gunst and his father had been remarkably reluctant to hold onto anything that might be considered archival.

"No, but I can recall it from what my father told me," Daddy answered.

"*Dear Jews,*" Daddy began. "I did not intend to order another shipment of your whiskey, but your Jew salesman was so insistent that I had no choice. As it is, I have no intention of paying you for this liquor."

"*Dear Christian,*" Henry wrote back. "Had your Christian associates been more able to vouch for your honesty and good character, our Jewish firm would have been delighted to ship you another order, even though you have not remitted payment for the first."

Henry sent his son to collect the debt. He got it. My father still had the pearl-handled forty-five Emmanuel carried that day. Now

Daddy used it as a starter pistol when he worked his bird dogs at field trials and when he laid them to rest. After he and Theodore Jefferson, Carrie's father, had dug the grave for one of his dogs, in the little cemetery under the holly tree at the bottom of the hill behind our house, Daddy would aim that pistol skyward and fire a single shot.

"Last time, old fella!" he would cry, swallowing his tears.

MY FATHER WAS so transfixed by the power and the glory of his ancestors that he could not stand for Mother to have any of her own. Whenever she brought up the subject of her relations, the Schaaps and Fishblates and Einsteins, hoping to tell me something of their history, Daddy shook his head as if she were a child inventing tales.

When I was twenty-something, Mother persuaded him to take a sentimental journey with her to Wilmington, to search the courthouse records there. She was hoping to drag him away from Glenda for a while, too. But Daddy was so ill-tempered and impatient the whole time they were there that Mother rushed through the records without finding anything. When they went to the cemetery in search of her grandfather's grave, she failed to even find that. Mother came home defeated, and my father was vindicated in his belief that this grandfather of hers, this ne'er-do-well with the ridiculous name of Solomon Fishblate, had never been the mayor of Wilmington, if in fact he had ever even existed. No one on Mother's side of the family was worth remembering.

eleven

HEN I WAS twenty, I fell in love. Ray was an artist, a painter of luminous abstract expressionist watercolors. He was five years older than I, and to me—a college dropout who had no sense of purpose—he seemed to know exactly who he was and where he was going. He was best friends with my sister Mary and her husband, so I'd been hearing about him for years. The weekend that we met at their home in New Hampshire, Ray was walking on air after a chance encounter with his idol, Willem de Kooning, at a gallery in New York. De Kooning took a look at Ray's slides while Ray stood beside him, all but holding his breath. "Hey, Xavier," de Kooning said to the gallery owner (in his inimitable combination of accents, Dutch overlaid with Brooklynese), "this guy is pretty good. You oughta give him a show."

If it wasn't love at first sight for me, it was close. Ray was tall and loose limbed, with a shock of tawny hair that fell across his high forehead; he carried himself with the ease of a man who took his beauty for granted. He was brilliant, a charismatic talker who went off on riffs of true genius, hysterically funny and sad, in the dark manner of Lenny Bruce. I was captivated by Ray, and the fact that he seemed tantalizingly indifferent to me only made him all the more compelling.

The family next door to Mary had six children, and they were all fierce riders. Their horses were hot-blooded thoroughbreds who'd been demoted from one racetrack or another around New England—not the kind you should ride without a saddle. But James, the eldest boy, dared me to a bareback race with him up the hill in front of Mary's house and I couldn't resist showing off. I came off that horse at a dead run and landed on my head in the hardpan dirt road. The last thing I remembered was trying to sit up, spitting the grit out of my mouth. Then I fainted.

❧

RAY CARRIED ME up to the house and the doctor came, diagnosing a mild concussion. I was put to bed in my white Victorian nightgown and Ray sat beside me for a night and a day while I raved, not exactly delirious but still unaware of what I was saying. When I came to, Ray gave me a wry smile.

"Oh, God," I moaned. "What did I say?"

"Oh, nothing too bad. You just kept grabbing my hand and begging me to tell you whether we'd slept together yet."

As it turned out, I must have been more appealing in an amnesiac state than I knew. Ray asked me to come live with him in northern California; he had just gotten a job teaching art at Humboldt State College in a town called Arcata. I had never heard of the school or the town. But, then, nothing about California interested me in the least. I believed New England was the center of the universe, whereas California was a Sahara of the mind, populated by moronic hippies who smiled no matter what and would pray for you if they heard you ate meat.

Nevertheless, I went. I was in love and besides, I had nowhere else to go. But I was lost and homesick from the moment I arrived, despite the foggy beauty of the redwoods, the seals barking on the rocks in the ocean just down the hill from our little cottage, and Ray's consuming tenderness for me. Nothing made me happy. I missed the East, my sister and her husband and their kids; my scene—such as it had been—in Boston, with its poets and readings and bookstores; the evening parties I'd dress up for in my silks and velvets, where I'd be admired for my wit and for my wild raven hair. I was wearing it long by then, letting it kink and curl and frizz its way around my head like an untamed ethnic halo (the word for it back then was a "Jew-fro.")

In our tiny fishing village, I had nothing to dress up for. Ray was totally absorbed in his teaching, so while he gave his classes on the beach, I'd pop one of my Dexedrines and clean house like crazy, getting in touch with my Inner Maid. Then I'd take my brand-new copy of Julia Child's *Mastering the Art of French Cooking* down from the shelf in the spotless kitchen and pore over it till I'd decided what to make for dinner that night.

Learning how to cook was a tremendous challenge for me; it was the one domestic skill that Rhoda had never taught me. Ray assumed I'd be able to turn out basic dishes, but the very thought of preparing an entire meal gave me an anxiety attack of massive proportions. I started by asking Mary how to do the simplest things and writing down, verbatim, what she said in a little book covered in bright, sixties-hip Marimekko fabric. I still have it, after all these years. It's filled with sad little notations like "How to Bake a Potato" and "How to Broil a Piece of Fish." Perfectionist that I was, and determined to advance beyond this level, I turned to Julia Child and began slowly but surely to transform myself into an accomplished—if slightly anal-compulsive—gourmet cook.

At first, I knew nothing about spices and herbs and other delicious aspects of being "creative in the kitchen." (Young women like me were taught that the kitchen and the bedroom were the only places we could actually create anything.) At our house, Claudine had been forbidden to use anything more exciting than paprika when she cooked, because Daddy associated onions and garlic with

Russians and Poles, those eastern European Jews whom he considered to be children of a lesser god than that of his own German
ancestors. Mother was forever "outing" him for this prejudice,
which he would vehemently deny. "Goddamn it, Evelyn! That is
not the reason. I simply can't stand the reek of garlic!" That was his
word, *reek,* and if you had been foolish enough to eat garlic and
then come into his presence, he'd screw up his face like a child
about to have a tantrum.

Cooking wasn't the only thing I was doing that year. It was 1970
and the first wave of the women's movement was breaking over us.
I read every feminist tract I could get my hands on—"devoured"
would be a better word. I consumed them, wolfing down those
angry, impassioned essays like they were food and I was starving.

Thankfully, we had no children—I would probably have thrown
them out a window and then put my head in the oven. I was overwhelmed by a rage I could not channel, and Ray and I began to
have the fights that were common as grass at that moment in time.
We had the Who-Is-Going-to-Clean-the-Toilet? fight, the Why-
Do-You-Leave-Your-Dishes-in-the-Sink? fight—all the charged,
symbolic skirmishes of a couple in the throes of attempting to dis-
mantle the sexual division of labor. ("Good luck," as they used to
say to young men setting out for the wild, wild West. "Write if you
find work.")

In desperation, Ray finally said we ought to hire a cleaning lady.
I blew up. "I'll be damned if I'm going to pay some other woman
to clean up your mess," I hollered, seeing Rhoda in my mind's eye.

Somehow, we hung together. But I was determined to leave
California and return to school. Somewhere in New England, I
told Ray. I had no idea where; with my 1.4 cumulative average
from Boston University, I sure wasn't "Radcliffe material" now. But
all those feminist books I'd been reading had convinced me of one
thing: I wasn't cut out to spend the rest of my life staging dinner
parties and entertaining Great Men.

Ray and I went to live in the caretaker's house at Mary's place in
New Hampshire, and Ray began to paint full-time; we lived on the

trust fund my father had set up for me with the proceeds from the poison flea collar.

One day late that summer, I drove the twenty miles to the Durham campus of the University of New Hampshire, to meet with an admissions officer. He took a glance at my transcript from Boston University, which resembled a tic-tac-toe board of zeros and x's and "Incompletes." I could hear the air escaping from his lungs.

"I'm afraid there is no way we could admit you at this time," he said. He saw that I was about to cry. "You'd have to prove yourself. We have an excellent night school here, and maybe you'd consider taking a few courses this semester, see how it goes? If you do well, we could think about letting you into our degree program, a year or so from now."

I swallowed my pride and signed up for two courses in European history. One was on witchcraft in the Renaissance, taught by a brilliant, quirky medievalist who understood that the witch hunts we read about were partly grounded in the ancient fear men had of women, especially the old ones who practiced folk medicine, healing, and the conjuring arts. His thinking appealed not only to my ardent feminism but also to my personal history, my times with Rhoda and Sophia, both of whom—with their "roots" and prophesying and firm belief in the spirit world—would probably have been burned at the stake in an earlier time.

The other class was on Elizabethan England, a time and place with which I had always been enchanted. Here I was again, going back in time to the exuberant half century that had carved my own Virginia from the shores of a new world. I reveled anew in the heady atmosphere of that splendid court, watching the Virgin Queen with the heart of a man bask in the devotion of her dashing courtiers—and outfox the plots on her life that they hatched. I came alive to the erotic delight of reawakening the past, an almost alchemical mystery. I could mix the cool discipline of research with the fire of my own passionate imagination, and with this scholar's potion, this combination of intellect and heart, I could all but bring the past back to life. This was a power greater than any I had yet known. In an ecstasy of reading, I went through most of the pertinent books in the university library and soon needed more.

"Why don't you use the libraries at Harvard?" asked my witchcraft professor casually, as if it was just another college down the road. "I'd be glad to give you a letter of reference to Widener."

Widener! He might as well have said Athens or Alexandria. But when I presented my professor's letter to the librarian at Widener, he did not scoff; instead, he quietly minted me a borrower's card to paradise. Not only could I get into the open stacks, like the Radcliffe girl I once dreamed I'd be; I could also use Houghton Library, where the university keeps its matchless collection of rare books.

Houghton was the spark that lit my scholar's fuse. It was also the most intimidating place I had ever been, a temple where all the priests were men and I was the only woman—except for the three-hundred-pound librarian who hovered behind her desk like a giant bird of prey. One morning, needing to consult the card catalogue, I stood up and left the little sixteenth-century octavo volume I'd been reading facedown on the table.

The librarian swooped down on me, her great bat-winged arms flapping. "Have you no idea how to treat these books?" she hissed in a whisper loud enough to make all the tweedy men look up. "You could have damaged the spine!"

After that, she scowled at me every time I came through the padded leather doors from Widener into Houghton. But I didn't care. Nothing could have kept me away. While the windshield of my car on Massachusetts Avenue bloomed white with parking tickets, I read until the light on the other side of Houghton's tall windows turned blue, oblivious to the world outside.

At the close of one long day, light-headed from having skipped lunch because I could not tear myself away, I opened a letter written in 1633 by a French inquisitor into an outbreak of demonic possession among the nuns in the convent of Loudun. A few grains of the sand that had been used to dry its ink sifted onto my table. Had it ever even been read before, I wondered? Tears sprang into my eyes, and suddenly I knew that this was what I wanted to go on doing forever:

to reach back across time and touch lives distant from my own. To glimpse, if only for a moment, the world through someone else's eyes.

୧

I STAYED AT the University of New Hampshire for three blissful years. In that time, I worked most closely with one mentor—a brilliant, mirthful, gay professor whose passion was the history of ideas. Of the many teachers I have loved, none was more dear to me than Donald Wilcox. His intelligence was matched by a capacious heart and a keen sense of play; he was one of those rare scholars who understand that thinking is the mind's purest joy.

Don shared a Victorian brownstone in Boston with three other men, and all of them were fabulous cooks who loved to entertain. Their finest hour was their formal New Year's Eve dinner, with the men in white tie and the women in evening dresses. We lolled around the long table in Don's dining room with its red flocked wallpaper, which looked like a New Orleans bordello and was hung with prints of the notoriously debauched Renaissance popes. We did our best to observe the requisite formalities till the hash brownies were passed. After that, all bets were off.

Don had gotten his doctorate at Harvard, and soon he began encouraging me to apply.

"Do you really think I have a chance?" I asked.

"My little Maimonides!" he laughed, his blue eyes twinkling merrily. That had become his nickname for me, after the twelfth-century Spanish Jew who refused to choose between reason and revelation and wrote a book with the audacious title, *The Guide for the Perplexed*.

"I'm not worried about your getting in. I just want you to be aware that it might not be all you think it is."

"Why? Why wouldn't I love it?"

Don tilted his handsome head and gave me a look that was both tender and sad. "I know your intellect will find its match there. But I'm just not sure a scholar's life is what you really want. And I think the sexism at Harvard is going to blow your mind."

But I was not convinced. I had a perfectly hilarious interview with the grand old man I hoped to study Renaissance history with; we sat in his office in Widener, piles of books and dusty documents threatening to topple and bury us, as I tried to impress him with my scholarly purpose (mindful that he was about to see my transcript from Boston University and would probably have some serious doubts) while he prattled on about the glorious cuisine of Florence, whence he had just returned after supervising life at I Tatti, Harvard's villa there.

I must have impressed him sufficiently, though, because I got in. When my letter of acceptance came, on a bleary March day in 1974, I kept reading it over and over and then slipping it back inside the watermarked envelope so I could take it out and read it yet again. I had to be sure there'd been no mistake.

"I'm sorry, darling," I kept hearing Mother say. "But I just don't think you're Radcliffe material."

RAY AND I got married. I was reluctant, already knowing that even though I did love him, we were more like brother and sister than lovers by then. I think he was afraid that if we didn't tie the knot, I'd be off like a shot in pursuit of all those brilliant, handsome Harvard men. The only one I wanted was Don Wilcox, but he was gay. Ray still had a point, though; he knew me well, and he knew that I was at a stage in my life where I was sexualizing every teacher I had. I simply couldn't imagine having their adoration in any other way, and it was just lucky for me that all the professors I ever worked with at Harvard were too ethical (or uninterested in me) to respond in kind.

Ray and I moved into a jewel of an apartment, the top floor of a house built in 1842 on Brattle Street, just a block from the Radcliffe Yard. It echoed with the ghosts of the Boston Brahmins and robber barons who had been guests there: Henry and William James, various literary Lowells, Fricks, Cabots, and Eliots. Our landlady, Hildreth Burnett, who occupied the rooms downstairs, was not a Brahmin—she was from Virginia—but she had the beautiful manners and perfect bearing of the born aristocrat she was. I loved hearing her trilling voice in the morning, when she let her Siamese cat out the front door and called hello to a neighbor who might be strolling by. I'd be in our bathroom, with its window right above Hildreth's front door, and sometimes I'd look down to see a little tour group staring up at the turrets and gables and rose windows of our historically important early Victorian house.

My first year at Harvard proved Don Wilcox right. There were thirty-six in my class of history graduate students and only four were women. Two of them had nervous breakdowns in the first month and never came back. This left me and a brilliant, sexy Jewish Bennington graduate by the name of Carol Lasser. She had an untamed mane of thick, curly black hair—I had cut mine short by then, in deference to what I thought of as a serious look—and the fine-tuned body of a swimmer, her sport of choice. She was living in a co-op with a crew of other graduate students, all of whom were politically left and socially active. I was newly and not all that happily married, and I envied Carol her freedom more than I dared admit.

But she and I made friends nonetheless, survivors that we were. She seemed so blissfully free of self-doubt, whereas I suffered from what's called the Impostor Syndrome, convinced of my unworthiness and sure I was going to be found out.

"Gunst!" Carol chided me. "Relax, for God's sake. You're doing great. No one's going to kick you out. You're just feeling out of it because you're doing all this sixteenth-century stuff. And all your teachers are doddering old men."

She had a point. Carol was on the cutting edge of the new social history, concentrating on working-class and women's studies, and her reading was a lot more exciting and immediate than what I was doing. I had gone to dwell in the long ago and far away, without understanding why I needed to put so much distance between what I studied and who I really was. I was escaping, although I did not know it. But it would not be long before events would conspire to bring me back home. Back to my own side of the ocean, instead of Europe. And back to that most American and southern of all tragedies. Slavery.

I heard the first whisperings of this, the sea change that was about to come for me, as I walked home from the library steeped in melancholy, my arms laden with musty-smelling tomes. Along Tory Row, as Brattle Street is so aptly called, I passed the exquisite houses where the eighteenth-century grandees lived, and as I walked I thought about how all that wealth and beauty had been bought with blood. All of them were slavers. They owned the ships that brought the captives to the markets of the South. They got rich from slavery, fattened like cannibals on the triangle trade in human beings from Africa and the New World commodities these Africans produced: rum and sugar, cotton, rice, and indigo that were sold in English, European, and American markets for the money to buy more slaves.

One day—in what seemed to me like a bragging, offensive homage to Brattle Street's worst tendencies—the Cambridge Historical Commission erected a concrete stanchion in the sidewalk in front of Hildreth's house. The thing was topped with a blue oval marker that said TORY ROW. Underneath was one sentence: WEALTHY FAMILIES LOYAL TO THE CROWN LIVED ON BRATTLE STREET DURING THE REVOLUTION.

Hildreth noticed the marker one morning when she let her cat outside and called me to come downstairs. The two of us stood on the sidewalk in our bathrobes, so angry that we didn't care who saw us. "Have you ever?" Hildreth fumed. "What an absolutely appalling sign. I've never seen anything in such poor taste. Wealthy families, indeed. As if that's what this neighborhood ought to be known for."

"I know," I answered. "It's awful, isn't it?"

"You know what we should do?" Hildreth's brown eyes were glinting with mischief. "Let's come out here tonight with a can of black spray paint. What shall we write?"

I thought for a moment. "I know! How about crossing out WEALTHY and writing . . . STEALTHY?"

Hildreth whooped with glee. "Oh, Laurie! That's perfect! That's absolutely grand!"

But I didn't have the nerve. The sign stayed the way it was.

◎

No matter how far I was from home, from Rhoda, she still lived inside me. I heard her voice in my ears and in my heart, and we talked on the phone several times a week. Ray and I separated in an amicable way, and now I was alone. Rhoda fretted over our separation even though I reassured her that I was doing fine on my own. But Ray had been the man she'd counted on to take care of me.

"How you doing up there?" she asked tenderly. "You getting along all right at that highest school of yours?" That was her phrase for Harvard.

"Oh, I'm okay, I guess," I answered. "Except that I miss you, Rhodie." I was thinking how I'd give this place up in a minute for one laid-back evening on Idlewood Avenue, sitting on her front porch and calling hellos to the neighbors next door. I would trade my "highest school" for her "high geraniums," as she called the ballooning purple hydrangeas that grew on either side of her front steps. Trade in all this cold, fierce book learning for a chance to listen to Rhoda and her friends from Bethel AME, telling stories about things that mattered. About the past, and their families, and the place they called home.

"I miss you too, child," Rhoda murmured, her voice soft inside the cradle of the phone. "When you coming home to see me?"

"Soon as I can."

Where was my home? It wasn't Cambridge; that I knew.

Rhoda in her late seventies, at her home on Idlewood Avenue.

twelve

HE PLACE I came to call home was another country, one so different from the land of my birth that at first I could not fathom why it felt so familiar to me. It was a fledgling nation in the peacock blue Caribbean, an island like the one in Shakespeare's *The Tempest*, "full of noises," all of which whispered insistently in my ears.

Jamaica.

Mother and Daddy and I went there to join Mary and her family for the Christmas vacation of 1975; they had rented a house in the hills above Montego Bay. Many of their friends, and ours, had warned us not to go there. "Jamaica is dangerous," they said. "It used to be so peaceful, but everything's changed now that Michael Manley is prime minister. He's a socialist, a big fan of Castro's. Jamaica has become a very violent place."

The only thing I knew about Jamaica was the advertisements that ran in *The New Yorker* for Douglas Cooper's exclusive jewelry store in Montego Bay. In these ads there'd always be a small,

affordable piece of jewelry and then an over-the-top ring or neck-
lace with a note that said "Price Available Upon Request." From
these ads and other things I'd heard about Jamaica, I pictured it as a
string of fancy hotels lined up along a glittering coast, where English
men dressed in dinner jackets and women wore flowered chiffon.

But from the moment we disembarked to the strains of a
calypso band playing banana-boat songs for the tourists, I saw and
heard another Jamaica. Standing at the baggage carousel, I stared at
the blaze of color and listened to my first phrases of island patois.
Years later, I connected this moment to the riff that Richard Pryor
did in *Live on the Sunset Strip*, when he went to Africa and saw that
everyone was black. In his parody of minstrelsy, Pryor widened his
eyes into saucers and said, "But you know what? I looked all
around me and I didn't see any *niggers.*" Because there were none.

Q

THAT WAS MY first shock. The second was language: The patois
everyone was speaking—Jamaica's rippling river of English that
sounds like no English I had ever heard—I understood immediately, as if I had been brought up with it in some other life. This was
inexplicable, since I had never heard it spoken before. Patois is a
daunting mix of English and West African words and syntax; it
almost always baffles newcomers to the island, yet to me it was
instantly comprehensible and made perfect sense.

I knew to listen for its rhythms, and then the meaning would
come clear. When we got into a taxi, I couldn't resist trying to
speak a little patois with the driver, not caring how I sounded. It
was like being able to sing, to free my voice from all hesitation.
Now my speech flew from its cage like an eager bird.

As we drove from the airport to our hotel, we passed a shantytown
with red graffiti dripping down its rusted zinc fences like blood.

"Socialism Is Love!" the graffiti proclaimed. "Under Heavy
Manners!"

"What that mean, sah, Heavy Manners?" I asked the driver. He
grinned at me in the rearview mirror.

"It mean say, Michael Manley control tings now. It mean we haffi' stan' firm fi' socialism. We cyan' go back to slavery days again."

Feeling the eerie sensation that I had been here before, I remembered that Christmas years ago, when Mary had gone to Jamaica with the Reynolds family and Mr. Reynolds had advised her to "Jew 'em down" when she went to the market in Montego Bay. The memory of that event had burned itself into my heart. When I thought of the snapshots Mary had brought home, of her and Glenny Reynolds sitting on the donkeys with those ragged children gathered around, I thought it was a good thing that Jamaicans wanted those days dead and gone forever.

But the echoes were not to be so quickly silenced. We arrived at our hotel just as a black Santa Claus careened up to the beach on water skis, chanting, "Ho ho ho." The beauty was overwhelming; green hummingbirds darted among psychedelically huge scarlet hibiscus, but thin children in rags were hovering around the kitchen at the far edge of the whitewashed terrace. Later that day, after we'd unpacked, Mary led me on a tour through the thronged market, where she went to buy her fruits and vegetables. The higgler women sat behind their little hillocks of tropical fruits, calling out good-natured greetings and stashing money in their brassieres.

"Does this feel strangely familiar to you?" I asked my sister. "I know you've been here before, but that's not what I mean. It's something else."

"Yes," she answered. "Don't ask me why, but it feels like home."

◎

THAT FIRST VISIT lasted only two weeks. But in that short time, I began to take the pulse of this new country, to meet some of the people Mary was getting to know, and to make some friends of my own. Even though people warned us not to go to Kingston—the capital where most of the current violence was— my brother-in-law and I very much wanted to see the city. We took a small plane across the island, hired a driver in Kingston, and spent two days there, visiting museums and libraries and meeting one of the island's historians at the national archives in Spanish Town.

We saw graffiti everywhere: red for Michael Manley's People's National Party and green for the opposition, the Jamaica Labour Party. Our driver explained that the JLP bore no relation whatsoever to England's Labour Party, but was in fact a right-wing group. He was reluctant to discuss politics, and his reticence made me realize how dangerous a subject this was. We drove through choking heat and clotted traffic past shantytowns that sprawled for miles. There were gullies strewn with trash and running with sewage. There were young men sitting in the shade of any tree they could find, their eagle eyes missing nothing. They reminded me of the hero of a movie I had just seen, *The Harder They Come,* which starred the handsome reggae singer Jimmy Cliff as a raw country boy come to town who had big dreams of making it as a singer but quickly ran afoul of the law. The character Cliff played was based on a real-life Jamaican outlaw from the fifties, a man named Rhygin who was a kind of Robin Hood hero to the "sufferers," as Jamaicans call the poorest of the poor. The young men on these Kingston corners were Rhygins, too, just waiting for a gun.

But amidst the rot and the stench of a Third World city, Jamaica's beauty still resolutely bloomed. I glimpsed it everywhere. In a schoolgirl sauntering down the rubbly sidewalk, her hair in ribboned braids, her body's ripeness not fully disguised by her prim khaki uniform. In the timeworn face of a Rastafarian elder, sitting in the merciful shade of a rum shop wall with his Bible on his lap, one eye on the word of Jah and the other on the cop with the red stripe down the pants leg of his uniform, which he slapped ever so lightly with his swagger stick as he strolled by. In the quiet dignity of a church woman, clad in stainless white with a matching head tie, holding herself like a queen as she picked her way through the goats and the pigs and the chickens, on her way to an all-night revivalist meeting at a tented Jesus tabernacle. This was Kingston.

This was the Jamaica to which I knew I would return—for reasons both political and personal, almost none of which I yet understood.

$$\mathbb{Q}$$

THERE WAS A certain synchronicity for me, a resonance between the self I was becoming and the outlaw ethos of this island I was beginning to know and to love. The "runnins" of the seventies, the glory days of Rasta and reggae when so many young Americans traveled to Jamaica, were famous for two things. Both of them touched me in ways that were—and still are—not easy to admit.

The first was ganja, which is the Weed of Wisdom to many Jamaicans and to almost all Rastafarians. Smoking it became—as for so many other young American visitors to Jamaica—my ticket to acceptance among the Rastas whose teachings had begun to be so significant to me.

This was not simply because the herb was pleasurable and went so well with the tropical life. Its power also derived from another source, something that perhaps you had to be inside of to really understand. For the smoking of ganja was, for many of us, a way of expressing solidarity with black people, with their struggle and their joy and the way they saw their world.

I know this sounds self-serving, inexcusably "ofay" nowadays when everyone is doing twelve-step penance for being who they once were. But the sharing of ganja felt like a sacrament to us in Jamaica, on those endless nights when we sat talking to new friends, who might be Rasta visionaries or simply good folk, trying to get closer to them and narrow the gap between our wildly dissimilar worlds. They, for their part, were trying to teach us about themselves, and the ganja made this instruction seem even deeper, more wondrous.

There was a knot tightly tied: between reggae music—surely one of the most potent forces the world has ever seen—and the ganja that propelled it. Both fueled the energy for protest that was catapulting this small island into the forefront of the Third World. And if the Weed of Wisdom sparked this vision, these songs of freedom, this righteous anger and grief at what the First World had made of the Third, it also united people of different races who might otherwise never have bridged this gap. In the passing of a ritual chalice, thousands upon thousands of young people, black and white, sought to find common ground. And for this there need be no apology.

I have never forgotten a visit with a Rasta elder I knew, a gray-haired prophet by the name of Bongo Sylvester. "Sylly," as everyone called him, lived in a seaside palace not far from Ocho Rios that was woven entirely of wicker. He sat me down in the airy upstairs room where he held court, surrounded by his many ardent followers, and handed me a spliff the size of a Monte Cristo that I knew I was supposed to smoke all by myself.

Sylly then launched into one of his mystical "irations," a lecture about slavery and colonialism and the longed-for Rastafarian repatriation to the African promised land. The smoke from everyone's spliffs billowed like the sails of a great ship, transporting Sylly and his devout disciples away from their Jamaican exile to a long-dreamed-of home.

I took only a few tokes, as much as I dared; I knew how strong this stuff was. When Sylly paused to gather his next words, I ventured to say that since I was white, I could not really appreciate what it would mean to go back to Africa.

"*White?*" Sylly growled through the cloud of smoke that obscured his lionlike features. "You not white, sistah!" He grabbed my sun-darkened hand and placed it on the bedsheet. "*This* is white!" he rasped. "You no' see it? You nah' white, sis! You dark like a Arawak!"

The Arawaks were the original inhabitants of Jamaica, a peaceful tribe that was exterminated within two decades after Columbus and his band of thieves arrived.

"You Arawak!" Sylly exulted. "Africa is fi' we, and Jamaica is fi' you! Is *your* land, this. You come to capture back your true-true home!"

⚲

GANJA WAS THE first of Jamaica's culture-straddling gifts to its visitors. The second was a phenomenon that is equally tempting to scoff at but which nevertheless changed a lot of lives: that of the white American woman who spent a two-week idyll on the island and fell (like lead) for a black Jamaican man.

This pattern got to be so familiar that it soon had its own name: "rent-a-dread." You'd see these couples careening by on motorbikes in every resort town from Port Antonio in the sleepy, laid-back East to Negril in the wild, wild Jamaican West. The white woman would be sunburnt a painful red, her hair in Bo Derek braids or ripped crazily by the sun and wind. Her man would be looking like he had just snared the trophy of all trophies, his long locks whipping her face as she held on behind him, clinging for dear life.

Sometimes, she never left. She'd stay with her rent-a-dread and go live in a tiny hut with a dirt floor, learn to cook "ital" (vegetarian) food, and have beautiful brown babies with exotic names.

Mary and I had a phrase for such women. We'd gotten friendly with one whose name was Barbara. She'd gone all the way, married her dread and gotten him a coveted green card, and when he came to the states he promptly left Barbara in the dust.

Mary and I nicknamed her "Two-Week Barbara" and shook our heads in sympathy, swearing we would never make the same mistake. I had my own reason for being so sure. In the South of my girlhood, men of color were so off-limits, so forbidden, that I knew I would never go against this aspect of my "raising," as Rhoda would have called it. And not because I didn't find black men decidedly beautiful, or desirable. But in the South I knew—and the one whose lessons still beat in my blood—a white woman who seduced a black man might as well have thrown the lynch rope over the pine bough, all by herself.

I had never forgotten the murder of Emmett Till in Mississippi, which took place in 1955, when I was six. Till was fourteen, from Chicago, and he was visiting his great-uncle for part of the summer.

On a dare from some local friends, he entered a store and asked a white woman if she would go out with him, then whistled at her as he left. The men who killed him were acquitted on a technicality: They mutilated Emmett Till's body so terribly that it could not be positively identified. *Jet* magazine obtained photographs of the body, and a copy of the magazine found its way into our house, where I saw it on the dresser in Rhoda's room. Enough said.

So every time I felt the tug of attraction to a Jamaican—even though I knew this was another country, a place where a black man might make love to me without risking being butchered—I talked myself out of it. I had seen too many pictures of the Strange Fruit dangling from Southern trees, and always my eyes went to the one place on the lynch mob's victim that I knew would be bloodiest, cut to pieces by their knives. Then my gaze traveled to the leering, jeering faces of the white devils in the night crowd, lit up into monsters by the camera's flash.

❧

AFTER THAT FIRST trip to Jamaica, I began going back as often as I could. The island became the place where I set free a side of myself that was shut down at Harvard. The rippling energy of reggae and patois, the intoxicating power of the Rastafarian "teachments" I hearkened to with a reverence that became more and more intense as they multiplied—I was caught now between two opposing worlds, and I could not reconcile them.

I was also courting danger in Jamaica. I had become transfixed by the secret symbiosis between the island's corrupt politicians and those Johnny-Too-Bad, *Harder They Come* outlaws whom the politicians armed and paid to control Kingston. All I wanted now was to get through my doctorate, earn those letters after my name, and leave Harvard for the work I really wanted to do: getting into the ghettos of Kingston, finding those legendary outlaws, talking to them, and writing the untold history of their lives.

I knew full well how perilous an endeavor this would be, but I wanted it—every bit as fiercely as I'd once desired Harvard. Some force was pulling me back to Jamaica, into its direst, most closely guarded secret. I never knew whose beckoning voice it was that I heard, but I think it may have been Rhoda's, even though she would have died of fright if she'd had any inkling of what I intended to do. The voice told me: "You don't have to be afraid. No one will hurt you. Just treat the people you meet with respect, as you have been taught to do, and they will treat you just the same." A laughable innocence that was, in retrospect, but I took this lesson to heart and, as it turned out, it was true.

"My own mother and father," I remembered Rhoda saying. "They were born in slavery." Sam and Julia. The bondage they had endured was still alive and well on the ghetto streets of Kingston. Slavery had not ended. I did not question why it was my work to witness this and chronicle it. I simply felt it. And, as Bob Marley said, "Him who feels it knows it, Lord."

I started asking questions of the new friends I was making in Jamaica about the island's dirty little war. They told me stories, vague as shadows on a wall, about this gunman or the other; their secret affiliations with Manley or his right-wing nemesis, Edward Seaga, leader of the Jamaica Labour Party. This was oral history: never written, only told. It was passed along in whispers from one sufferer to another, and whenever one of these outlaws was gunned down, his life became the stuff of legend. But the facts, the details, were lost. A people's history died every time a Robin Hood bandit was killed. It was this history I meant to salvage.

But I was wrong to think I'd be able to simply observe. There was an entry fee, or so it seemed to me, to this outlaw world. And the price of the ticket was drugs. When the storytellers I was coming to know in Jamaica imparted their secrets to me, we were almost always high. The ritual sharing of ganja came with the territory of my inquiry. It came with being a supplicant, a student instead of a teacher. With being a white outsider, a stranger knocking on the gates. I believed that the only way I could partake of their afflictions was to share the herb that gave them their brief respite from a pain-filled life. I wasn't so arrogant that I believed I could ever know what they knew. Whatever arrogance I owned took another form.

I started smoking in ever-increasing amounts, and soon I was smuggling ganja when I returned home. I'd slit the seam of my out-size pocketbook and stash a well-pressed pound or two between the lining and the leather. I was so sure I'd never get caught and that if I was, my white privilege would keep me out of jail.

One sultry afternoon, as I was packing for my return to Boston at the house my sister and her husband were renting above Montego Bay, he watched me sew the ganja into my bag. He sauntered over and clamped his hand down on my shoulder.

"Are you willing to risk this?" he asked.

"What's *this*?" I shot back, cocky as always.

"The sinking sensation you're going to have when a customs officer collars you at Logan Airport and says, 'Come with me, please.' You ready for that? Because if it happens, it won't just mean a fine, kiddo. It'll mean you might never be able to come back to Jamaica."

"Oh," I answered blithely, "I'm not going to get caught."

Mercifully, I never was. The trap I was laying for myself would be sprung in other ways.

@

DETERMINED TO KEEP Jamaica in my heart, I began to seek out Caribbean students at Harvard. The one with whom I soon became close was Karen Ford, a Jamaican woman who embodied everything I admired about her country.

She reminded me a little of the American folksinger Odetta, with her dark skin, strobe of a smile, and hair cut short enough to show off the shape of her elegant head. She was built like the country women from whom she descended, with arms strong enough to lift just about anything: a baby, a market basket, a personal computer. Maybe even a country, if it came to that.

The Christmas after we met, Karen invited me to come home with her to Kingston. Her parents were waiting for us in the line of people at the gate after we'd cleared customs, and she flew into their arms. I could see the pride and delight they took in their daughter, and as I stood there, waiting my turn to be introduced, I felt a pang of envy, wishing my own parents loved me in such an unrestrained way.

We drove back to their apartment in New Kingston through streets that had become familiar to me. Upstairs on their little balcony, with the outline of the Blue Mountains rising in the milky moonlight and the streetlights of Kingston twinkling beneath, I could still hear the night sounds of crickets and tree frogs. We sat up very late, talking and laughing and telling stories, until Karen said she had to sleep. We tumbled together into her double bed. But I could not fall asleep. I lay awake for hours, listening to a sound system in the neighborhood that was so loud it threatened to take down the walls. I was remembering a story Mother had told me, years ago, of an event in her own life when she was young.

It was about exactly what I was doing at this moment, sharing a room—not to mention a bed—with a friend whose skin was a different color. Not a nurse or a maid, a *friend*. Mother's story was from the forties, when she went to hear Marian Anderson in concert at Hampton Institute. Anderson had refused to sing before a segregated audience in Richmond.

"I went with a dear friend of mine," Mother recalled. "Her name was Anne Gelman. She and her husband belonged to Beth El." Beth El was Richmond's Conservative synagogue, and most of its congregation were Russian Jews, unlike our Beth Ahabah, where almost all the families were of German descent. I knew the difference, believe you me, and Mother knew I did. It meant that my father heartily disapproved of her friendship with this Anne Gelman.

"Oh, she was the most marvelous woman!" Mother went on. "Very political. She and her husband had Negro friends. I mean real, true friends, not just people they went to meetings with. They socialized. I wanted so much to, too, but Daddy would have died . . ." Her voice trailed off. "Well, anyway, Anne and I kind of sneaked off to

Hampton to hear Anderson. I think I told Daddy we were going somewhere else. We had to spend the night, and we shared a dormitory room there with two colored women.

"I know this sounds pathetic, but at the time that seemed like the most radical thing I had ever done. To share a room with a Negro woman who wasn't a maid."

Now, in this velvety Jamaican darkness, lying beside my friend, I yearned for Mother. I wished we could have shared this moment, what it meant for me and what it might have said to her about the changes that had come with time. When I finally drifted off to sleep, I had a startling dream.

I was being interviewed by a young white man who was dressed in the baggy pants of the thirties. I was wearing a faded calico apron, and when I looked down at my hands, I saw they were black. Suddenly, I realized who we were. The young man was one of those WPA writers who went through the South during the Depression, interviewing former slaves. I was one.

He asked me something about when freedom came, what that had been like. "No, sah," I heard myself say, in a voice not my own. "We was still in slavery then."

I woke with a start and fumbled for the bedside lamp. My heart was beating hard and I was damp with sweat. Next to me, Karen slept on.

"Who *was* that?" I asked myself in a whisper as if there was someone in the room with me. "Whose voice was that?"

☙

BY THEN, I was shuttling every couple of months between Harvard and Jamaica. I was finished with all my course work and was reading for my dissertation. Under the influence of Jamaica, I left the Renaissance in a cloud of dust and metaphorically set sail for the Indies, deciding to write my dissertation on the beginnings of African slavery in the Spanish Caribbean. It wasn't quite Jah Rastafari, but it was close enough. I'd begun studying with a wonderful professor, a swashbuckling English historian by the name of

John Horace Parry, who had the most adventurous spirit of any man I have ever known. He would have been a rare find anywhere, but at Harvard he was a treasure. The first time I traipsed into his Widener office, my skin dark from the island sun, I was met by a vitally handsome man in his sixties with silver hair and a patrician bearing. Parry cocked his head and listened closely to my idea for the dissertation and then drew a monocle up to his eye.

"I say, Miss Gunst!" he boomed. "You're not actually *from* Jamaica, are you?"

He went on to explain that he was only hoping I was, because the island was perhaps his favorite place in all the world—and Parry was a man who had seen most of it. "I was the first head of the history department at the University of the West Indies, you see," he explained. "At the Mona campus in Kingston. I don't think I've ever lived anywhere quite so beautiful. Or quite so very sad."

I knew that I had found a friend.

Parry's love of adventure, his passion for cross-cultural exchanges of all kinds, proved to be contagious. That fall, determined to make my Cambridge life into as much a replica of Jamaica as I could, I embarked on one of the wilder group-living experiments of my life and invited a Rastafarian couple I'd become friendly with to come live with me.

Geraldine Robbins was an accomplished artist, a green-eyed Jewish American Princess with dreadlocks down to her knees. She had gone to Negril ten years before, on one of those two-week vacations that turned into the rest of her life. While she was there, she met a Rasta elder named Iyah Brown and they soon got married. Geri's parents in Pennsylvania sat shiva for her—the Orthodox ritual of mourning—as if she were dead. Just in case she rose from the grave, they told her never to come home again.

Standing four foot ten in his bare feet—and he didn't like to wear shoes—Iyah was a pygmy prince with dreadlocks. He had a mouth full of excellent teeth, which he flashed all the time because he loved to smile and to laugh. His locks were much shorter than Geri's because the weight of his dreads had pulled many of them out over the years. But most of the time, Iyah hid them underneath one "crown" or another, as Rastas call their outsize hats. With his favorite crown of bright red, gold, and green, striped like a barber pole, you could see Iyah coming from three blocks away.

He was a bush doctor of no mean skill. He knew how to concoct tonics and potions from just about every tree, bush, and plant that grew in Jamaica, and from the time he and Geri married, he had been bringing all the force of his herbal wisdom to bear on one major project: helping her conceive the baby they both yearned to have.

Finally, Geri had gotten pregnant. She was visiting my sister in New Hampshire when she got the news, and she intended to stay in the United States till the baby was born; she knew enough about Jamaica to want her child to be an American citizen. She also meant to go on welfare while she was pregnant, to get money to help cover their expenses while they were with me. We knew that after she had notified the welfare office, an inspector was going to come knocking on my landlady's door, since Hildreth was the owner of the house.

"You all," I said to Geri and Iyah, right after she'd been approved for public assistance, "I'm going to have to explain the plan to Hildreth. It's her house, after all, and I can't do anything behind her back."

"Yes, Dawtah," Iyah drawled, letting out a cloud of smoke from the eight-inch spliff of the very finest sinsemilla I had just bought for him, at a hundred dollars an ounce. "You mus' speak the truth, always."

I put on a nice skirt and a cashmere sweater and walked by that blue historical marker bleating out its message about WEALTHY FAMILIES LOYAL TO THE CROWN, and timidly rapped the heavy brass knocker on Hildreth's door.

She ushered me into her parlor with its tall windows looking out onto Brattle Street, and we settled into her little French armchairs covered in very old tapestry. With an eggshell-thin cup of tea poised on my lap, I launched into the saga of Geri and Iyah. Hildreth's beautiful brown eyes widened in wonderment.

"My *deah,*" she breathed, bringing her hand with its fiery opal and diamond ring to her throat. "Do I understand you to say that this woman is about to have a baby, and her own mother wants nothing to do with her?"

"Yes," I answered. "That's about the gist of it."

"How ghastly!" Hildreth exclaimed. "How absolutely frightful." She paused. "Well! Of course, they must stay here with us! With you, I mean. And how wonderful you are to open your home to them. We shall all have the most exciting winter!"

⌇

IT TURNED OUT to be one of the coldest on record. Geri stayed indoors most of every day, painting and drawing and stuffing herself with delicious sweets from the patisseries of Harvard Square. Iyah and I went everywhere together, to natural food stores and reggae concerts and crowded, rundown flats in Roxbury and Dorchester, where Iyah's Rasta brethren hailed him as a Prince of Dread. His locks functioned like some kind of radar, sending out a signal to every Rasta within a radius of fifty miles, and sooner or later all of them found their way to Tory Row.

I was in heaven. All day long and deep into the night, I'd be reasoning and arguing and speaking patois with these men—there were no females; all the women were tending to the babies. But since I did not get into a sexual relationship with any of them, they made me into a kind of honorary male, which suited me fine. With Iyah as our tutor, we'd delve deep into "the History and the Mystery," the four hundred years of slavery and colonialism that had landed Jamaica in its current travail. Finally, it seemed, I had found a way of bringing Jamaica and Harvard together.

Hildreth proved to be the angel downstairs. She never complained about the large numbers of fierce-looking Jamaicans who routinely showed up at my door, which was right across from her kitchen window. She said she liked the sound of the records by Bob Marley and Burning Spear and Toots and the Maytals that Iyah blasted and I kept trying to turn down. And she didn't seem to mind the smoke from the ten or twenty spliffs that we burned each day. The smoke was so thick that it went right through the priceless Fortuny curtain hung across the upstairs door between Hildreth's part of the house and mine. When her daughter came to visit, she caught a whiff and told her mother we were smoking only the very best.

In February, the whole East Coast was blanketed by a record-breaking blizzard. It turned Brattle Street into a Brueghel land-scape, everyone on foot and children with their sleds. All our neighbors were desperate to have their driveways and sidewalks cleared, so Hildreth introduced Iyah to her many Brahmin friends; she knew almost all the neighbors who lived in those resplendent mansions where I had never so much as set foot.

Iyah shoveled snow as energetically as he tilled his provision ground on the rocky red-clay hillside back home.

"Whoy!" he beamed, stepping back inside to get more coffee for his thermos. "What a sight, eh? Come like Jamaica!"

"Iyah! You're crazy. There's ice in your beard. What do you mean, it 'come like Jamaica'?"

"Is all one Creation, dawtah! You no see it? Jah Majesty is the same everywhere!"

The neighbors stepped outside to chat with Iyah while he worked. He gave them his "teachments" about vegetarianism and nonviolence and the Rastafarian way of life. Soon, these sweet-natured souls—who had no reason to be afraid of anyone or any-thing, so cosseted by wealth were they—invited Geri and Iyah and Hildreth and me to tea in their sumptuous drawing rooms.

We perched on velvet chairs while I tried not to stare with too much naked envy at the gorgeous antiques and wonderful art. Geri brought her knitting, the tiny sweaters and baby blankets she was working on, and the clicking of her needles was background music to Iyah's talk. He took the grandeur of his surroundings in stride. Since he knew he had a hotline to the Creator, he felt it was only his due to be treated with the utmost respect.

In the spring, Geri gave birth to a boy. They named him "Ital," which means "natural." Geri's only regret was that Ital's skin was lighter than she had expected; she had wanted to have a baby whose skin matched Iyah's.

"Oh, but darling!" Hildreth murmured, cradling Ital as she spoke. "He's the most beautiful baby! And, Geri, who knows? His skin might grow darker in time!"

Like I dreamed for a second time that my skin was, one night a few weeks after my Rasta holy family went back to Jamaica. I woke and shuffled to the bathroom, looked into the mirror, and was shocked to see I was still white.

thirteen

I MISSED THEM SO much after they had gone—Iyah with his fulminating eloquence, his warmth; Geri with her almost constant kvetching that had nevertheless come to feel very motherly. And, unexpectedly, I missed Ital very much. I'd grown accustomed to kissing the top of his head and to how he smelled of milk. I think I knew even then, though I was only thirty, that I'd never have a baby. It just wasn't in the cards.

In my loneliness, I ought to have realized how vulnerable I was. Adrift from any human anchors, I was more susceptible than ever to the dubious solace of substances. Someone I knew bitingly referred to Harvard as "the drug-riddled underbelly of academia," and he knew whereof he spoke.

A couple of months after Geri and Iyah left, on a glorious, lilac-scented May afternoon, the dealer from whom I'd hitherto bought nothing stronger than ganja dropped by with a gram of pharmaceutical-grade cocaine.

He and I were setting out for a concert by Bob Marley at the

Harvard stadium in honor of the independence of Zimbabwe. He took a tiny vial from his pocket, shook a little pyramid of coke onto the miniature mirror he was never without, and said, "Here. Just do this one line."

"No," I answered. I was still a virgin when it came to snorting anything; the idea was as frightening to me as sticking a needle in my vein. "I don't think so."

"Oh, come on," he urged, giving me a Mephistophelian grin. I looked at him and then at the mirror. The powder wasn't really white, I noticed. And it was flaky, iridescent like mica. It was actually a beautiful shade of pale pink, like mother-of-pearl.

"How come it's that color?" I asked.

"Because I don't whack it," he answered. "I don't cut it with baby laxative or Xylocaine like the other dealers you know. It's too good for that."

He prided himself on what he called his "product," on having the best drugs in town, and gloried in his power to get everyone around him high.

Well, I thought to myself, *if it's pure, why not?*

The scorching burn didn't last but a second, and what followed soon thereafter was enough to tell me that I'd found my drug. Ganja had been pleasurable, sure enough. But this stuff was something else. For the first time, I knew how it felt to rule the world.

"So . . ." The dealer's voice sounded like it was coming from a faraway place. "You think you could get into a little Marley now?" That devilish grin again. He knew just what he was doing; oh, yes he did.

"Don't ask me," I answered, cool and surging with my new, secret power. "I can do *anything.*"

Except imagine living without this sensation, ever again.

FROM THAT DAY on, cocaine was my constant companion. It meshed so splendidly with my outlaw identity, the need I had to cut myself out from the straight and boring Harvard herd. It went perfectly with the person I was becoming, the woman all alone in her proud tower on Tory Row, the woman who thought she needed no one but herself.

Driven as I was, I still managed to keep working on my dissertation. I was deep into my subject, the life and times of a tortured Spanish reformer by the name of Bartolomé de Las Casas. He had sailed to the Indies with Columbus on the admiral's last voyage and was given a number of Arawak slaves—my ancestors, if you believed what my old friend Bongo Sylvester in Jamaica had said—to work his fields and mines on the island that is now shared by Haiti and the Dominican Republic; the Spaniards called it Española, which means "Little Spain." But Las Casas couldn't square his conscience with the horrors he saw—the massacres and forced labor and starvation that were bringing about the destruction of an island world that had been close to paradise before the Spaniards arrived. In 1516, Las Casas came up with what seemed to him like a good idea at the time. He proposed to the Spanish crown that a small number of Africans be imported into the islands; their slave labor would serve as a "remedy"—Las Casas's word—for the native Arawaks, most of whom were already dead.

John Parry, my much-loved mentor, was tremendously excited by this subject; he had been waiting for years for someone to debunk Las Casas. For generations, historians had seen the man as a saintly priest, the "Defender of the Indians," the title bestowed on him by the Spanish crown. Now Parry had a graduate student who was finally going to expose Las Casas's dark side, his tragic mistake: defending the liberty of one race while advocating the enslavement of another.

In our weekly meetings and at wonderful dinner parties that John and his wife, Joyce, gave, we talked endlessly about the Caribbean, the different histories of all the islands, the ways in which colonialism still haunted the region. And as I trudged home every night from the library, my head full of terrible images from this brutal past, I somehow never realized just why this whole subject was emotionally devastating for me. I was strangely blind to the personal implications of what I was uncovering, to how the history of slavery made my stomach churn. I was reading about the heritage of those I loved.

I think this was one of the reasons I sought to numb myself with cocaine. I'd manage to go without it for a couple of days, and then the weight of sadness and depression, the near hysteria I was feeling over what I was reading about, would come flooding back over me and the next thing I knew, I was speeding down Memorial Drive to the filthy apartment where my dealer lived, to score another few grams of oblivion.

His apartment was directly across the street from the Cambridge police station, but this was just part of the daring, the risk. He lived on the third floor; there was a rickety staircase up to his back door, and the steps were skittering with rats who fed from the garbage cans on the landings. I'd rap lightly on the rotting wood door, knowing I would find him awake no matter what time it was. He and his friends—*my* friends now—would be hovering around the pilot light on his grease-encrusted stove, stoking a freebase pipe.

I never lingered—I couldn't stand the chaos and the dirt—but stayed just long enough to get my gram. Enough to carry me through the morning, till I was in such a state of wired misery that only sleep could comfort me. But sleep would never come.

◎

DRUGS HAVE A way of obliging you to cut the traces to your straight life. I had a secret to keep now, and keeping it was a lot easier if I hung out mostly with other users. I canceled tutorials, told my students I was sick. I stopped going out to parties or clubs because I'd start snorting lines before I went, and then get so wired I couldn't be with anyone but myself. I'd lock myself into my garret of a study overlooking Tory Row and pound away on my IBM Selectric, composing letters that I never sent (thank God). Or I'd phone all my friends who lived in California and might still be awake, since it was three hours earlier on the other coast.

One night, I heard a faint scratching noise on the other side of the door across the hall, the one that led down the stairs to the street. *Oh God,* I thought, *someone's broken in.* In a panic, I stashed my coke and mirror in the desk drawer and dialed 911. Two squad cars arrived within minutes—one of the perks of living on Tory Row. When I flicked on the light in the stairwell, I could hear the cops laughing.

"Jesus, Joseph and Mary!" one of them called out to his commanding officer. "*It's a bat!*"

"Wait!" I hollered. "I'll be right down." I've loved bats ever since I was a child, and I didn't want them to hurt it. We always had some in our garage and when they flew into the house, Daddy would take care to get them safely back outside. He was forever telling us what helpful, insect-eating, plant-pollinating creatures they were.

I took a broom and got the little fellow safely back outside. The cops drove away into the dawn. *Bats in the belfry,* I said to myself as I climbed the stairs. You've got bats in the belfry, old girl.

❧

THERE WERE STILL friends who never let go of me, and one of them was my Jamaican soul sister, Karen Ford. She knew what I was doing, but she also knew I needed to be reminded that there were things in life besides cocaine. She and I were both great admirers of Jimmy Cliff, the reggae singer who starred in *The Harder They Come.* Cliff lived just up the street from Karen's home in Kingston, and whenever she and I were there together, we'd drive to his house and see if he was there. He'd stroll out to the car, lean into the window, his face as beautiful as a Benin bronze, and chat with us for a while.

In the fall of 1979, Cliff came to Boston to give a concert, and Karen and I threw a party for him at my place. I never thought he'd come, but he did, and his entire band did, too. It was such a fabulous party that from then on my friend Luke Ehrlich—a white Jewish Rasta and a favorite deejay on the Boston reggae scene—dubbed me the Pearl Mesta of Rasta. Luke was at the party, of course, as, for the first time, were friends from both the Harvard and Jamaican halves of my life.

It was one of those starstruck nights no one ever wanted to end. I sidled through the packed crowd from one room to another, reveling in the energy. Don Wilcox, my teacher from New Hampshire, stood in the kitchen with his new black lover, sharing a spliff with the keyboard player from Cliff's band. Don put his arm around my shoulder.

"My little Maimonides," he smiled. "Whoever would have thought?"

In the hallway stood my landlady, Hildreth, quite at home in this multicultural pageant that had taken over upstairs. "Wonderful party, darling," she said. "Don't you wish that Geri and Iyah could be here? They are, you know. In spirit."

In the living room, my old friends from the Rasta community in Roxbury and Dorchester were holding court for a worshipful audience of Harvard undergraduates who were hanging on their every word. Karen Ford was in my bedroom with a small group that included Cliff and my friend Luke who intended to do an interview that night with the singer for his Boston radio show. My sister Mary, newly divorced, was sneaking down the steps with the drummer from Cliff's band, which was aptly called the Jamaican Experience.

There were copious quantities of ganja being smoked everywhere, but the cocaine users had the good taste to stay in my bedroom. My dealer had taken the bathroom mirror down from the wall, laid it on my bed, and was now busy cutting lines ten inches long.

Jimmy Cliff sat deep in a wing chair in the corner, sipping a nonalcoholic drink I'd made for him from pineapple and ginger. His face showed his exhaustion from months on the road, but—being a Muslim and therefore not a taker of drugs—he still looked a hell of a lot better than the rest of us. Every time I bent over the mirror, I'd straighten up to see his eyes on me. There was no flicker of judgment in his even gaze, only a mild boredom with the antics he observed. My dealer kept prancing over to him, lowering that mirror under Cliff's nose like a waiter with a tray. And every time, the star looked up at him and politely declined.

"No, mon," he murmured, laying one graceful, long-fingered

hand lightly across his throat. "Mi' voice, you see? I haffi' protect mi' voice."

Until that moment, I had never seen anyone refuse cocaine. By then, I was familiar with the way coke strangled my own voice, paralyzing it in my throat and leaving me to stammer. A new thought blazed its way into my brain. I'd always associated coke with being hip, and being hip with being black. Here was one of the brightest stars in the world of black music, turning it down. Maybe he knew something I didn't know.

The gray light of dawn was breaking into the bedroom, and Jimmy's eyelids drooped. But he was still politely answering questions from Luke, who then turned to me. "Is there anything you'd like to ask Jimmy?" he offered.

I did have one question. By then it seemed foolish, but I felt like asking it all the same. "I've always wondered," I said, "why you never locksed up." I paused, suddenly ashamed of asking such a personal question. "It's just that, well . . . it seems like every other Jamaican artist is a dread. So, I wondered why you aren't."

Cliff threw me a dazzling smile. I blushed. "Well, dawtah," he whispered, his voice hoarse from all that singing. He paused for a moment, considering what he wanted to say, "Let I tell you. Mi' dread's so long, you cyan' even see it. It's invisible! Indivisible!"

We both laughed. Then he leaned forward, speaking so softly that only I could hear. "You must check for the dread in the heart, you know. Not for the locks on the head."

⚬

CLIFF'S WORDS TO me were his gift in parting. It was a kind of blessing, and I might have known it was a summons to live another way. But as things stood, I was still ensnared in the web I had woven, and it was not quite time for me to come unstuck.

This was the time when Rhoda's life, her light, began to flicker and die out. The thought of losing her was beyond my comprehension. She was in her eighties now and no longer living on Idlewood Avenue. Her house had been torn down for an expressway and her old neighborhood destroyed. The new road was called the Powhite, which was pronounced "Pow-Hite." But Mother and Daddy and I referred to it as the "Po' White," and I refused to use the new highway when I went home. There was a tollbooth where Rhoda's house had been and most of Idlewood Avenue had ceased to exist.

Mother found a new apartment for Rhoda that was not too far away; it was closer to where we lived. She moved in with all her old furniture—the beautiful mahogany bed and the polished shelves for her whatnots, as she called them, her collection of china figurines. But although her new home was lovely, with a porch overlooking the tree-lined street and a window sill in the kitchen consecrated to her prized African violets, it was not the same as her old house on Idlewood. No sooner had she moved in than the flight of steps she had to climb began to be a problem for her. She began to have small strokes that left her hands shaky, so she could not write well anymore. The words seemed to tremble on the page, the lines went every which way. But I could still read them.

"Dearest Laurie," she wrote, after I had sent her money for her birthday, "I see the Pony Express has come It remind me of the Old Days. And it will be used wisely. Your Mother is wonderful to me. She is good in so Many Ways. We all had a lovely time."

I knew she meant her birthday party at our house. But somehow that sounded to me like a farewell; as if she were saying that her whole life with us had been "a lovely time."

"Dear Laurie," another letter read, "I miss you so much. I hope you are well and happy. I am thinking of you I am fine Your mother took me to the Doctor He gave me a good report. Take care of yourself and keep happy. What are you thinking of? I love you. Rhoda."

What are you thinking of? Slavery, Rhoda. The sea change and the four hundred years. I'm thinking of you, my love. Of a little girl in Summerville, South Carolina, with a mother named Julia and a father named Sam. *Born in slavery.* I'm also mindful of myself, Rhoda. Up north, here at the "Highest School." Living in my self-made prison of cocaine.

◎

ENDINGS ABOUNDED. IN June 1982, I received my doctorate. Two months later, John Parry died of a heart attack on a scholars' cruise he was leading through the fjords of Scandinavia. With his death, not only did I grieve the loss of a true friend, I also realized that I was mentorless in academia and would have to chart my professional course alone.

I cobbled together a series of courses to teach, a postdoctoral year hanging on at Harvard in the Program for History and Literature, and then a semester teaching at my old alma mater, the University of New Hampshire. But my heart wasn't in it. I'd stopped wanting to be an academic, to spend the rest of my life doing research and publishing books that only a few people would ever read. The world was on fire: Ronald Reagan was in the White House, Edward Seaga had become the new right-wing prime minister of Jamaica, and the island was bleeding from the mounting violence of its gangs. I did not belong in Cambridge anymore. But I was afraid to leave. Absurd as it may seem, when I asked myself the mocking question, "Is there life afer Harvard?" I honestly wasn't sure that the answer was "Yes!"

I spent as much time as I could with Rhoda in Richmond. I'd go to meet her at her apartment and then the two of us would slowly descend her front steps and walk up Cary Street to a restaurant called The Track. They had Rhoda's favorite dish, soft-shell crabs. I'd put the pillow we'd brought on the seat in our booth and the two of us would sit holding hands across the table. The waitress would bring us Cokes and menus, and we would exchange smiles.

"We know what we want," Rhoda would say.

One day, waiting for our soft-shell crabs, I tried to forget the fight I'd had with Mother that morning, about putting Rhoda in a nursing home. I insisted that we take care of her ourselves. She could live with us, I said, in the room over the garage—the former maid's room that Mother had turned into guest quarters now. She said I was out of my mind.

"Honey. Listen to me. I'm old now, too. I can't be taking care of Rhoda here in this house. We're just not set up for it."

"So get *up!*" I yelled, in a white-hot rage. "What do you think all this fucking money is for?"

"Don't use that kind of language with me, please."

"I can't believe this!" I was crying now. "She's taken care of five generations of this family, and now you're going to stick her in some godforsaken place where she'll sit in a wheelchair all day long and no one will care? I can't believe I'm even related to you. I don't want to *know* you, Mother!"

Sophia was in the kitchen with us. She stepped over and put her arm around my shoulder.

"Sugar, your mama knows what she's talking about. Believe me, she does. You just don't have any idea of the work it takes, having an old person at home. Rhoda will be better off in a nursing home, I swear. And we'll all go to visit her, I promise."

They won, as I knew they would. There was no way Mother was going to take care of Rhoda at our house. Sitting with her now in our booth at The Track, I tried to get the terrible thought of her being in a nursing home out of my head.

"What are you thinking of, Rhodie?"

"Oh, I'm remembering this old friend of mine from Summerville. A girl by the name of Mamie. We grew up together. She's still there. But she's old and ailing now. Just like me."

An idea took hold. "Let's go and see her, Rhodie! You and me."

"How we gonna get there? It's a long, long way."

"Can't be more than two days' drive. We'll just get in the car and go."

Rhoda shook her head. "I'm not sure I can make it, honey. Much as I would love to see Mamie. I just don't think I can make such a long trip."

◎

THAT FALL, RHODA moved into a nursing home called Westport Manor. It was in the West End, not far from our house. Mother and

Sophia were as good as their word; they did go to visit her often, and we hired a private-duty companion to be with her so that she would be well cared for. But I could still see how Rhoda resented the intrusion of this stranger, the indignity of having to be "toileted" and wiped like a child.

"Life everlasting!" she would say as I bent to kiss her. "I'm just so glad to see you, child."

"I brought you a hydrangea. For your windowsill. And some really good ham and candied sweet potatoes that Sophia made."

Rhoda ate hungrily and afterward she ran her tongue across her teeth.

"They're all mossy." She frowned. "I can't floss them anymore, my hands shake too bad."

"I'll do it for you."

Rhoda leaned her head back and I went to work, holding my breath against the smell as I was sure she'd held hers countless times when she changed my diapers. What goes around comes around.

The photograph of Rhoda, the one taken in Harlem that I adored, sat on her dresser next to the picture of her first husband, Willie Lloyd. I held the two framed faces in my lap so we could look at them together.

"You're still beautiful, Rhodie." I smiled. "You haven't changed a bit." I remembered how she and Granny would always tell each other that when they met at the train station. Now, looking at those photographs, I knew what Rhoda was thinking before she said it.

"Don't you worry. I'll always keep you and Willie together, like you said. I promise."

Rhoda turned to me with that Gioconda smile. "I know."

❧

I WAS STILL going to Jamaica every chance I got. Only now I was serious about getting a job there, at the University of the West Indies in Kingston. I interviewed with the head of the history department in the spring of 1983 and he phoned me soon thereafter to say that one of their professors was going on leave the following fall, and would I be interested in filling in?

I said yes immediately. But I didn't tell him what else I planned to do that year. Had I told him that I intended to get into the Kingston ghettos and interview the gang leaders for a book about the bitter history of Jamaica's tribal war, he would never have offered me a job.

When I went to visit Rhoda for the last time before I left, it was summer and my skin was several shades darker from the sun. A young aide was in Rhoda's room when I walked in; she was new at Westport and so we hadn't met before.

"Is this your daughter, Mrs. Lloyd?" she asked.

Rhoda and I exchanged a conspiratorial look.

"Yes," I answered. "This is my mother."

fourteen

I LEFT CAMBRIDGE FOR Kingston in the late summer of
1984. Those first few months at the University of the
West Indies were some of the most difficult I ever had.
For starters, I quit cocaine cold—finally heeding the lesson I'd
been given by Jimmy Cliff years before. Now I was working too
hard to waste time.

I moved into a little ground-floor flat on the university campus.
In those first months, my loneliness was so intense that I ques-
tioned whether I could last. Karen Ford was off the island, at law
school in Barbados with her new husband, a brilliant playwright
named Earl Warner. Her absence cut deep. My teaching was all-
consuming; I had over a hundred students in a course on the history of the United States, which was not a field I knew all that
well. Many of my students were women, working mothers who
came to class hungry because they had used all their meager
income to feed their children, and they were often so exhausted
that they fell asleep in their seats.

The ghettos of Kingston, where I hoped to find people who would guide me into the gang world, might as well have been on the far side of the moon. There was a yawning abyss between uptown, where the university was, and the downtown slums where the sufferers lived. This wasn't just a matter of geography. There was an unwritten law that said the boundary between rich and poor in Jamaica was a line never to be crossed.

"None of us has any reason whatsoever for going down there," one of my new faculty colleagues warned me, referring to the ghettos. "If we do, we get what we deserve."

One afternoon, I took a drive into the hills above Kingston to visit a beautiful botanical garden. The guide led me on a long ramble through the grounds, proudly showing me the flora: frangipani with its white blossoms drooping, scarlet ornamental ginger, the spiky red-and-purple bird-of-paradise, and majestic traveler's palms. It was unearthly quiet, cool in the shade from all those trees. Suddenly, the guide bent down and touched his finger to a tiny circle all but hidden in the mossy ground.

"Look here, miss," he said. "Do you know what is this?"

Instinctively, I did know. No creature but a spider would be capable of such stealth.

"Is the nest of a trapdoor spider, this," the guide said, justifiably pleased with himself for knowing where it lay. I shivered. There was no arachnid visible, but I knew it was down there, waiting for its hapless prey.

On the way home, I thought of that hole in the ground as a metaphor for what I was seeking: the hidden funnel down which I would tumble, to find an unseen world.

❧

MY HOLE INTO the ground opened up not long thereafter, through one of those coincidences that turn out to be not so coincidental after all. I met a man with whom I fell in love, and it was he who led me in.

Homer was an actor who was starring in *Woza Albert and the*

Boys, a play by Percy Mtwa, Mbongeni Ngema, and Barney Simon. I'd recently gotten to know a very sharp graduate student named Nadi who was an old friend of Homer's and he invited me to the play. Nadi and I sat in the front row of the tiny theater, close enough for me to see the sweat trickling down Homer's bare chest. The part called for him to wear only a pair of red sweatpants and a ridiculous red rubber ball on his nose, the clown's mask he wore for the white world. From time to time, when his rage overwhelmed him, he'd yank the ball from his nose and become a man again. I kept wondering who it was that Homer resembled, and then I realized it was Frederick Douglass.

His skin was the chestnut brown of the log-wood honey that country folk sell on the Jamaican roadside. He was only in his thirties, but his hair was shot with silver. He was small of stature, not much taller than I, the kind of person of whom Jamaicans say, "Him lickle, but him tallawah." Small, but full of strength. And he had a voice to match, deep and rich and hinting at a river of mirth that ran beneath his serious demeanor.

Nadi took me backstage afterward. Homer was surrounded by his admirers, most of whom were women, so I stood off to one side. Nadi managed to introduce us and Homer said he'd like to "pass by" my place the following night, for the three of us to have a drink.

Nadi stayed for an hour and then Homer suggested that the two of us should take a walk. "It's such a beautiful night," he said. I hadn't ventured out alone after dark, even to stroll around the campus, because I could hear gunshots ringing out from the nearby shantytown called Poco Flats. But the grounds were very beautiful in a haunted way: The campus had once been a vast sugar estate, from which it took its name—Mona—and there were ruins everywhere. My flat was a stone's throw from the tumbled-down remains of an aqueduct once used to carry water to a brick building where the cane was pressed into juice. And right next to the aqueduct was a grove of ackee trees, their psychedelic orange pods hiding the plump, pale yellow fruit within. Ackee, brought to Jamaica from West Africa in the eighteenth century, became a dietary staple for enslaved Africans and, by virtue of its connection to their homeland, took on a sacredness all its own. On the Mona estate, a little village of slave dwellings once stood beneath these trees. Some said they buried their dead within this grove because the ackee trees were a reminder of home.

Homer and I sat down on a block of rubble in the moon shadow cast by the aqueduct. It was early December and the air was damp and chill; I began to shiver.

"I'll warm you up," Homer said, and took me in his arms. That first kiss sent a wave of heat through me that was like a swig of brandy, fire traveling from his velvet mouth down to my groin.

"Homer!" I murmured. "My students . . . what if one of them sees us?"

He drew away and gave me his deep, booming laugh. "You think they'd be shocked?"

"I don't know," I answered. "But it doesn't look right, all the same."

We stumbled back to my flat in the dark, laughing like a pair of mischievous children, and made love while the cheeping of the frogs in the ackee trees and the whistling of night birds muffled our cries.

"I can't see you," I whispered afterward, in the inky tropical darkness.

"That's all right, "Homer said. "You don't need to."

"Oh, yes, I do."

"So turn the light on."

"I can't. You're still on top of me."

More laughter. "You've never made love with a black man, I take it?"

"Ah, Homer. If you only knew." I was thinking about where I came from, of the consequences and penalties this one act would have inflicted on both of us in the kingdom of the South. Even now, at the end of the twentieth century, it might still have cost us dearly.

Homer was thinking his own thoughts, having bedded many a white woman in a country so different from mine. And yet, Jamaicans are colorstruck in their own way. "I shouldn't call myself *black,* though," he said, reaching for one of his cigarettes and lighting it. The match flared in the darkness and illuminated the smile on his stern face. I noticed the gap between his two front teeth and thought of Carrie Jefferson's.

"You know how we are in Jamaica," Homer mused. "When I was a little boy, I used to spend the summers in the country with my grandmother. She was the grandchild of a master and his slave, so her skin was light brown. Believe me, she never forgot it and she never let me forget, either. Almost all the other people in her district were well and truly black, and when I'd come back from playing with my little friends, she'd tell me to be careful or else their skin would rub off on mine."

"Amazing, isn't it?" I said. "How far we haven't come."

"Nadi told me all about you, you know, before you came to see the play."

"And just what did he say?"

"He said he knew a woman who would love me to death. But she was white."

"So what did you say then?"

"I told him I didn't mind." I could see his sly smile in the cigarette's glow.

I can't say that being with Homer was just like being with any lover; that I was not mindful of the color of his skin. I was transfixed by it. On the many nights that followed, I'd lie beside him and study our two naked bodies, the way we didn't match and the different textures of our hair. But there was something about Homer that was familiar, nonetheless.

"You remind me of Rhoda," I said.

"Who is Rhoda?" Homer asked.

"My mother."

"Excuse me?"

"I'll explain it to you, in time."

HE HAD GROWN up in Central Kingston, the waterfront that stretched away to the east from the city's original commercial heart. Central had once been Kingston's most cosmopolitan neighborhood, open to the sea and ships and sailors from around the world. This was the stronghold of the People's National Party; the dockworkers who proudly plied their trade on the wharves were loyal to the PNP because it had been the first party to struggle for independence from England. In 1962, the right-wing Jamaica Labour Party punished the neighborhood by tearing down the old wharves and rebuilding them close to its own garrison, West Kingston. After that, Central began to wither and die. Now it was a ghetto, its stores and once-fine cottages turned into tenement yards or torched into rubble by the fires of tribal war.

Homer's mother was a nurse and his father ran a shop; they were strivers and made a decent living. They'd been able to send their bright son to a preparatory school and then to university at Mona, so Homer was one of those fortunate youths who left his old neighborhood before it crumbled. He had never returned. But he nursed a deep affection for the people and the culture downtown, and he had stayed in touch with a man he knew from childhood.

"You need to meet Brambles," he said to me one evening as we sat on my front steps. "He's a photographer, one of the best. He used to work for the island press service, the Agency for Public Information. When Seaga took over, he thought that sounded too Cuban so he changed the name to the Jamaica Information Service. But I think Brambles is still there."

When Homer introduced us a few weeks later, Brambles was hesitant to take me into his confidence. He had been Michael Manley's personal photographer in the seventies, when Manley was prime minister and the gangs were running so hot that Manley never knew whether he might get shot at—even in Central Kingston, which was his constituency. Brambles still lived there, in a tenement yard a few blocks from the sea. Homer and I went to visit him there one Saturday morning. The three of us sat on the concrete veranda, where Brambles spoke of seeing a wounded gunman shot dead during the vicious election campaign four years before. At one point, Homer and I went outside. He hunkered down on his

Homer and I on the north coast of Jamaica; winter, 1985.

haunches for a moment on the sidewalk beside a rivulet of raw sewage coursing down the lane. He gazed up and down the narrow street, at the half-clad children and the rum shop blasting reggae into the morning air. He turned to me with a look so full of rage and regret that I suddenly felt afraid. I realized that this neigborhood had once been his home. But it was lost to him now and I could see the anger he felt over this relinquished sense of belonging.

Little by little, Brambles befriended me. The more we talked and walked side by side through the lanes and yards of Central, the more he came to believe in the book I hoped to write. At first he could not be convinced that I wasn't a spy.

"Who it is you *really* work for, sis?" he'd ask, a frown knitting his wide brow. He wore a well-trimmed mustache and a little goatee, and when he frowned he looked slightly devilish. "CIA?" he asked. "DEA? FBI?"

But after a few months of this, he quit asking. We'd been in several scrapes by then. We were at a street dance where gunfire broke out and twice we were tailed by police. To Brambles, my determination not to let these mishaps get in our way was proof of my seriousness. One by one, he began introducing me to the men he knew who had connections to the gangs.

And then—maybe because this work was opening my heart and mind to a world I'd hitherto not known—a child from the streets walked into my life. A boy of twelve.

℘

HIS NAME WAS Steve Miller, and he lived in the shantytown called Poco Flats near the campus. He came into the dirt yard in front of my flat late one afternoon, begging for food. Homer was with me, and his presence seemed to bolster the boy's confidence. He had the look of a child who'd been on the streets for some time, with wary eyes and a crooked nose that had obviously been broken. He was wearing only a pair of threadbare running shorts and his dark, spindly legs were gray with dust. At first, I couldn't tell how old he was; he had the haunted, ageless face of battered children the world over.

He stared up at me, quiet as a bone. I went inside and got a plate of food, which he ate sitting on the steps.

"Wash your car, miss?" he said.

"After you've eaten, sure. My name is Laurie. What's yours?"

"Steve, miss."

"You don't have to call me miss."

"Yes, Miss Laurie."

I KNEW THE shantytown where Steve lived; Homer occasionally bought ganja from a man there. Poco Flats was a warren of narrow lanes and scrap-board dwellings, and the sounds emanating from them—shouts and laughter, oaths and curses—rang out onto campus, night and day. The homeless boys from Poco Flats subsisted by scavenging through the garbage dumps behind the dormitories and faculty flats like mine, picking through the refuse for edible scraps.

I was more afraid of them than I was of the gunmen Brambles was taking me to meet downtown, even though these shantytown boys were only children. But there was a malevolence in them that chilled me. They stoned any dog or cat they came across, sometimes to death, and fought each other with venom, like grown men. They picked most mercilessly on the smaller boys like Steve. Now I felt protective of him. I could not think what more I could do but feed him and give him small change for washing my car. Where was his mother? He seemed not to have one. He never mentioned a mother or a father, either.

"Why you let that dutty boy come into the yard?" pouted the Indian woman, a lecturer in the French department, who lived upstairs. I had a feeling that she was afraid of Steve, as I was of the other boys who roamed the campus. But Steve seemed different from them to me. "He will tief you, you know," this woman warned. "Steal whatever he can lay his hands on. And when he does, don't come crying to me!"

But as it happened, I had made friends with a wonderful, motherly woman who came each day to clean and wash for the faculty members who lived in our block of flats. Her name was Merle Eccleston and she lived in August Town, a tight-knit neighborhood nearby. Merle had seen Steve around for years—"from mornin'," as she said—and she knew his mother, too. So now at least a part of Steve's mystery was solved. But it wasn't good.

"That is one worthless 'ooman!" Merle sucked her teeth in the Jamaican expression of contempt. "Oh, yes, I know Yvonne. Seem like she take up with a different man every week." Merle paused to look for a clothespin in her apron pocket, reminding me of Rhoda. "You know what that mean fi' Steve?" she went on. "New man a' yard don't want to see no boy pickney 'round the place. So Steve cyan' stay there no more. He haffi' ketch as ketch can. You watch out, Miss Laurie. He will soon be axin' to come live with you."

Slowly, irresistibly, Steve wound his way into my life, and Homer's, too. He was an excellent runner, so we began taking him with us when we went every morning at first light to jog around the Mona reservoir. "The Dam," as it was called, was the place to see and be seen, where everyone from reggae superstars to ranking politicians (and their pistol-packing bodyguards) put in their laps before the blistering sun rose. Steve outran them all. I bought him a silver-gray tracksuit and a pair of Adidas.

He told me he wanted to go to school. But where? He had no fixed address, no one but me to pay for books and tuition—primary education in Jamaica is supposed to be free, but it isn't. Now that the Jamaican dollar was becoming virtually worthless and the wages of the working poor were plummeting to new depths, none but the middle and upper classes could afford to educate their children.

But Steve had a plan: He thought that maybe because he was such a good runner, he could convince the principal of the nearby elementary school to let him in. Sports are such an obsession in Jamaica that a principal might accept a child if he or she showed promise as an athlete.

"I gwan' win nuff-nuff trophies!" Steve vowed.

When I told this to Merle, she shook her head. "Is not right, Miss Laurie. You cyan' jus take responsibility fi' a child like that.

Make we go an' see his mother. Is time you an' she make four eyes. She mus' know is you lookin' after her boy."

The next morning, Merle and I walked to Poco Flats. Yvonne was standing in the bright sun at the door of her one-room house, with only an old sheet covering the entry. She was a sinewy woman with deep lines etched into her forehead. The muscles in her arms were corded like a man's. She tried to give me a smile, but it froze on her lips well before it reached her eyes.

Steve was nowhere around. "I don't really see him, more than so," said Yvonne. Meaning almost never. Her man stepped from the shadows of the room and said a sullen hello. The four of us stood in the merciless glare and tried to make conversation.

"I'd like to help Steve with school," I ventured to Yvonne. "If that's all right with you?"

She nodded. And that was that. But then her man, whose name was Reid, said something ominous.

"Disya' one rough place, miss." Reid gestured toward the sandy lane and the scrap-board dwellings. "When I come here from country, I bring me goat an' cow. But the goat soon dead. An' then the cow take sick an' die."

Reid paused, waiting for me to get his meaning. "You unnerstand?"

I did. He was talking about *obeah*—black magic—and letting me know that someone in Poco Flats envied him so much that they cursed his animals to death.

It was a warning, of course. Not to meddle where I didn't belong. But I was too blind to heed it. Steve had already become the child I hoped to rescue. For hadn't someone once rescued me?

❧

STEVE GOT INTO school and quickly became the star of the track team. The relay was his best event. When the other boys fumbled the baton, dropped it in the dust, he was always there to retrieve it, making up the lost time and tearing across the finish line first. But he almost never smiled, never relinquished his air of cool detachment.

This boy knew not to care about anything too much. Especially victory. He knew it was an illusion. I was the one who failed to understand.

One night, with Homer sleeping beside me, I had a terrifying dream. I looked out through the louvers by the bed to see a tribe of famished children in the ackee grove behind the flat. A garden had mysteriously sprung up beneath the trees—where I'd been told the graves of slaves were hidden. Suddenly, in that nightmare logic of dreams, I reverted to being the classic white bitch, the kind of woman who barks orders at black people as if they were dogs. I screamed at the children to get away, and they fled. But one remained, and when he rose from the ground, I saw with a jolt of horror that this was Steve. He stood among the trailing, dried-up vines and gave me a bitter look. Before my eyes, he became as thin and withered as one of those vines. And then he vanished into the earth.

I woke drenched in sweat, gasping for breath.

"What is it?" Homer murmured, still half asleep.

"I don't know," I answered. "But something bad is about to happen."

Three days later, in the first heat of morning, Steve staggered to my door. He was holding a ratty pink towel to his head and his eyes were streaming with tears. My cat took one look at this specter and tore off into the bushes like he had smelled something dead.

"Oh, Jesus, Miss Laurie," Steve sobbed, sagging into my arms. "Me head hurt so bad, me cyan' hardly breathe!" I managed to get him into the car and we sped to the university hospital. On the way, between bouts of crying, he told me what had happened, in disconnected bursts. From what I pieced together, the police were doing night sweeps in Poco Flats now, and a boy from the lane had accused Steve of being an informer. This boy, Robbie, went after Steve with an ice pick. Yvonne had wrestled Robbie to the ground and Steve got the ice pick away from him. This goaded the boy into a frenzy and he went after Steve with a rock. Steve said he was cut badly, just above his left ear. But I couldn't see any wound.

The doctor at University Hospital could find none either. He scoffed at Steve's story. But not at the fever of 103 that Steve was running or the other symptoms he had. "I think it may be meningitis," the doctor said. "He needs to be admitted. Unfortunately, we have no beds open here. You'll have to take him to Kingston Public Hospital. Get there right away. And you come back uptown before dark, you hear me?"

No one went to Kingston Public unless they had no choice. The hospital was on the border zone between turf that belonged to rival gangs from the PNP and JLP; gunmen often shot their way into the wards to finish off wounded foes.

"Miss Laurie!" Steve moaned. "Don' take me there. Please. Please! I gwan' die in that place. Is only sick people an' dead in that 'ospital. Is nothin' but a dead-house, that."

"Steve, I don't know what else to do. You're running a high fever and it has to be brought down. This is an emergency. We have to do what the doctor said."

Steve and I waited for the rest of the day and into evening at Kingston Public for a doctor. None came. The corridor where we sat on a newspaper I luckily had—there were no seats—reeked of urine and something else that I knew was blood. Steve gripped my hand so tightly that my arm went numb. Finally, after dark, a nurse admitted him to one of the wards. The iron beds had no mattresses and I could see wedges of smoky sky through holes in the roof.

"Don't leave me!" Steve begged, sobbing.

"I'll be back as soon as I can. I'm going to August Town to find Merle. She'll know what to do. We'll bring you some food and a blanket and we'll get you out of here once your fever has come down. I promise."

THANKFULLY, MERLE WAS home. She and her man, Thomas, were sitting beside the cook fire in the yard of their house. They had a new baby boy, Matthew, whom Thomas was holding in his lap while he stirred the wood of the fire.

"Oh, Miss Laurie . . . ," Merle sighed, after I had told her the story. "I don't know what to say." I knew she was trying to think of some way to explain the situation to me, since she understood it but as I was not likely to.

"Merle, I think I know. So does Steve. He says it's *obeah*. Just like Reid said. Someone in Poco Flats wants him dead."

Merle exhaled slowly. "Ezzactly," she whispered, as if the fireflies flitting through the deepening dusk might be listening. "You don' really know what life is like, Miss Laurie. You 'ave a good heart, fi' true. So you don' understand how some people feel when they see luck come fi' another and not fi' them. They will kill because of that. Pure murder."

"You know what Brambles calls it, Merle?" I remembered something he had said to me only a few nights before, about how the people in the ghetto would do anything to keep each other there. "He calls it 'crabs in a barrel.' Says as soon as one crab tries to crawl out, the others claw him back down again. But I don't like to believe that. I mean, sometimes it's that way. But not always."

"True-true," Thomas offered. "But Steve is sick now. An' no matter what cause it, is only you and Merle him can really trust."

"The doctor says it's meningitis, and if it is, he could die," I said.

Merle and Thomas cut their eyes at each other.

"Miss Laurie," Merle asked softly, "you know what is a balm yard?"

"Yes. I've been to one before, in the country. Is there one you go to?"

"There's a woman I know by the name of Mother Ramsay. She keeps a yard downtown. On Elletson Road. Sundays are when she sees people."

It was Friday night. "I'll get Steve out of KPH tomorrow. He can stay with me till Sunday."

When I went back downtown to the hospital, with a dish of food and a pillow and a blanket, Steve was wide awake. He was too sick to eat, and his head was blazing hot. The only thing that calmed him was the promise of getting out of there, going to the balm yard and having the curse that had been laid on him lifted.

Sunday morning dawned bright and it was hot by seven. But a breeze stirred the branches of the majestic tree in Mother Ramsay's swept-dirt yard. It was a *lignum vitae*, which means "tree of life," the hardest wood in Jamaica. It was blooming with tiny pale lavender blossoms and they were alive with white butterflies. In the shade of this tree, Mother Ramsay's female helpers came and went like angels of mercy, bathing the feet of the sick who sat quietly on rough wooden benches. An old woman, milky eyed from glaucoma; a young girl with withered legs; a child with fever crying fitfully in his father's lap.

When Mother Ramsay appeared, I took her for a priestess. As if by magic, she materialized from the cool shadows of her cottage and stepped onto the wide veranda. She was wearing all white and her head was tied with a bandanna in the old Jamaican pattern, a plaid of blue and red. A long-stemmed clay pipe was clenched between her teeth, reminding me oddly of the portraits I had seen of eighteenth-century gentlemen. When her eyes fell on me, it was clear that she was wondering who this white stranger could be. But then Merle waved at her, and her face broke into a smile of recognition. Her mouth was full of gold.

She stepped down from the porch and strode over to us, bowing ever so slightly. "You are welcome, milady." She turned to me. "Now, please to fetch a Q of white rum for me? There's a shop on the corner."

An offering for the spirits, such as I had seen made before. I trotted off and when I returned with the half pint of 181-proof rum, Mother Ramsay was ready. She cupped Steve's face with one large hand; in the other she held the little bottle while she unscrewed the cap with her teeth. She took one good long pull and then spewed it out in a sun-dazzled shower across the ground. The spirits had been fed. Now they would help her in her work.

Mother Ramsay closed her eyes tight and began to snort. She

winced and shook her head from side to side, her body shivering with the effort of taking whatever evil had invaded Steve into herself and then disarming it. Steve sat on the bench before her, his eyes closed, too, but a smile playing around the corners of his mouth. I could tell that the pain in his head must be abating.

Suddenly, Mother Ramsay opened her eyes and looked straight into mine. "Please to come with me," she breathed. Merle and Steve and I followed her to a private spot behind the house, where she planted herself on a three-legged stool and opened her Bible.

"Cross her palm with silver," Merle whispered to me.

The fifty-cent piece was already in my hand. I had no idea why I knew to do this—part of the offering, like the white rum—but I did know, the way I would have in a dream. I think I *was* in a kind of trance by then. Mother Ramsay tucked the coin, which bore Marcus Garvey's face on it, into her apron pocket and looked into her Bible. Steve began to cry, more with relief than anything else.

"Stop yu' noise, boy," Mother Ramsay said gently. "Them cyan' hurt you now. You safe."

And then she turned to me. Her face was stern but kind. "Is not your fault, milady. This sickness, I mean to say. But is you cause it, still. You understand?"

"I believe so," I answered.

"Is you whey give this boy what him nah' supposed to get," she said.

Simple as that. I had given Steve what he wasn't supposed to have.

"Yes, Mother. I understand. But I was only trying to help."

"I know. It no matter now," Mother Ramsay said, her hand on Steve's head. She bathed his arms and legs in a red-tinted water scented with herbs. Then she handed him a small bottle of tonic to take home and drink.

"You must keep the boy with you," she said to Merle and me. "Don't let him go back where he was." She turned to Steve. "There are people in that place who want to harm you, boy. So you mus' stay away from them, you hear me? An' you mus' leave this city. Is too-too dangerous for you here."

❧

STEVE STAYED WITH me for the next two weeks, and he got well. His fever was gone and his head pain never came back. But Poco Flats was getting more dangerous by the day. The police shot three young men dead, in cold blood—their way of dealing with almost any situation—and others had been "roped in," rounded up and sent to jail. If Steve was detained, nothing and no one would spring him. He would lie in a four-by-six-foot cell and rot until he was beaten to death by the police.

I was due to leave Kingston for good in a month's time. The gangs I had been tracking with Brambles had almost all moved north, migrating to cities across the United States and muscling in on the crack-cocaine trade there. Strangely, I did not understand—yet—how much the fire in my belly for telling this story derived from my own still-secret time of bondage to cocaine. I did not fathom why I felt such an affinity for the posses (as Jamaicans call the gangs) and for the world in which they lived. Had I known, I doubt I could have admitted it. No one would have understood; it was preposterous that a privileged, educated white woman would have seen even one iota of herself in the faces of men and women who had known nothing but poverty and desperation all their lives.

When I left Kingston, I knew only that I would be going next to New York City, following the trail of the posses there. Brambles vowed he was coming, too, in search of work. As was Homer. Who would watch over Steve when all of us were gone?

He told Merle and me that he had a sister in Montego Bay, and he could go live there with her. But he did not want to leave Kingston.

"I is a *town man,*" he proclaimed. All of thirteen now, but he already knew that Jamaica is divided into two halves; there is "town," meaning Kingston, and everything else is "country." "Country" meant the dead-end torment of labor in the cane fields, dirt-floored shanties with no running water, and the ever-present reminders of slavery days. Kingston, despite its poverty and danger, looked like paradise compared to that.

"Steve," I pleaded. "You have to go. Remember what Mother Ramsay said? I know Kingston is home. But it's dangerous for you here. MoBay is a town, too. You'll make friends there. And you'll be safe."

As if leaving his mother and everything he'd ever known could make a child feel safe.

Steve loved airplanes, and he insisted on coming to the airport the day I left. Brambles and Homer came, too, to see me off. Ours was a momentary parting; I knew I'd see both men again, and soon. But leaving Steve felt like a final goodbye.

The four of us waded into the crowd inside the terminal. Sullen-faced customs officials barked orders and pushed people from one line to another, reveling in their authority. How they loved their work, weeding out the lucky ones with visas and American passports from the throng of sufferers who would never leave. Like Steve.

He had given me his sister's address in Montego Bay, and I promised to write to him as soon as I got to New York. He had a bicycle now and was riding around looking for work as a gardener here and there.

"I'll carry mi' bike on the bus to MoBay," he said, turning his face away shyly when he feared I might try to kiss him goodbye. "I be all right, Miss Laurie. I is a big mon now, an' I can take care o' meself."

The last glimpse I had of Steve was his tiny, distant figure in a hot pink shirt, standing on the observation deck and waving to the plane.

I wrote to him two days later, care of his sister in Montego Bay. That letter and all the others came back to me unopened, stamped Addressee Unknown.

That October, a hurricane swept through Kingston. It hit the city harder than the rest of the island, drowning fourteen people, laying waste to entire neighborhoods—all of them the poorest ones—and ripping ancient trees up by their roots. After the storm had passed came the looting; most of the stores downtown were smashed.

I went to Kingston a month after the hurricane. It was hard to imagine what the deluge must have been like, now that the heat and flies had set in and the flattened lawns and gardens of the university neighborhood were caked with mud. The first person I needed to see was Merle, for I was dreading what the storm might have done to her house. I held my breath as I drove down the little hill into August Town, till I saw that her house was still standing and that its roof was intact. I parked the car and let myself in by the swinging gate, calling out her name. She hollered back to me and ran out into the yard with her arms flung wide. Even amidst her joy at our reunion, I felt that mystical Jamaican calm: The people of that island are so accustomed to partings with loved ones and to unheralded returns that they all but take it for granted that one of these days, an old friend or lover, a prodigal son or daughter or husband or wife, will simply reappear. Will come back from England or Canada or the United States, after an absence of years. The new arrival will unlatch the gate and step right up onto the veranda, greeting you as if it was only days since you and he "made four eyes," saw each other last.

Merle and I hugged and kissed and cried a little.

"You're not surprised to see me?" I asked playfully, drawing away from Merle to put my arms around the children first and then Thomas, when he came out from the house.

"Oh, Miss Laurie!" Merle grinned. "We knew you would come back."

She and Thomas and I sat by the fire in the yard. I listened to the well-remembered sounds of a Kingston neighborhood as evening fell: greetings called and dogs barking and the music from a rum shop nearby. But the peace of the moment kept being broken by the looks that Merle and Thomas were exchanging. I knew they had something bad to tell me and neither of them wanted to be the one who spoke. By then, I knew what it was.

"Do you hear anything from Steve?" I asked. Thomas let out a mighty sigh and glanced at Merle, as if for her permission to be the messenger.

"Lord have mercy, Miss Laurie," he murmured. "Steve's dead."

The three of us just sat there for a moment, and then I whispered, "How?"

"Police," Merle answered. "Them shoot him downtown jus' after the storm. Them say he was with a crowd of youths looting a shop."

I let go slowly of the breath I was holding. "He never went to MoBay, did he, Merle?"

"No. I saw him a few times after you left. I warned him he should go. But I knew he never would."

fifteen

IN THE WEEK that remained to me in Kingston, I went every morning to police headquarters on Hope Road, trying in vain to find the one who had killed Steve. On each of these visits, I was ushered down a long, dim hallway into one office or another, where a constable sat behind a desk piled with files and dusty papers.

"We have no record of this boy's death," the constable would say. "None whatsoever. Are you certain of his name?"

I repeated the story time and again, but I knew that the police would never admit anything. They commit roughly one-third of Jamaica's homicides, tallying in the hundreds every year, and they have become the executioners of their own people. But the government of Jamaica stands behind them, and so they are never reprimanded, let alone brought to justice.

I was seeking absolution for having failed this child. And for meddling where I did not belong, as Mother Ramsay had warned me. If I had wanted to rescue Steve from his world and from whatever was to be his fate, I would have to have adopted him and taken him home with me. But the truth was, I had not loved him enough to do that. I wondered if I had it in me to love a child that way. Did I even know how? Had I ever been shown what such love was? Even with two mothers—as everyone was so fond of telling me I had—even with Rhoda and Mother, I was still nobody's child.

❧

RHODA DIED ON the sixth of October 1986. I was not with her. She died in her sleep, and her nurse, Shirley, found her in the morning. Mother called me in New York and asked if I intended to come home for the funeral. She was crying softly into the phone. I was too sad to be angry with her for asking if I would come. As if I would not be there, to honor Rhoda and to help send her home.

As I packed a small suitcase with black clothes, I was brokenly singing an old Jamaican folk song that I loved. "One fine morning when my work is over, I will fly away home." I remembered the painting Rhoda and I loved, *Swing Low, Sweet Chariot,* of the black man dying in his cabin and the chariot coming for his soul. Rhoda knew there was a heaven. I wished I did. But my two years in Jamaica had made me think of heaven in another way. For many people there, heaven was Africa. The promised land. As it was and is for millions, some long dead and some still living, whose ancestors stood on the shores of whatever lands slavery had brought them to—Brazil, the islands of the West Indies, the tidewater inlets of the American South—and looked away, across the water, off to where the ships had stolen them from. They believed that if their spirits were strong enough, their bodies would follow. Would rise into the air, sprout wings, and fly away home.

Maybe Rhoda is already there, I said to myself. With those of her people who have gone on ahead. But *her* going had drawn a veil of silence over all the questions I should have asked her. Now it was too late.

And if I had asked her to tell me what her life had really been, what it was like to grow up poor and black in Jim Crow South

Carolina, would she have told me? With her dignity and sense of privacy, would she not have wanted to keep her bitterest memories secret from me? Perhaps because I was white and a child of privilege, she knew I could not have understood.

It seemed to me that all I had left was those two given names of her parents: Julia and Sam. But Sam and Julia *who?* With a bitter pang of loss, I realized I did not even know their last names, or Rhoda's. I had only ever known her as Rhoda Lloyd. Now that she was gone, how would I find her again? How would I search for her in the archives, in the records? For I knew that I was bound to try.

©

THE FUNERAL WAS very small; there were so few friends left to bury her, and no family members. But Rhoda had one dear friend, Louise Howard, who was quite a bit younger than she. Louise belonged to Bethel AME. She and Mother planned Rhoda's funeral together, decided it should be held not at the church, as I'd hoped, but at Chiles Funeral Home.

"Rhoda told me she didn't want her pallbearers carrying that heavy casket up and down those steps at Bethel," Louise said. "She was worried they might stumble and fall, and what a terrible thing that would be."

Rhoda's casket was open, propped on its catafalque at the front of the little room at the funeral home. I wanted to kiss her goodbye. I had never touched a dead person, and so I stood gazing down at her stony face with some misgivings. But the desire to feel her skin beneath my lips overcame them, and I bent down.

Her cheek was icy, hard as marble. I drew back with a shudder from that calm, sweet, so-very-dead face. She was gone, that I now knew. Nothing left of the warmth and the soft flesh that had once folded me into itself. I fought the urge to put my hand over my mouth, as if I could wipe away the memory of that coldness, that hardness, from my lips, and bring back the sensation of pulsing life that I wanted to remember as Rhoda.

I turned slowly and walked back to the row of folding chairs where Mother and Daddy were. Neither of them made a move to touch me. They were deep into themselves. I knew what Daddy must be thinking. Rhoda had been a constant star, the longest-lived of any woman from his wife's past. He had not known Rhoda as he might have, surely not the way I did. He had always called her "the Last of the Mohicans," even though Mother never liked that; it was paternalistic, she said. But I knew what he meant by it, and how he must be feeling at this moment, saying goodbye. Now, the Last was gone.

Reverend Walker, the pastor I had known at Bethel, was long since gone, too. The new pastor was Reverend Reed, and he did not know Rhoda all that well. He had asked me to give the eulogy. I had never delivered one before, and I had not written it out; foolishly, I thought that when I stepped to the lectern, the right words would come. But now I faltered, overwhelmed by the enormousness of what I needed to convey.

"Rhoda was like a mother to me," I heard myself say. *Like?* I looked over at my "real" mother, seeking permission to betray her, for Rhoda's sake. But Mother's face was a mask.

"She was born in South Carolina," I stumbled on. "Her mother's name was Julia and her father's name was Sam. When I was a little girl, Rhoda told me they were born in slavery."

The mourners shifted uncomfortably in their seats. In a flash, I saw myself as they must be seeing me: a white woman delivering some kind of history lesson . . . to those who had lived it all their lives. What presumption. How could they know what Rhoda's revelation meant to me? I gave up, then and there.

"I love you, Rhoda," I said, tears breaking into my voice. There was nothing more to say. "I will always love you, and I will never forget your life."

We drove to the cemetery and stood by the freshly dug grave in a stiff October wind. I kept a tight hold on myself while Reverend West read the last words. Ashes to ashes, dust to dust; we hope in the Resurrection and the Life. I was concentrating on how the groundskeepers unwound the canvas tape and cranked Rhoda's casket slowly into the grave. It wasn't until they began to shovel clods of earth onto her that I realized this was it. She was in there, forever, alone, in the cold and the dark, and I was about to leave her. We mourners were going to Louise's house for the funeral meal. I wanted to cry out, "Can't we bring Rhoda?" As if I were a child again and we were all going somewhere, but she was staying behind.

Louise was standing beside me and I sagged against her shoulder.

"We can't leave her here, Louise," I sobbed.

She put her arms around me. "She's not here, Laurie. She's gone home."

immediate family

sixteen

RHODA HAD ONE parting benediction for me that was her favorite. But she rarely got to bestow it, because for almost all her life, I was alone, and her blessing had to do with being part of a couple.

"You all take care of each other," she would say when I was with my first husband, Ray, and we three said goodbye. I was such a proud, solitary tower of a woman, even though I was married, that Rhoda's simple, tender advice embarrassed me a little. I would say to myself: "Why do I need someone to take care of me? And why would I want to take care of him? What an old-fashioned idea." But I never said this out loud, because of the sweet look on Rhoda's face. She glowed with the assurance that her "baby" had someone now. Someone to watch over her.

Rhoda did not live long enough to see me grow into the woman I've become. I'm a ridiculously late bloomer, and it has taken me almost half a century to understand the beauty and the strength in taking care of a man I love, or in his taking care of me. Rhoda was eighty when Ray and I divorced, and she did not live to meet the man who would become my second husband. What I regret even more is that Jonathan came into my life too late for him to know Rhoda, because if he had, she would have changed his hopelessly unreconstructed Yankee mind. Made him see another side of the South.

$\backsim$

I KNEW THAT Jonathan and I were meant for one another before we even met. He had a personal essay in *The New Yorker* in the summer of 1993, just as my book about the Jamaican gangs was about to find a publisher. His essay was called "Survival in the Night," and it was about being robbed at gunpoint in his SoHo loft by a man who was black. I was then struggling in isolation with my own particular feelings about racism and its relation to the violence of the city, and the vulnerability of black and white to this ever-present fear. I had spent the last five years with Jamaican gang members in Brooklyn, and had found precious few individuals outside that world with whom I could talk about what it was like. The piece in *The New Yorker* blew me away; whoever this Jonathan Rubinstein was, he wrote from the heart about the rage and sadness of the city, and every word rang true.

My sister Mary called a few days after I had read the essay. "What did you think of it?" she asked. When I told her that I was about to sit down and compose a fan letter to the author, Mary said, "I know him. Not well, but we've met a couple of times."

"*You know him?*" I all but shouted into the phone.

"Well, kind of. All I really know is that he's an ex-cop with a doctorate from Harvard."

I felt faint. "What in?" I asked.

"I'm pretty sure it's history."

"Mary. This is a serious thing. I have to meet this man. Do something. Find a way. Call him up."

"I don't know where he's living at the moment. He moves around a lot. I think he has a girlfriend in Boston but he isn't living with her. He may be in New York."

Jonathan and I at the rehearsal dinner, at which Esau and I arrived almost two hours late because we went to see Gone with the Wind.

Esau and I in the garden.

It was another eight months before Jonathan and I met, at a gallery downtown where a mutual friend was having an opening. He was standing on the sidewalk, smoking a cigar, when Mary and I drove up in a taxi. "There he is," she said. My heart lurched. He was older than I, and bald, with a body that spoke of good discipline. Decidedly sexy, but in a way completely unlike any man I had ever been attracted to before. In other words, he was Jewish. He was from the tribe. Instead of one of those gentile pretty boys I was always falling for—other than Homer, my former lover from Jamaica, the only exception to this time-honored rule of mine.

"Uh-oh," I murmured to Mary. "Here we go."

I walked up to Jonathan and we began to talk. Two hours later, when we left the gallery for a party, we were still at it. We couldn't stop; there was just so much to say. We went into a huddle at the party, so obviously smitten with each other that the young woman Jonathan was with felt obliged to take me aside in the hostess's bedroom and politely inform me that she and he were together. I thought, but did not say, *That's very nice. But you aren't his destiny. And I am.*

℘

As IT TURNED out, I was right. We've been together since that April night in 1994.

But we're a marriage of truly opposite minds. Jonathan comes from a Jewish world diametrically opposed to mine. He's a child of the Holocaust whose parents got out of Lithuania in the nick of time. His mother was eight months pregnant. Jonathan was born in September 1939, a month after his family arrived in Boston. With the exception of one elderly cousin, no one in the family survived but Jonathan's parents and his two elder brothers, one of whom now lives in Israel.

They settled in Winthrop, just outside Boston. Jonathan grew up with a firm belief that territory south of Mason-Dixon was the devil's stomping ground. Not that he'd ever *been* there; at least, not much—other than to visit an old friend, Reuben Greenberg, the African American and Jewish chief of police in Charleston. But Jonathan had never set foot in Richmond.

I brought him home with me for the first time about a year after we'd begun living together, to meet Mother and Daddy and see the city where I was born. We drove down Monument Avenue, with its statues (in order, from west to east): Stonewall Jackson, Jefferson Davis, Robert E. Lee, and J. E. B. Stuart.

"Good God!" Jonathan gasped. "*War criminals!* I can't believe it. You people put up statues to war criminals."

I heaved a sigh of resignation. "I know. I'm with you a hundred percent. Just for God's sake don't let Daddy hear you say that."

℘

WE WERE MARRIED three years later, in 1998, in the garden of my family's house in Richmond. I had my heart set on being married there. My father, however, all but offered me money to have the wedding in New York—even though he knew full well that if I did, neither he nor Mother would be there. She was eighty-seven and much too frail to travel; he was ninety-three and no longer the gracious host he had been. His worst side came to the fore, all his selfishness and narcissism.

Jonathan stood by me, knowing how much I wanted to be married at home, even though my father ended up virtually dictating the guest list—and I, to my lasting shame, went along with this.

"It's okay, love," Jonathan said. "He just can't stand the idea that he won't be the center of attention."

The guest list was so small that the only members of Jonathan's family who were invited were his two grown sons, Gabriel and Max.

I told Jonathan that Mother and Daddy had not always been as he saw them now; that once upon a time, they had loved nothing more than giving grand parties. I told him about the only other wedding that took place at our house: Carrie Jefferson's, in the summer of 1976.

"You should have seen it," I said. "We had more than a hundred guests. All the men were in *Saturday Night Fever* white suits with wide lapels and the women were wearing skirts up to *here*. Daddy spent two hours before the ceremony hanging out in the kitchen with Theodore, Carrie's father, drinking champagne with their arms around each other, three sheets to the wind."

"So your father was okay with the idea of a hundred black people coming to a wedding at your house?" Jonathan asked incredulously.

"Not at first. Mother had to convince him. He was nervous about what the neighbors would say. But he thought for a few days and then came back to Mother and said he thought it was a wonderful plan. 'Anyway,' he said to us, 'I *know* what the neighbors will say.' 'What?' Mother asked. 'That the Gunsts must be having one hell of a party if they need that many in help.'"

$$\mathcal{Q}$$

BETWEEN US, MARY, Jonathan, and I still managed to work up a great guest list. It included Sophia Norrell Beal, now seventy-three. I told Daddy that if Sophia wasn't coming, neither was I.

"You're having Glenda," I said. His mistress of some thirty years was coming; by then, Glenda had grown accustomed to being included in every family event. "So I'm inviting Sophia. Period."

When I told Sophia about Glenda, she scowled. "You all still as crazy as ever. All right. Just don't sit me anywhere near that thing," Sophia warned me. "Just keep me and Ole Dead Chicken as far apart as you can. Or there's no telling what I might do."

I invited Claudine Leake, who was almost ninety. She and I had gotten close over the years and I went to visit her whenever I was home. She was sharp as a tack but physically frail, and incontinence made her nervous about leaving her apartment. "You know I can't hold my water like I used to," Deanie said. "I don't want to have to worry about wee-weeing in my pants. Tell you what . . . just bring me a slice of the cake."

There was one remaining hurdle. Mary had been living with a Jamaican Rastafarian named Esau Kerr for the past ten years. Esau and Jonathan and I had become close friends, and Esau and Mary were about to marry, but he had never been invited by our parents to Richmond. This caused Mary a great deal of pain, and for years before my wedding, she and I had spent long hours bemoaning the situation.

"What do you think I ought to do?" Mary would ask.

"I don't know," I answered. "If you make a crusade out of it, everyone's going to be unhappy."

"But why can't Daddy see the light?"

"Listen. Our father was born a mere forty years after the end of the Civil War. He's a son of the Old South. Stood on his front porch as a little boy and watched the Klan parade down Monument. Think about it. We can't expect the man to be exactly overjoyed that his daughter is *shtupping* a black Jamaican with dreadlocks down to his waist."

"True-true," Mary said.

But when the time came for our wedding, Jonathan said there was no way Esau wasn't going to be with us; Jonathan wanted him to be one of the four people who each held a pole of our *huppah,* the traditional Jewish wedding canopy.

"Daddy," I said, "the time has come."

"Well, sugar," he answered, giving in like he had for Carrie Jefferson, "I reckon you're right."

THE DAY BEFORE the wedding, I noticed in the paper that *Gone with the Wind* was playing in town. It had been a long time since I'd seen it, and I had a sudden hankering to see it again. It's one of those southern institutions that I'm always pondering, and I had recently read an article about how David O. Selznick, the movie's Jewish producer, dealt with the racism in the script. In response to the refusal of the great Hattie McDaniel, who played Mammy, to participate if the word "nigger" was used, Selznick took it out, even though Margaret Mitchell used it throughout her book. The article also described how McDaniel had kept her dignity in the midst of being pointedly excluded from the segregated festivities surrounding the movie's Atlanta premiere.

As it happened, Esau expressed an interest in coming, too. "I hear nuff' ting 'bout that film," he said. "But I never get to see it yet."

"Well," I answered, "I promise, when you do, you'll understand just about everything there is to know about my father's personality."

Esau smiled. "Mek we go, then."

The line snaking its way around the theater was four deep. There were only two other black people I could see, besides Esau. He and I got the only two seats left. People tried hard not to stare at us, but they couldn't help themselves. I was sure the younger ones in the audience had seen a Rasta before, but the old-timers were in a state of awe.

"Yes, I'm from Jamaica," Esau said gracefully to the old lady with blue hair sitting next to him. "I'm here to celebrate this daughter's wedding, tomorrow evenin'."

"This is your daughter?" the old lady gasped.

"No," I offered. "He's my sister's fiancé."

I thought she might faint. But then that Old Virginia politesse kicked in.

"Oh, how lovely," she said, nodding and smiling. If she'd had a fan, it would have been fluttering like a moth around a flame.

"The rehearsal dinner is tonight," I told her, "at the Jefferson. It starts at five, and I'm wondering if we'll be late, because I know this movie is very long."

"Five hours, honey," said the woman sitting behind us. She had one of those low-pitched whiskey-and-cigarettes voices that reminded me of Granny. "If you count the intermission. And if you need to leave, you'd best do it then. Because if you try and get up in the middle of part two, we're going to stone you."

I had a feeling she meant it.

No matter how many times you might have seen *Gone with the Wind*, if you're white, you haven't ever really experienced it until you view it with a person of color. Only then do the movie's pernicious stereotypes hit home. Even though Hattie McDaniel and Butterfly McQueen (as Prissy) are magnificent, they are still caricatures from another place and time.

Sitting next to Esau, I was alive to the movie's cheerful racism in a way I'd never been before; even though I'd always seen Mammy in

the light of Rhoda, and therefore revered her, now I saw the conde-
scension with which she was portrayed. When Scarlett slapped
Prissy in the face, for lying about knowing how to birth babies, I
cringed.

The lights came up for intermission. I asked Esau what he
thought.

"It's *cute*," he answered gravely. When a Jamaican uses that word, he
doesn't mean "adorable." He means "sharp," as in the blade of an axe.

"Do you feel like leaving now?" I asked. "While we still can. . . . "

"No, mon! I want to know what happens. We haffi' stay through
to the las' reel!"

I went to the pay phone and called Jonathan. "How are things at
the house?" I asked, feeling guilty about abandoning him with all
my relatives. "Can you hold down the fort till we get to the
Jefferson? We're going to be at least an hour late."

"Absolutely," Jonathan answered. I could hear his smile over the
phone. "Anything for the Cause."

It was close to six-thirty by the time Esau and I got to the
Jefferson. All the guests were seated at the table, and we entered the
private dining room to a round of relieved applause. My aunt Alice,
Mother's sister from Washington, gave me a kiss and said, "I cannot
believe you almost missed your own rehearsal dinner to see that
god-awful movie."

The next morning, Esau was helping Jonathan assemble our
huppah, while I tied silk ribbons to the corners of the four poles.

"So, Esau," I said, "I want to know what you thought of *Gone
with the Wind*. Really and truly."

"Well, sis." He pondered for a moment. "Me haffi' say, you took
me into that part of America fi' the first time. And that film let me see
a couple of things. One was the relationship between the African and
the white. And the other was the liberation of the woman."

"You mean Scarlett?"

"Yes. I respect her for the way she struggled."

"But what about when she slapped Prissy?"

"Was a kind of passion, that. Like she knew it was wrong to

d'weet, but she a' lose control. People 'ave power, you no see it? An' them don' really know how to handle it. People did them things in them times. If you were not really heartical, it was considered an okay thing to do."

Esau held up one of the *huppah* poles for Jonathan to hammer in a tack. "That time was that time," Esau went on. "And the person who got slapped has to get over it. Make sure that slap don't come to him again. We all haffi' take responsibility fi' ourself. You no see it?"

"I don't know," I mused. "I'm not sure history works that way."

Esau gave me one of his great smiles. "Your mind is like an old clock, you know that? Been ticking for three hundred years! You jus' haffi' stop it, one o' these days."

That evening, at the wedding supper, everyone offered their toasts. My brother, Dickie, was there and so was my sister, Susan; it was only the second time that she had come home to see my parents in twenty years. When Esau's turn came to give his toast, he rose from his chair, elegant in his tweed jacket and tie. He scanned the upturned faces in the dining room and then gazed lovingly down at Jonathan and me. He raised his glass, smiling as if he had a secret.

"I wish you tolerance," he said.

☙

TWO DAYS LATER, Mary and I were draped across the twin beds in the former maid's room, going through a box of old photographs. As always, no matter the countless times we'd done this, we magically managed to come up with ones that neither of us had seen before. This time, Mary found a treasure.

It was a family group—Mother, Daddy, Granny, and my aunt Barbara at Virginia Beach. With Rhoda. In it, they're all sitting on the sand, and Barbara's hand is resting lovingly on the head of our mixed-breed Scottie, Fella. Mother's beaming jubilantly and Daddy has a goofy grin. Granny, all of sixty-five, is wearing a flirty little two-piece number and her breasts are tumbling out. Behind them,

Rhoda is kneeling, glancing sideways down at her white folks with that Gioconda smile, as if to say, "What *couldn't* I tell!"

"I remember that summer," Mary said. "I remember that bathing suit of Granny's. You had just been born. That was a pretty intense time for Susan and me, because we hadn't ever thought that Mother would have another baby. She was nursing you, it was the first time I ever saw that, and I was fascinated by her breasts being full of all this milk. I asked Rhoda and she explained that women had lots of milk when they had babies."

"Mmm," I said absently, preoccupied with how Rhoda was smiling in the picture.

"One night," Mary went on, "when Rhoda was putting me to bed, I asked if I could see her breasts. She thought about it for a minute, then said, 'Okay' and unbuttoned her uniform."

"God almighty!" I exclaimed. Mary had my full attention now.

"Well," she said, seeing how shocked I was, "I was a very curious kid. And very sexual, I guess. I asked Rhoda if *she* had milk, and she said no, that you only got it if you had a baby. Then I asked if I could touch her bosoms and she said yes."

I was appalled. "I never even *saw* Rhoda's breasts. Even in all the times we shared a bed. She was so modest, Mary. God. What an invasion of her privacy."

"I was only eight! I didn't think I was being naughty. But then, this thing happened."

"What?" I couldn't believe there was more.

"Her breathing changed, like she was aroused. At that point, I knew something was wrong, that we shouldn't be doing this. So I stopped. And a couple of days later, I told Mother. I must have felt guilty. She said it was okay, that if I wanted to touch *her* bosoms that was fine, but I shouldn't have asked Rhoda to do something she didn't want to."

"Poor, poor Rhoda!" I said.

"I guess. But of course I didn't think of it that way then."

"But how awful for her, all the same. She must have felt like she

238 | LAURIE GUNST

had to say yes, and maybe she even wanted to, for reasons of her own. But still . . . "

"True," Mary conceded. "But who knows? Who knows what she was feeling?"

❧

MARY'S STORY STAYED with me like a cat with its claws dug into my arm. It filled me with shame. Some of this had to do with my never having had children, with being ignorant of all those milky, maternal feelings that only women who've birthed and nursed can ever comprehend. This was a bond my mother and my sister shared, and I realized it was one from which Rhoda and I were both excluded. She'd had a baby born dead, and I had had more than my share of abortions.

I had finally met the man with whom I would have had my babies. But I was too old now to conceive. It was too late.

The last night before Jonathan and I went back to New York, I was going through a box of my own old things. I found five teacups crocheted from multicolored yarn, a present Rhoda had given me, made by a woman from her church. At the time, I hadn't thought much of these little cups, but now I knew I'd cherish them for the rest of my life. I plumped them lovingly and set them in a row.

I went through the other things in the box: photographs and diaries and love letters from my high-school sweetheart, Frank. At the very bottom was a page torn from a notebook. I opened it and read.

I have so much to thank god for I was barn in a small town where they were not registering Black Babyies I was born in 1894 I was found in Summerville S.C. at 6 years old.

It was Rhoda's shaky handwriting, and I remembered when she wrote it. Not long before she died, I'd asked her to write me something about her growing up. And this was it.

"*Found,* Rhoda?" I said, into the silence of the room. "You weren't found in Summerville. You were born there, to Julia and Sam." But then I wondered. Could she have been an orphan? Adopted? Was she someone else's child, and did Sam and Julia take her in?

I shivered in the warm room as if I'd caught a sudden draft. I thought of how Rhoda had wanted to make that one last visit to South Carolina, not long before she died. I remembered the name of her girlhood friend, Mamie, the one she'd wanted to see again; I said to myself, *Mamie must be long gone by now.*

Rhoda must have heard me. "So?" her ghost whispered. "So what if Mamie's gone? We don't ever really leave, do we? An Old Head like you knows that!"

"Are you still here, Rhoda?" I whispered.

"Sure I am. All you have to do is come and find me."

"But where are you?" I breathed.

"Everywhere you are, child. Everywhere I was. You could start down in Savannah, or Summerville."

"But I don't even know your maiden name. You only ever went by Lloyd. All I have is Sam and Julia. How can I find you?"

"You and your *words!* Stop worrying about all those words. Been so long now, I don't even remember why I wrote *found.* I just meant that Summerville was where I came to know myself, as a child. It don't matter anyhow. You just come look for me, you hear?"

"But where?"

"What? You mean to tell me, all that learning of yours, and you can't even figure out where to find my name? On my marriage license, of course, Willie's and mine. Down there in the courthouse in Savannah. We got married in Savannah, remember?"

My heart began to race. "I didn't call you Old Head for nothing, did I?" Rhoda laughed. "Now you get on down to Savannah and find me. I'm right there, waiting. I've been there all along."

And then she was gone. The room was silent again, empty but for me and my box of old belongings and a suitcase yawning open, waiting for Jonathan and me to pack it and leave for New York.

"I have to go to Savannah," I told him when he walked into the room.

"Right this minute?"

"No," I said, "but very soon." I took a couple of deep breaths. "I just had a sort of . . . interview, with Rhoda."

"I believe you," he answered, flinging himself down on one of the twin beds. "This place is clamoring with ghosts. It feels like the whole twentieth century breathes in and out through the windows of this room."

"Is that all?" I laughed, nestling into the crook of his arm. "What about the nineteenth?"

Ask, and you shall receive. But before I could get to Savannah, the buried past of my own family surfaced. With a vengeance. The ghost of my great-grandfather, Solomon Fishblate—the mysterious mayor of Wilmington—rose from his unquiet grave.

seventeen

OLOMON FISHBLATE'S RESURRECTION—and my awakening to the role he had played in one of the worst
racial massacres in the history of the South—began not
long after Jonathan and I were married with a telephone call from
my aunt Alice.

I was in Richmond for one of my increasingly frequent visits to
Mother and Daddy. He was still his protean self, remarkable for his
ninety-three years, but Mother was growing more frail by the day,
and her memory was failing. She spent most of each day in bed,
propped up on a raft of pillows, dozing and waking, not wanting to
leave the sanctuary of her bedroom. I had taken to sitting with her,
on the chaise across from her bed, with a notebook open on my lap
and a tape recorder beside me. Even though her short-term memory was dim, she remembered the distant past very clearly, and this
became the subject we most often talked about. She loved to reminisce about her girlhood in Wilmington, and since Daddy was usually not with us—he would most likely be sitting in the den down-

stairs with Glenda, who came to see him every day—Mother could give free rein to her memories without his mocking interference.

On the night that my aunt Alice phoned, it was dinnertime and I was in the kitchen, standing at the stove and making hollandaise sauce, Daddy's favorite, for some fresh asparagus I had bought. Mother had come downstairs for dinner, her one descent of the day, and she was in the den with Daddy, having a weak Scotch and soda. It was she who answered the phone, and I heard her chatting amiably with Alice. The two of them had a somewhat thorny relationship, still full of sibling rivalry, but there was a lot of love between them all the same. After a few minutes, Mother called for me to pick up the extension in the breakfast room.

"I'm glad you're there," Alice said, her voice strong as ever. She was in her late seventies but had lost none of her mental energy, which had always included a passion for liberal politics and for the history of her and Mother's family. "You're going to be very interested in something I've found out," she said.

Alice went on to explain that she had just read a recently published historical novel about Wilmington. It was called *Cape Fear Rising*—the Cape Fear is the river that runs through the city—and its author, Philip Gerard, was a professor of English at the University of North Carolina's Wilmington campus.

"This is a hell of a book, Ev," Alice was saying to Mother. "It's about a race riot in Wilmington in 1898. Did you ever hear of this before?"

"God, no," Mother answered. "How would I?"

"What do you mean, how would you? From our mother, of course. Or from Fannie."

Fannie Schaap Fishblate, my great-grandmother, was the wife of Solomon, the mayor. He was in office around that time; my grandmother would have been ten years old.

"Neither of them ever said a word to me about it," Mother said. "I don't understand. What does this novel have to do with us?"

Alice took a long slow breath and then exhaled. "There's a character in it named Solomon Fishblate, Ev. And it's *him*. It's our grandfather. This man is the mayor—I mean, he *was* the mayor until just before this riot happened. He's Jewish, and his name is real, of course, so there's no mistaking who he was. And he isn't a very appealing character."

"Tell me more," I said, staring at my hollandaise as it curdled in the pan.

"Well, from the way this novel tells the story, Solly—that's what the author calls him—was one of the men who helped plan this thing, this race riot. It wasn't really a *riot*. I'm using the wrong word. It was a massacre. The whites had it all planned out beforehand."

"Lordy," Mother said softly. "How awful. Why would they do such a thing?"

"Ev," Alice said witheringly, "since when does there have to be a *reason* for a racial massacre in the South?"

"Um . . . Alice," I whimpered, with a sense of dread, "I've got to read this novel. Can you send it to me right away?"

"Yep. I'll mail it tomorrow morning. And after you read it, maybe you can fill me in on some of the history. Because I'm in the dark here. I know so little about that time, the background to this thing."

☙

WE HAD THE asparagus for dinner, without the hollandaise. Afterward, Mother and I went upstairs by ourselves and Daddy stayed in the den to watch a football game on television.

"So," I began. "Sounds like we've got a skeleton rattling in the closet."

"A villain," Mother answered. "A *racial* villain. The worst kind of all."

"And you never heard a word about any of this?"

"No, I swear. I'm shocked."

"Do you think it could have been the reason why Fannie never talked to you about Fishblate? You've always said she acted as if he had never existed."

Mother did not know her grandfather; he died the year she was born.

My great-grandmother, Fannie Schaap Fishblate, "a noted belle of Richmond."

"I don't know if the race riot was the reason," Mother mused. "Fanny wasn't all that interested in the real world. She was so involved with Christian Science and all that spiritual stuff. But I do know, from Mother, that there wasn't any love lost between Fannie and Fishblate. Mother always said Fannie only married him because she was afraid of being an old maid. She was all of twenty-three when they met, but that was considered kind of past it, in those days, for finding a husband."

"How come we don't have any pictures of him in the album?" I asked. "We've got all those beautiful ones of Fannie. I mean, he was the mayor, for God's sake. That's a pretty remarkable thing, for a Jew in the South at the turn of the century. There must have been at least a few photographs of him."

Mother gazed up at the ceiling and sighed. And then she casually let fly one of the genealogical bombs she was fond of dropping, out of the blue.

"Well, there must have been quite a few pictures. Because Mother said that Fannie burned every single one of them after he died."

◎

I READ *Cape Fear Rising* in two sittings, mesmerized and horrified. Not only was the novel very well written and its subject all too close to the bone, it also delivered into my waiting gaze the long-lost image of my own great-grandfather. There is something slightly unreal about discovering a blood relation, an ancestor of whom you know next to nothing, in the pages of a novel written by a pluperfect stranger. I kept wanting to raise Solly from the grave so that I could ask him: *Was this really how it happened? Did you help foment one of the worst racial massacres in the history of the South?*

And these were only the easy questions. The hard one, the one that made me really sick with fear, was: *And if all this is true, how could I be your great-granddaughter?*

Solly made his first appearance in *Cape Fear Rising* at the secret meeting when Wilmington's oligarchs began to plot the massacre. This was not long before the crucial, bitterly contested statewide elections in November 1898; the plotters intended these elections to put an end to what they considered the "Negro misrule" of the South. This was, of course, a white supremacist delusion as to the political power of black people; the truth was that Reconstruction had already been dead for thirty years, but Confederate blood was running hotter than ever. The Wilmington oligarchs were cotton barons whose fortunes had taken a downturn after the financial panic of 1897, only a year before, and now they were determined to get some of their old clout back. Who better to blame for the mess their speculation had landed them in than Wilmington's black strivers, who had managed to buy commercial property and were now running some of the city's most successful businesses? Oh . . . and while we're casting around for a scapegoat, let us not forget our age-old adversaries, either: those sneaking, underhanded, money-grubbing Shylocks. The Jews.

It is at this moment in the novel when Solly Fishblate is first mentioned, at the meeting when the Wilmington oligarchs are trying to decide who should be included in their plot.

"Solly Fishblate wants in," one of the conspirators mutters.

"Solly's part of the reason we're in this mess," another sneers. "If he'd shown more backbone as mayor. . . . Anyhow, we don't need any Jews. This is Anglo-Saxon business."

(As I read this exchange, I heaved a small sigh of relief. It seemed as if maybe Solly was a good guy after all, might have made some enemies because he was a little *too* liberal, in fact. But then I read on.)

"Solly's got some pull with the Red Shirts," a third member of the conspiracy pipes up.

I looked up the "Red Shirts" and found out who they were: none other than North Carolina's homegrown version of the Ku Klux Klan.

At that point, I phoned the author of *Cape Fear Rising*, the University of North Carolina professor Philip Gerard. I told him who I was, and that no one in my own family had known much of anything about Fishblate until my aunt rediscovered him in the pages of the book. Gerard was not surprised.

"Most of the descendants of the characters in my novel didn't know much about their ancestors, either," Gerard said. "And I can tell you that they haven't been real happy with what I wrote."

"But I'm not like that," I said. "I want to know everything you found out about Fishblate. I don't care how bad it is."

"Well, as you can see from the book, for my purposes he was a minor character. But of course that doesn't mean he was, for you. He was a shadowy figure, always hovering in the background. But he *is* mentioned in almost all the sources."

"Like what?" I asked. Suddenly, I knew that Wilmington was bound to be hiding a treasure trove of undiscovered information about my great-grandfather, and that the ill-fated trip Mother had made there years ago might have yielded untold secrets, had she known where to look.

"Oh, newspaper stories about the massacre," Philip Gerard said. "Old diaries, letters, memoirs, that sort of thing. Your great-grandfather was a very well-known character in Wilmington at the time. And from the looks of it, he was also very popular, right up to when they ousted him as mayor."

"Why did they do that?" I asked. "Did it have anything to do with his being a Jew?"

"I don't think so," Gerard answered. "Even though there was always that southern good-old-boy Anglo-Saxon anti-Semitism floating around."

I knew I was going to like this Philip Gerard; I could tell we shared a certain gallows humor about history and about the South.

"It wasn't being Jewish that got him in trouble," Gerard went on, "as much as running out of money."

"Running out of money?"

"Yes. Fishblate had always been a high roller, one of those glad-handing politicos who was able to hand out contracts to his supporters, bribes here and there. I have a feeling he was using his clothing store to sort of bankroll his political career. But he went bankrupt in the panic of 1897. By the time the plot was getting hatched, he was in real trouble. As were the men who were behind the thing. What they really wanted to do, under cover of the white supremacist propaganda, was to run all the black businessmen out of town and steal their property. That was why Solly wanted in."

I couldn't think of anything to say. On the other end of the line, Philip Gerard must have heard my silence for what it was.

"I know," he said. "It isn't pretty. But I do think there was another side to your great-grandfather. In the 1880s, when he was mayor for the first time, he was friendly with Wilmington's black leaders. His constituency was a neighborhood called Dry Pond, and it was racially mixed. So he had to have been on good terms with his black constituents and with the black men on the board of aldermen. The aldermen were the ones who chose the mayor. But then something must have happened. I'm just not sure what it was. The man was an enigma."

"I wonder if you know how bizarre this is for me, Mr. Gerard?"

"Philip."

"Thank you. It's just that I have this ancestor no one in my family knows anything about, and suddenly he pops up in a novel. My hitherto-unknown great-grandfather turns out to be a massacre-fomenting white supremacist with ties to the Ku Klux Klan. You don't know my family, of course, but if you did, you'd appreciate the black humor—excuse the expression—in this situation."

Philip laughed sympathetically. "If I were you, I'd come down here and root around for yourself. There's a whole lot more about Fishblate than what I put in this book. Believe me, you aren't the only one who's freaked out by what I dug up. People here, black as well as white, have tried to forget this thing ever happened. They've buried it for a hundred years."

I ARRIVE ON a Sunday in late March. Living in New York City as I do, with its interminable winters and its slow-coming springs, I have forgotten what this month is like in the South. The breeze wafting up the hill from the brown-and-sapphire Cape Fear River is warm instead of whippingly chill, as it would be in New York, and I'm sweating through my urban black, the only color I seem to be wearing these days. I find a shop that's open, buy a white cotton shirt, put it on, and start walking.

Wilmington is gorgeous. Some of the old wood houses downtown remind me of Jamaica; they are painted in pastel colors and have wooden louvers on their windows, along with the one architectural feature—an upstairs porch running the full length of the house—that never fails to make me weak with desire. (Till the hundred-percent humidity descends in April, that is.)

Camellias bloom everywhere. My grandmother's favorite flower. The strong sunlight glints off the river. The wharves are silent now. No more cotton-laden paddle wheelers waiting for the tide. I pause before the flyblown windows of the empty store on Front Street that once belonged to Solomon Fishblate. I can see a few pool tables gathering dust inside.

I walk on and imagine how this street must have looked and smelled and sounded in . . . say, 1863, when Wilmington was the only port in the South that stayed open in the face of the Union blockade. Somewhere I had recently read how much money one successful run to the Bahamas would net, from just one ship packed with bales of cotton, for the hungry mills of Manchester and Birmingham, England, returning full of contraband French brandy and desperately needed chloroform for the Confederacy's wounded men. A cool quarter-million dollars, in gold. Crazy money, just like smuggling cocaine.

I would give anything for just one hour, walking down this street in that now-distant time. But I don't have to yearn for long, because the ghosts have already started whispering in my ear.

"We're so glad you've come," they say, their garments rustling ever so softly. "We've been waiting for you all these years." They are all here: Solly, with his soul-destroying lust for politics. A man imprisoned in the double loneliness I know he must have felt: first, having a wife who loathed him; second, being a Jew among gentiles in the fusty, Bible-thumping South.

And here is Fannie, in her trailing widow's black. Which I know she wore even before she was widowed; that was her color. She strides purposefully past me, carrying her copy of *Science and Health* by Mary Baker Eddy, on her way to a Wednesday night testimonial of healing. She has left her two little daughters—my grandmother, Alice, and Alice's baby sister, Bessie—at home with the maid.

And here, too, oh! Here, most vividly of them all, are Granny herself and Rhoda. My grandmother is stepping out, on her way to a card party or a tea dance at the club. She takes no notice of me, standing here on the sidewalk; she is busy pulling on her three-button white kid gloves. And where will I find Rhoda? I know. She is where I am going later in the day, in the house where she helped to raise my mother. But, for now, I have one other errand.

⌒

I DRIVE TO Oakdale Cemetery where I know Solomon Fishblate is buried, to look for his grave. I want to find it for Mother's sake, as well as mine. But there is no one at the gate to direct me and the cemetery is big. I drive up and down the paved paths, past plots dripping with camellias, until I see a dapper man with a waxed mustache, walking an English sheepdog. The dog is panting and the man wipes his glistening pink brow with a handkerchief.

I lean from my car window. "Excuse me. Can you tell me where the Hebrew section is?" (I know this is what it's called.)

"You're almost upon it," the man answers. "May I ask if you're looking for anyone in particular? Perhaps I can direct you."

"Yes. My great-grandfather. Solomon Fishblate."

"Ahh . . . Fishblate!" he sighs, as if the two of them had parted only a few minutes ago. "One of our most intriguing characters. By the way, have you seen his house on Sunset Hill? It's a very fine example of the Italianate style. Built in 1878, when he was mayor for his first term."

He sees me gaping, smiles forgivingly. "I hope I didn't take you by surprise. It's just that I feel as if I know him, I'm such an admirer of his house. I fear it's fallen on hard times, though. Seems to be deserted now. But you won't have any trouble finding it. Corner of Front Street and Nun, overlooking the river."

I step out of the car. The sun beating down on my head makes me think I might faint.

"The Hebrew section is right over there." The man points. "You can see the wrought-iron gates. Fishblate's grave is just beyond them." I thank him and we say goodbye. The granite obelisk must be twelve feet high. I can't imagine how Mother and Daddy missed it. The inscription says Solomon Fishblate has gone to be with the angels. He was born in 1843 and the date of his death is February 22, 1910: thirty-nine years to the day before I was born.

I drive to Fishblate's house on Sunset Hill. It is every bit as lovely as the man in the cemetery said, a miniature riverboat of a house, with tall, triple-sash windows and delicate wooden tracery around the porch. The man was right; it does seem to be deserted. The louvers, their once-green paint now chipped and fading, are drawn tight across the windows. I wander to the backyard over-looking the river. There's a carriage house and two beautiful trees. Before I know it, I'm imagining that I live here. Just me, single again, no Jonathan to talk me out of coming here and wafting around these haunted rooms like Blanche DuBois.

"I could turn that into a study," I muse, gazing up at the carriage house. "And I'd put a hammock right here between these trees. Looking out across the river."

The white ghosts are laughing softly. "Not so fast," another voice breaks in. It is Rhoda's.

"See that river, child?" she says. "Take a good look at just how wide it is. Well, they said this river was so full of dead people after the killing was done that you could walk across it on them. Like logs."

Not so fast. As Rhoda says.

◯

I AM WALKING slower now. It is late afternoon and the light has begun to slant. I cross a couple of streets that run parallel to the river and go up a gentle hill to Fifth Avenue, where Mother has told me her childhood home was. I know the number, 111, and from the other houses on Fifth, I'm expecting hers to be like them—lovingly restored antebellum wood-frame houses with flowers in front and wrought iron gates. But I am wrong: Number 111 South Fifth is a graceless two-story apartment house of dark red firebrick. The roof is rotten and about to collapse. A sign warns of impending demolition. KEEP OUT, it says.

I creep past the dead-eyed windows on the side of the house to the backyard. Still standing, miraculously, is the magnolia tree beneath which my mother and Rhoda sat by the hour. Somehow, it has survived in all its loveliness. But around it now are mounds of trash.

I am overwhelmed by an emptiness so deep that I lean my head against the tree and cry.

"Rhoda?" I call to the distempered yard, the dirty back fence hung with vines. She materializes from the gloom, wearing her white uniform with the safety pins on her apron. She gives me a sad smile.

"You think nothing changes, honey? You thought you'd come here and this old place would still be looking the way it did a hundred years ago? You know better than that! Go on now. Don't be troubling me. I'm tired."

I walk back down the driveway, my feet crunching on the broken glass. I pause at the front steps and notice a faded wood sign with the street number 111 by the front door. I remember that Rhoda took the number down from her front door on Idlewood Avenue before her house there was demolished—it was 1502. She kept the sign in the drawer of her nightstand in the nursing home. What became of it? I wonder now.

Carefully, I step across the sagging floorboards and pry the plywood number from the wall.

◎

I WALK BACK to the inn near the waterfront where I am staying and phone home. Richmond, that is; the place I still think of as "home" even though I have not lived there in forty years.

It is dinnertime, and I know that Mother will be sitting in the den, having her Scotch, while Daddy waits for the weather report to come on TV. I picture her in the chair she always sits in; now that she is incontinent, the seat cushion is beginning to smell slightly of pee. I see her little gnarled feet in their lace-up shoes, planted on the rug and turned inward like those of child.

"Hi, Mom!" I say, when she answers the phone.

"Where are you?" she asks. She is always confused these days as to my whereabouts.

"I'm in your home town!" I explain. "Remember? I told you I was coming down to Wilmington? Well, here I am."

"Oh, honey, how wonderful! You have to tell me how it looks. I always wanted to get back there, but I don't think I can now."

"I know. I'm doing my best to see it for you. And it's just beautiful, Mom. It's one of the prettiest cities I have ever seen. All the old houses are still here, and so many have been restored. They don't look anything like Richmond. They're more like the islands. Remember how there are palm trees?"

"Oh, yes! I sure do." She sighs. "It always was the loveliest place. I don't care how everyone raves about Richmond. You can have it!" I can hear Daddy grumbling in the background.

"I've just come from your old house," I say.

"It's still there! How does it look?"

"Well," I hesitate, not wanting to tell her the truth. "It's fallen on hard times. Looks like it hasn't been lived in for a very long time. But the magnolia tree is still there, out back. Fine as ever."

"Oh, honey. I can't believe you're really there. If you only knew . . . I still have dreams about Wilmington. Can you imagine? Even after all these years. . . . "

"I found Fishblate's house, too," I say. "And his grave, at Oakdale. And the house is so lovely, Mom. It sits on a little hill above the river. I felt as if I'd been there before."

"What does his grave look like?"

"It's very imposing. There's a tall granite obelisk with his name and his dates."

I hear her breath on the other end of the line. "Thank you, darling. I feel so good, knowing you found it. At last."

When I hang up, I know that this conversation is a kind of goodbye, a parting before the final one. My coming to Wilmington is my farewell gift to her. A return to the place of her birth, and a retort to my father's endless dismissals.

What Mother said about her dreams must have worked its way deep into my subconscious, because that night, I dream that I go into Fishblate's mansion on the river. The first room I enter is the front parlor, where I am astonished to see a massive pier glass still in the room, a gold-framed mirror tilted slightly forward from the wall between the front windows. The mirror must be close to ten feet high, because it reaches up to the molding, and the ceilings are perhaps fourteen feet. Dwarfed by the vaulting space, I am staring fixedly at my own reflection when a bald gentleman wearing a black frock coat steps out from the silvered glass. I am frightened, but also fascinated. I know this is Solomon Fishblate.

I drift away toward the rear of the house and see that the kitchen is in bad shape, its walls stained dark from water. I go back to the parlor and look again at my reflection in the pier glass. With a start of horror, I see that I am not myself. The face in the mirror is my great-grandmother's. And I know that she is dead.

℺

IN THE MORNING, before I set out for the library, I phone Carrie Jefferson. She is Dr. Carrie Jefferson Smith now, married and divorced, a tenured member of the faculty at the School of Social Work at Syracuse University. Over the years, she and Mother have become closer than ever, and Carrie always comes by the house to see her and Daddy when she returns to Ashland or to Richmond to visit her relatives there.

Carrie and I have begun to feel our way tentatively toward a friendship of our own. But we are still pretty formal with each other; the polite African American woman and the polite white woman, walking on eggshells. We hadn't really started getting down yet. I wasn't sure we ever would, but I didn't worry about this. It just meant so much to me that we knew each other.

I had told her previously what I had discovered about Solomon Fishblate, and that I was going to Wilmington to dig further.

"This is your evolution, girlfriend," Carrie had said. And then she paused, thinking. "Your evil-oution, if you know what I mean."

I didn't laugh. "You sound like one of my old Rasta friends," I had said. "The way they remake words."

"Yes, well . . . " Carrie had continued. "It is your evil-oution. It's the working out of your history. Of the evil in your family, hard as it is for either of us to imagine that."

This morning, when I call Carrie from Wilmington, I tell her that I found Mother's house and Solly's grave, and that the ghosts were not only whispering in my ear as I walked around but now they have invaded my dreams.

Carrie drops into the vernacular, as she does every now and again. "Yeah, well, a couple of strange dreams ain't nothin' com-pared to what's gonna happen after you get into those archives."

"Thank you," I answer. "I'm scared shitless, to tell you the truth."

"I hear you. But you don't really have a choice, do you? I mean, you are who you are. Nothing's going to change what has been. And you know something? This whole race thing . . . all this lying and keeping secrets and telling half-truths. Don't you think that maybe, just maybe . . . someday . . . if enough of us can tell the *whole* truth, the whole sad, ugly, pitiful truth, we might be able to lay this burden down?"

IN THE FOLLOWING week, I read so many documents, letters, memoirs, and newspaper stories of the massacre that I'd come out from the library at the end of the day in a daze, blinking into the blinding sunlight like a toad. It was hard to believe how much doc-umentation there was, slumbering in the archives for a hundred years. And I did not have to do this culling by myself: Wilmington is blessed to have had a native son by the name of Bill Reaves who took it upon himself to comb through every old newspaper and make files of clippings on all the notable families of the city. I did not have to scroll through endless spools of microfilm.

The files on the Einsteins and the Fishblates were each an inch thick. From them tumbled stories and anecdotes, social notes and descriptions of what the Fishblate daughters, Alice and Bessie, wore to this party or that dance. The image they presented, of the life of this turn-of-the-century southern city, were so rich and plentiful that I would get lost in the precious details and have to remind myself of the grim events I had come here to uncover.

The news stories about Solomon Fishblate began appearing long before the massacre of 1898. They started in 1869, when he arrived in North Carolina from New York. Like so many other Jews, he was peddling dry goods, riding the railroad from one depot town to the next. His first stop seems to have been Kinston, and not long after he arrived there, he got into an altercation with a man named Thornton, who pulled a gun. The bullet passed through Solly's jacket, leaving him unharmed.

"Scrappy little bastard," I whispered to myself when I read this story in the Fishblate file. I could see that he didn't shrink from a fight. And in many of the stories that followed, I could sense the threat of violence, the fear and vulnerability that Solly lived with, the constant insecurity of an outsider. This was the same feeling I got from those stories Daddy used to tell me about his father and grandfather always carrying a gun. About that letter some irate saloon keeper sent to Emmanuel Gunst that began "Dear Jews . . ."

Always vulnerable. Always needing to be on guard. For this was the era when Jews in the South ceased to be as welcomed by the white oligarchy as they had been before the Civil War. Back then, white plantation owners had smiled upon the scattered Jews who made their way into the southern countryside, and even those who gathered in the region's few large cities, to buy and sell and bank. The Jews were welcome then because not only were they white— in a society where whites were a minority—but also because of their mercantile skills. They did not seem to be a threat.

But after slavery ended, a slow transformation began. Now, the

Jew ceased to look quite so *white* to his Christian neighbors. He began to seem . . . *different.* By the 1880s, the economic dislocations that placed poor southern whites ever further out on the periphery of survival had given rise to a fierce new nativism. As more and more Irish immigrants and those from southern Europe began to pour into the South from the cities up north where jobs were scarce, the Ku Klux Klan started to lump together Catholics and Jews in its paranoid vision of the "foreigners" who were menacing the purity of the Anglo-Saxon race. As the price of cotton plummeted and textile mills sprang up across the South—their northern owners lured by dirt-cheap labor—more workers left impoverished rural areas and went to work in these dirty, often dangerous mills. Many of them were women, and this infuriated southerners for whom the ability to "protect their women" was a cornerstone of what they believed to be their chivalric way of life.

Some of the foremen of these new factories were Jews. And now the Jew came to be perceived as one of these "foreigners" who had their capitalist hands around southern throats. Wasn't his skin sometimes suspiciously dark? Wasn't the texture of his hair a little curly? Did he not have strange ways, rituals, and dietary rules that separated him from everyone else?

Slowly but surely, the age-old hatred resurfaced, with a vengeance. The tide of anti-Semitism rolled back into Dixie. Solomon Fishblate had come to North Carolina just in time to feel the waters rise.

❧

STILL, AS I read on, I began to see that Solly did make some friends, the gun-toting Mr. Thornton from Kinston notwithstanding. Not long after that fracas, Solly had saved enough funds from peddling to move to Wilmington and open a dry-goods store of his own. Four years later, in 1873, he had become prosperous and popular enough to be elected to the board of aldermen, a stepping-stone to the mayoralty, which he won for the first time in 1878.

But there were mutterings all the same. "Mayor Fishblate was a

Jew," wrote a magnate from Wilmington by the name of John Bellamy, Jr. "And he had many enemies among the people, but only for that reason. I must say that in my business dealings with him, I found him to be always honorable and fair."

Be careful, Solly; they're watching your every move, I said to myself. *You're walking the southern Jewish tightrope.*

Not surprisingly, Solly had many friends among Wilmington's black citizens. They were a slight majority in the city and a very definite one in his own political constituency, the neighborhood called Dry Pond. They were important players in the city's economy as well as in its politics: Even before emancipation, some of Wilmington's enslaved people had been able to save money by hiring themselves out as workers. When freedom came they were ready, and they purchased homes and businesses. (Some of the city's free black men and women had done this even before the end of the Civil War.)

Such successes, modest though they often were, aroused deep resentment among the city's whites. But it seemed that my great-grandfather was not among them, at least not at first. The evidence suggests that he may have even had an appreciation of black culture, especially its Caribbean soul.

There was an African revel known as Jonkonnu, celebrated at Christmastime; it was brought to Wilmington and other seaboard cities of the South long ago (by way of the West Indies) by enslaved people. I had seen Jonkonnu in Jamaica, when I waited eagerly for Christmas morning and the appearance of brightly costumed actors on the Kingston streets. They danced and sang to the music of flutes and tambourines fluttering with bright ribbons, wearing fantastically painted masks in gorgeous African patterns. Jonkonnu can get rowdy—the actors ask for money and flirt suggestively with women in the crowd—and in 1888, when my great-grandfather was mayor, Wilmington's white leaders asked Fishblate to ban the revel. He refused.

I don't know why; maybe it was just clever politics on his part. Perhaps he was savvy enough to know he had to stay in the good graces of the city's black majority. But when I read the newspaper story of this episode, I felt a sudden burst of kinship with my great-grandfather. He and I, separated by a century, had witnessed—and he had affirmed—an African celebration that linked the Motherland with my own two places, the Caribbean and the American South.

I am your flesh and blood, Solly, I said, my voice a whisper in the quiet reading room. *Now: Tell me what went wrong.*

҈

IN THAT SAME year, 1888, Solly went up to Richmond on a business trip and came back with a wife. "Miss Fannie Schaap," the newspaper said, "a noted belle of Richmond."

I had to smile. How my vain, social-climbing great-grandmother must have loved reading that! *A noted belle of Richmond.* Hardly. Fannie was no southern belle. She had grown up above her family's dry-goods store in the Shockoe Bottom ghetto, taking care of younger siblings while her parents waited on customers downstairs. Mother told me that all Fannie ever wanted was to go to college; she worshipped books, lugged them home to her family's garret by the armful, and read them in the evening when her work was done by the dim light of a kerosene lamp.

"You are so very like her, Laurie," Mother used to tell me. "You, with your love of books and ideas. And your spiritual inclinations. Fannie believed in reincarnation, you know, and sometimes I even think you *are* her, come back to life."

This always sent a little shiver of excitement down my spine. And guilt, as well, because I wondered what my life would have been like had I been born in 1866, like Fannie was. As it was, I did not have to marry to get away from my family or to have a life of ease, which was what Fannie thought she was getting by marrying Solomon Fishblate. But she was wrong.

He started having financial reversals almost as soon as they got back to Wilmington. Business went soft; he was running his store on credit and—as Philip Gerard suggested—he was living in a bubble that was about to burst. Fannie, for her part, had no interest whatsoever in her husband's political career; she disdained his friends and looked down her nose at the rough hurly-burly of Wilmington. She soon withdrew into her own world, a fantasy of southern gentility. Her best friend was a society woman named Mary Bridgers, who founded the Christian Science Church in town, and she converted Fannie to the new faith. They became inseparable, traveling to Boston to worship at Mary Baker Eddy's Mother Church, and to religious meetings around the South. Fishblate went to his suppers and rallies alone.

"Mayor Fishblate is an exceedingly popular figure in Wilmington," one paper said; the year was 1895. "Having served sixteen years as alderman and four terms as mayor, he is spoken of as the most available candidate for Congress in his district, which includes the important cities of Wilmington and Charlotte. Mayor Fishblate's wife is a queenly woman and one of the most beautiful in the South."

Ah, yes . . . that rarely seen belle of Richmond.

But two years later, Solly's fortunes went south. He was forced to declare bankruptcy after the financial panic of 1897. Almost immediately thereafter, he was ousted from the mayoralty by the same Wilmington power brokers who were plotting to take back their city from the Negroes and Republicans they believed had stolen it away. The conspirators had enough firepower from the local arsenal to blow up the entire city, and behind them stood a white militia—backed by the Red Shirt mob—who'd been spoiling for a rematch since 1865.

Where was my great-grandfather in all this? He must have thought he saw his chance. The "Redeemers" who were going to retake Wilmington would redeem his fortunes, too. But there was a more insidious temptation. If he stood with them, then perhaps the whispers about how he was a Jew and an outsider, too much of a friend to the Negro—maybe these accusations would be silenced, once and for all.

On a chilly autumn night two weeks before the massacre, Solly stood before a mob of drunken Red Shirts at a torch-lit rally in his constituency, Dry Pond. The crowd liked Fishblate—he'd been their mayor, after all—and so he told them what they wanted to hear.

"The choice in this election," he shouted, "is between white rule and Negro rule. And *I* am with the white man, every time!"

Are you really, Solly? Or is it that you think you have to shout this from the rooftops, because you are afraid? Because you know it has been subject to debate, just who you're "with." Maybe you're a *nigger lover,* Solly. Maybe you've lost your old touch. Everyone knows you've been cuckolded by that high falutin' wife of yours, and she hasn't even left you for another man. She's dumped you for a *church!*

I think I know why you're up there tonight, Solly, on that platform. With the light from all those pine torches flickering across your big-nosed Jewish face. Pledging your allegiance to the white man. *Every time.* You hope and pray you can convince them that it's true.

But you're going blind, Solly. This I know. The metaphor of blindness is all too terrifyingly apt: The newspaper file has told me that there's something wrong with your eyes. The papers say you're suffering from an undisclosed affliction, your eyes pain you all the time. But you won't know why, won't be diagnosed for another ten years, when you finally see a specialist in New York. He will tell you that you're suffering from Bright's disease, a slow necrosis of the kidneys. One of its worst symptoms is persistent pain in the eyes. By then, you won't have long to live and you'll be in such agony that you can barely see, or think, or move.

THE WILMINGTON MASSACRE began the day after that night rally in Dry Pond, on the morning of November 9, 1898—election day. Although there was no doubt in anyone's minds that the Redeemers would sweep the polls, they were hell-bent on killing as many black people as they could.

In the week I spent in Wilmington, I read the many accounts of the massacre, studying it in great detail. I researched it so thoroughly that I almost lost sight of the one person I was trying to focus on, in there with the white supremacist horde. I would keep finding Solly only to lose him again in the horror of what I read.

I did some of my research at the Lower Cape Fear Historical Society, lodged in an antebellum house on Fifth Avenue not far from that grim dwelling where my mother was born and raised. The downstairs rooms of the historical society reminded me strangely of a coffin, maybe because the horsehair furniture was tufted like the inside of a casket and each of the tall Victorian windows was shaped like one as well.

Upstairs, in the library, I opened a memoir of the massacre written by a man named Harry Hayden, a Confederate veteran who thought the bloodletting was an excellent thing. I was alone in the room except for one other person, a pink-cheeked gentleman wearing a bow tie who was engrossed in a pamphlet titled *Etiquette Before the Civil War*.

"Six negroes were shot down near the corner of Fourth and Brunswick Streets," Hayden wrote. "One of them had fired at the whites from a negro dance hall in the Brooklyn section, and he was shot fifteen or twenty times. A member of the shooting party later exclaimed, 'When we turned him ovah, Mista Niggah had a look of surprise on his face, I ashure you!'"

I slammed the book shut. Suddenly, a childhood sensation I'd all but forgotten swamped me like a tsunami: a terror I used to feel in the part of my body Rhoda always called "my privates." It would come over me whenever I heard Daddy and his friends talk about killing, about hunting the frail birds they loved to shoot down out of the sky. I would feel this same shiver of helpless shame and fear, listening to the secret glee men took in the spilling of innocent blood.

I couldn't read any more. I fled down the stairs of that Confederate coffin of a house, out into the sunlight where the birds were fluting obliviously in the trees. But after a short walk, I forced myself to go back. I was not finished yet. In the library, I found a letter written several days after the massacre to President William McKinley. The writer of this letter was an anonymous black woman from Wilmington. She told of women and children fleeing from the mob into the woods surrounding Oakdale

Solomon Fishblate as a Knight of Phythias, ca. 1908.

Cemetery, the very place where Solomon Fishblate's bones now lay. This woman told the president of the United States how her people froze to death in the November cold, too terrified to return to their homes. She asked the president to intercede, to send help for the survivors. And then she named the three men who, in her opinion, were primarily responsible for the massacre.

One of them was Solomon Fishblate.

⌀

SOLLY DIED A pitiful death. After the collapse of his political career and the bankruptcy of his store, he tried to rebuild what was left of his life by operating a railroad hotel in Kinston, his first home in the state. But this venture failed and he returned to Wilmington, broke again and broken. He was all but blind by then from Bright's disease.

He died in the winter of 1910. By then, he was close to penury. He left Fannie all of a hundred dollars, barely enough to cover the expenses of his burial.

The archivist at the Wilmington library eventually found a photograph of Solly, buried in the records of a fraternal organization he belonged to, the Knights of Pythias. The picture was taken in 1902. Solly was as bald as an egg and was wearing pince-nez, so I couldn't see his eyes. They were clenched in a fierce frown behind his glasses; his disease must have been so bad by then that he was in constant pain. He had a thick walrus mustache that hid his mouth, and his nose was very large, like Daddy's. So were his ears, which were also like my father's; they reminded me of an elephant's.

"Hardly a rival for John Barrymore," Daddy said when I showed the picture to him and Mother. This was the first time she had ever seen her grandfather's face. Daddy's spitefulness threw her and me into a momentary silence, as always. But after he trundled off into the den, Mother took a good long look at the photograph.

"I think he has a good face," she said. "Very Jewish. And strong."

The Fishblate clothing store on Front Street in Wilmington, around 1890. Solly is standing behind the horse's rump.

The Wilmington house Solly built in 1873. It still presents itself to me, in dreams.

eighteen

OTHER WAS OLD by then, in her late eighties, and in some way she was past caring what Solomon Fishblate had done. But I was not.

I had nightmares after I got home to New York. Dreams in which I saw my great-grandfather as a corpse, his teeth bared in a mocking grin. I dreamt of Rhoda; she and I were walking hand in hand through a piney woods, as we had done when I was a child before all the houses were built on Wilton Road. But in the dream we heard the sound of gunshots barking through the trees.

"Run, Rhoda!" I cried. "We have to run."

"I can't, child," she answered. "I'm too old."

I knew I couldn't save her.

I woke from these dreams with no clear understanding of what they meant, only a feeling of heavy sadness. Sometimes, I woke Jonathan and we'd talk for a while. Eventually, I realized that my journey of discovery to Wilmington had not laid one single ghost to rest. Solomon Fishblate's skeleton was rattling even louder in my soul's closet, and I knew he'd never leave me. I was stuck with him now, with the truth of what he had done.

But if I had Solly's blood running in my veins, I also had Rhoda in my heart. Even though she was not my real mother, she had made me what I was. Hers was the good that counterbalanced the ancestral evil Carrie Jefferson Smith spoke of. And because of what I had unearthed in Wilmington, I felt a heightened sense of urgency to search now for Rhoda. Finding out what I could about her early years in South Carolina, her youth in Savannah, and her marriage to Willie Lloyd became an obsession. I knew this was a quest for myself as well as for her. Those were the places that had shaped her life, and until I walked in her footsteps, I would not know who I was either.

℘

A FEW DAYS before I left New York for Savannah, I was strolling home one evening through Central Park to our apartment on the Upper West Side. It was twilight, the "blue hour" that is my favorite time of day, and the lights were twinkling on in the old apartment buildings along the western edge of the park. I was thinking of Rhoda; she had lived in this neighborhood with my grandmother when Granny moved to New York from Richmond in 1936.

My grandmother had left Richmond under a dark cloud of tragedy and scandal. Her husband, Arthur Einstein, had committed suicide in 1930, gassing himself in the attic of the family home on the Boulevard. He had lost everything in the crash of 1929 and had sunk into a depression to which he could envision no end but death. But he had another reason for taking his own life. Granny was having an affair with his business partner, a man from one of Richmond's prominent German Jewish families, named Gus Schwarzschild. Arthur knew all about his wife's infidelity. Six months after Arthur killed himself, Gus Schwarzschild took his own life, in exactly the same manner and place as my grandfather. Gus went upstairs to the attic of the Einstein home on the Boulevard and turned on the gas. His suicide left no doubt in anyone's mind—if indeed there had ever been any—of just what the relationship had been between him and my grandmother.

It was this devastating event that Granny was speaking of to Claudine on that morning so many years ago, when I was eight and came upon the two of them commiserating in the kitchen. Claudine had been weeping over the sudden death of her lover, a married man, when I overheard my grandmother saying to her, "Don't cry, Claudine. You aren't the first woman to fall in love with a married man, and I promise you won't be the last."

I did not hear the full story of Granny and Gus Schwarzschild till I was in my twenties; it was my aunt Barbara who told me. But I had never forgotten that moment from my childhood, and after Barbara told me, I understood why, at my grandmother's funeral, Claudine had wept so hard and said, "She knew we're all the same, underneath our skins."

My mother and father had just married when Gus Schwarzschild killed himself; they returned from their honeymoon to the news. Even though Mother had been devastated by her father's death, she had a new husband and a home of her own. But my aunts Alice and Barbara were eleven and four, and for them there was no escape from the horror and the stigma of their father's suicide. When it happened, Rhoda was not there. Rhoda had not gone back to work for my grandmother after Willie Lloyd's death and her move to Richmond—I do not know why. It may have been because Rhoda found other work, since Nannie Robinson was employed by Granny to look after Alice and Barbara, who adored Nannie and were determined not to part with her. In the aftermath of their father's death, the two younger Einstein girls spent virtually every hour of the day with her, and Barbara all but lived at the farm that Nannie and her husband, Charles, owned in Zion Town, west of Richmond. When Barbara went to the farm, she slept in the same bed with Nannie—Charles moved into the room across the hall—and Barbara spent the days playing with her best friend next door, Lillian Purvoyle, who came from a family of twelve children. When Barbara and Lillian played marbles together, Barbara would look down at her friend's hands, dark against the pale sand of the Purvoyles' yard, and wish that she were "colored" too, so that she could look just like Lillian.

Rhoda did not return to the Einsteins until 1936, when Granny remarried and left Richmond for New York City, her new husband's home. Nannie Robinson stayed behind, and Rhoda went with the family to New York. Granny's second husband was Edgar Asch, a button manufacturer who Granny was fond of describing as "from the New York Asches," as if they were a prominent family, which they weren't. Barbara despised her new stepfather. In fact, no one except Granny liked him. They shared a passion for parties and they were out almost every night, so Barbara and Rhoda spent a lot of time together. They went to the movies on Saturday night, stopping on the way home to buy the Sunday *Times,* which Barbara loved for the comics.

Barbara is eighty now, and when we talk about that time in her life, she says she was a very independent child—almost a teenager by then—and that she often went by herself to Central Park and other places in the city. But when she needed a mother, it was Rhoda to whom she turned, because her own mother was never there.

℘

I WAS THINKING about all this as I walked home through the park that twilit evening, feeling Rhoda's presence and wondering if she had trod this same path. Suddenly, up ahead, I heard the sound of wailing and saw a little boy trundling along behind his nurse. He was crying, and she was clearly exasperated, walking resolutely ahead of him and ignoring his tears. I knew that she was one among that legion of women from the islands who raise the children of the city's affluent white families. I was certain that she had children of her own, too, far away.

"I want my mommy!" the little boy sobbed. "*You're* not my mommy. I want my *mommy.*"

My heart cracked in half. Part wanted to rush to the child and comfort him. The other half went out to this woman, not his mother but compelled to act the part. I could see how tired she was—as tired as Rhoda must often have been of me—and I imagined that she must be missing her own child or children she had had to leave . . . where? Jamaica? Grenada? Trinidad or Barbados? I thought of Merle, my friend and confidant from Kingston, who I knew was in New Jersey at this moment, taking care of someone else's babies while her man, Thomas, looked after their seven children at home. Without the U.S. dollars Merle sent to him, they would have starved.

The little boy here in the park this evening wiped his eyes and nose and followed the black woman home. He had no choice in the matter, and neither, I reflected, did she.

☙

WHEN I ARRIVED in Savannah, I remembered a poet friend who once remarked to me that being there was like waking up beside an old southern whore: warm and frowsy, not too good-looking, and tired.

But it was the sixties when he said that, and Savannah doesn't look that way anymore. Northern money and tastemakers started coming in around that time, restoring the old houses and the splendid little squares that James Oglethorpe laid out when he designed the city. And then came "that book and the movie," as the locals refer to *Midnight in the Garden of Good and Evil.* Now trolleys full of sightseers roll along the shady streets while tour guides give gossipy little spiels about decadent Savannah. And patrons flock to the riverfront nightclub where the Lady Chablis, the fabulous black drag queen who stole the movie, gives midnight performances one weekend a month.

Hardly the Savannah Rhoda knew, or the one I had come to find. Savannah is a closed society, like all old southern cities, and I would not have been able to penetrate its secrets had I not been very lucky in the one person there I knew to call. He was an African American octogenarian by the name of Westley W. Law, and I learned of him from an old friend of Jonathan's, Dave Epstein, who used to be Savannah's chief of police.

"You have to contact Mr. Law as soon as you get there," Dave told me. "He's the heart and soul of black Savannah. Used to be a mail carrier but he's long retired now, and he has dedicated his life to preserving the city's black heritage. There's a civil rights museum in Savannah now, and it's there because of Westley W. Law. He knows every notable figure, every street, every landmark." I could hear the smile in Dave's voice when he delivered his next piece of advice. "He doesn't own a car, and he walks everywhere. Let me warn you that he walks fast. Doesn't have any time to waste. And doesn't stomach fools gladly. He's seen more than his share."

WHEN I REACHED Mr. Law at his home, he was courteous. "Of course, I remember Dave Epstein," he said. "He was one of the best chiefs we ever had. I'd be pleased to meet you. No, I don't need you to come collect me. I'll be downtown anyway. Meet me at Nita's, on Broughton Street. She has the best food in town."

Mr. Law was small, slight, and imposing. His white hair was cut close to his head and his eyes were huge and doleful, as if he had seen it all. No doubt Rhoda would have recognized him as another Old Head. His manner was Old South, courtly and deliberate, although he almost never smiled and was given to raising his voice almost to a shout when making an important point.

"I'm a Geechee," he proudly proclaimed, as Nita, the restaurant's proprietress, came over to our table to greet him. "Just like this lady here."

Nita was perspiring from the heat in her kitchen, and she wiped her brow with a towel tied to her ample waist. "How you keepin', Mr. Law?" she asked tenderly, giving him a hug.

Geechee is the local Low Country pronunciation for Kissi, the West African tribe from which many of coastal Georgia's black people are descended. Mr. Law knew whence he came, and let no one doubt this. We tucked into our fried chicken and greens and cornbread, which Mr. Law ate delicately and sparingly; he did not finish what was on his plate, and Nita packed it in a little container so that he could take it home.

After we had finished eating, I reached into my bag for the photograph of Rhoda I had brought, the one taken in Harlem. I thought that when Mr. Law had seen it, he would understand how compelling a presence Rhoda had, in life and death. I handed it to him across the table.

"Goodness!" he breathed reverently. I told him who Rhoda was to me and explained that I had come to Savannah to find out whatever I could about her life here.

"I understand," he said. "Had I known such a woman, I would turn heaven and earth for her."

As always when I spoke about Rhoda to an African American, I was at pains not to sound as if I had a bad case of what's known as mammy-itis. This is a common affliction among white people from the South, and it almost always has no symptoms that *we* (whites) can see; the signs—acute sentimentality and an atavistic yearning for the mammy, along with a pervasive tendency to say that she was "just like one of the family"—can usually be recognized only by people of color. The white person in question doesn't see anything wrong with him or herself.

I did not want Mr. Law to think that I had mammy-itis. I also knew that the more "the lady doth protest," the more guilty she would sound. You can't win for losing on this one.

"Rhoda was a person to me, Mr. Law," I said. "She wasn't 'just like one of the family.' She knew so much about us, but I never knew who she was, and that's part of why I'm looking for her now."

While Mr. Law was considering what I'd said, I handed him the other picture I had brought, the one of Rhoda and me when I was two. I figured he had better get the full force of the thing, and that I wasn't doing him or myself any favors by pussyfooting around.

He looked at the photograph for a moment and then leaned forward across the table, fixing me with a blazing look. "*All right!*" he boomed, slapping one hand down on the table so that the water glasses jumped and the other diners at Nita's turned around to look at us. "This is the South! And the simple truth is—and I don't care how uncomfortable this makes black people or white people or anybody in between—no white person got where they did without the help of someone black. *All right!* But the reverse is also true. Do you understand what I'm saying?"

He did not pause for me to answer; he was on a roll.

"Listen to me! Look at the black men and women who became our leaders after slavery. Our teachers and churchmen, doctors and lawyers. Not one of them got there without the help of someone white. Maybe it was even a former master. Maybe it was a benefactor from up north or from right here, someone who had the vision and the decency to endow a college. You see? My point is, you can't divide black from white so easily."

"Yes, sir," I answered. I didn't think I was in any position to argue.

"And I take it from what you have said that this is exactly the nature of your love for this lady." Mr. Law touched the photograph of Rhoda and me. "That she was the African soul who set *your* soul on its path through life."

"Yes," I said again.

"Indeed," he murmured his assent. "This is exactly what I'm talking about. Where would you have been, who would you have grown up to be, without her? And what do you think her life would have been like, had she not been given you, to love?"

I was a little uncomfortable with the second half of the equation, and I told him so. "I'm not sure she wouldn't have had a perfectly fine life without me, Mr. Law."

"Nonsense!" he shot back. "Look at the expression on the woman's face. If that isn't love, I don't know what is."

I did not think that this required a rejoinder, so I offered none. We rose from our seats and said thank-you to Nita. "All right," Mr. Law said, yet again. "Let's go find Rhoda now."

THE AIR-CONDITIONING was running full blast in the room at the Savannah courthouse where the marriage records were kept; it was so cold that it made me think of a morgue. My hopes of finding the marriage license of Rhoda and Willie Lloyd began to crumble in the icy air. What if theirs had been a common-law marriage and there was no legal record? But Mr. Law would have none of that.

"Where's that photograph?" he demanded. I took the Harlem picture of Rhoda from my satchel. "Put it up here on the table," Mr. Law said. "We need her with us."

I was not sure of the year they were married, but I began with 1923; that was the year when Granny and Arthur Einstein moved to Richmond from Wilmington and when I thought Rhoda might have returned to Savannah. I pulled the enormous, heavy folio of 1923 marriage licenses from its wire rack and quickly noted that there was a helpful index at the back. Mr. Law gave me a meaningful stare.

"You see the letters 'col.' after some of the names?" he said. "All the 'colored' licenses are separated from the whites. Ironic, isn't it? But Jim Crow is going to make our work that much easier."

THE FOLIOS FOR 1923 and 1924 turned up nothing. "Keep going," Mr. Law said. And then, in the index for 1925, "William Lloyd, col." appeared. Holding my breath, I turned to the page where the index said the license would be, and there it was. On the first day of October 1925, Willie Lloyd and his beloved were wed. Her name was Rhoda Cobin.

I bent my head over the folio and began to cry. Mr. Law placed his hand, warm with life, over mine. When I lifted my eyes to Rhoda's face in the photograph, her expression seemed to be ever so slightly changed. The sadness in her smile was gone, and in its place was a little glow of triumph.

My mother's name was Julia, and my father's name was Sam.

"I know your name now, Rhoda!" I whispered. "And I know theirs. This is the beginning. From where I am now, I can find you. And your people, in Summerville. Because I know some of them must still be there."

Mr. Law was sitting quietly across from me at the table. He nodded toward the photograph. "Thank you, Rhoda Cobin Lloyd."

$\sim$

FOR THE NEXT two days, he and I combed through more records and roamed through Savannah. We walked the streets down by the riverfront, the oldest African American neighborhood, and found the house where a city directory told us that Rhoda had lived with her sister, Lizzie, in 1924. We stood in front of the old frame dwelling and I relived that night when Rhoda defied her bossy older sister and went out dancing with Willie, only to find when she came home at dawn that Lizzie had thrown Rhoda's clothes out onto this very sidewalk. When I told Mr. Law the story, he laughed.

I had also brought the photograph of Willie, the one that Rhoda had asked me always to keep with hers, and I showed it to Mr. Law. He noticed what I had always seen, too.

"He was as handsome as she was beautiful," Mr. Law said. "But no two people could have had such different features. You know what I say? No light-skinned woman would have fallen so in love with a man whose skin was as dark as Mr. Lloyd's unless she had a good amount of racial pride." Mr. Law's face was almost as dark as Willie's. "Believe me," he went on, "women of that era—not to mention this one—who looked like Rhoda didn't often cleave to black-skinned men. I know this for a fact, from when I was a younger man."

"It's not so very different in Jamaica," I said. I had told him about the years I spent there and presented him with a copy of my book. He said he had been to Jamaica several times.

"You must have seen the side of that island that she does not want the world to see," he said. "And still you love it?"

"Yes, I do. In many ways, it's very like the South."

"Indeed it is." He thought for a moment. "Do you feel the connection here, between the West Indies and Savannah?"

"Yes," I answered, "very strongly. And I felt it in Wilmington, too."

"Well," Mr. Law began, "as you probably know, many of the Africans who began their lives as slaves in the islands found their way to the Low Country. This went on for two hundred years. They came from Jamaica, from Barbados. Bringing their songs and their words and their foods and their baskets. Their gods and their memories of home. And it is truly wondrous how much of this has endured."

"Gullah," I offered, referring to the language of the Sea Islands south of Charleston, which is not unlike the patois of Jamaica. "Gullah-Geechee."

"Exactly!" Mr. Law answered, looking pleased. "But let me tell you something else. Since slavery ended in the English islands a good thirty years before it did here, the West Indies was a hot ticket for African Americans in the 1830s and forties and fifties. When things were getting worse and worse in the South, if they could get to the islands, they would be free. The people who made it to Jamaica and Barbados and so forth saw a whole different way of life, and after the Civil War some of them came back and brought these ideas with them. So you had this great back-and-forth among very talented people—preachers and teachers, artisans and doctors and nurses. Tremendous exchange of cultures going on here. Right on through the turn of the century and Marcus Garvey's Pan-African movement in the nineteen-teens."

"I don't know why," I said, "but somehow I have this feeling that Rhoda picked up on that. Even though she was very Old South with my family, kept to 'her place' when she was with us, I used to get these glimpses of a different Rhoda when I was with her and her church friends, for instance. I think she was a race woman, in her heart of hearts.

"And maybe," I said, more to myself than to Mr. Law, "that Caribbean vibe she felt in Savannah—she might somehow have passed it along to me."

I could not help wondering now if Rhoda had had something

to do with my Jamaican journey; if she had breathed some of that sea-softened island air into my own infant lungs, along with the songs we sang together. Taught me to speak and sing a language I had not yet even heard.

Later that afternoon, Mr. Law and I found Willie's death certificate. He died in 1927, a year and a half after he and Rhoda were married. On it was written his mother's name and place of birth. Her name was Clarissa, and she was born in 1844. In Africa.

&

MR. LAW AND I had discovered the address where Rhoda and Willie lived during their brief marriage. We looked it up in an old city directory at the Georgia Historical Society. Mr. Law could not suppress a smile when we walked up to the reference desk and the librarians greeted him as if he were a visiting dignitary.

As soon as we were out of earshot, he said, *sotto voce,* "When I was young, I couldn't even set foot inside this building. Absolutely no black people allowed. And I mean *none.* Not even by the back door. Makes it kind of hard to know your history when you're not allowed to read it."

We looked through a couple of file boxes full of photographs of old Savannah, on the off chance that we'd strike gold and find another one of Rhoda or of Willie, perhaps in a photograph of a church group or a fraternal organization. When our search turned up nothing except (for me) a deepened appreciation of black Savannah, we left the library and drove to the outskirts of the city, on the other side of the old Chesapeake and Ohio railroad tracks where Rhoda and Willie had once lived.

"Don't get your hopes up," Mr. Law advised. "A lot of our older houses have burned over the years, or been torn down. We might just get to Paulsen Street and find an empty lot."

Sure enough, Rhoda's house was gone. The lot where it had been was overgrown with weeds. But the cottage next door was still standing, and even though it was run-down, I was thrilled to see it because I figured that Rhoda's house had probably been like this one. It reminded me of the old settlers' cottages I loved in Jamaica. Weathered wood with a porch running along the front and a kitchen in the back that Mr. Law observed to me was probably separate from the house at some point, to minimize the heat from cooking and the risk of fire.

A man was sitting on the porch in the late afternoon sun, sipping a cold beer. Mr. Law frowned in disapproval at the condition of the house and said something to him about fixing the place up.

"Hey, bro'," the man replied. "I got better things to spend my money on. I got seven kids."

Whereupon Mr. Law launched into a lecture about birth control, while the man shook his head, as if we had been sent by Planned Parenthood to ruin his peaceful afternoon.

I bade a reluctant farewell to Mr. Law the following day; I felt sure that we would meet again. In parting, he told me that one of his projects was the restoration of the African American section of the Savannah cemetery, Laurel Grove. Willie Lloyd's death certificate had said that he was buried there, so Mr. Law suggested that I visit the cemetery before I left and see if I could find the grave.

I had several hours that afternoon before my flight departed, and I spent them wandering among those graves. It was late in the day, so there was no groundskeeper in the little gatehouse. But I was content to walk around on my own. I have always loved walking through cemeteries, pausing to read the inscriptions on the tombstones and letting my imagination recreate the lives of the dead.

I had meandered a good ways from the farthest rim of the graveyard when I suddenly became aware that the names on the headstones had changed. Abraham, Isaac, and Jacob; Leah and Rachel and Sarah. I had crossed over into the Jewish section. The "white" people—the Christians, that is—were buried on the other side of a chain-link fence not far from where I stood. I remembered seeing a map at the gatehouse that explained that Laurel Grove was divided into two sections—rather like those marriage licenses at the courthouse that had "col." after the names.

I walked around and read the stones. I found several Einsteins and wonder if they might have been distant relatives. I paused before the miniature headstones of the infants, as I always do, and thought of who they might have grown up to become.

It happened to be Friday; in an hour or so, the Sabbath would begin. I would be on an airplane, far from any observance of this holy hour. With a pang of sadness, I wondered if the Einsteins who had turned to dust beneath my feet had been dry-goods merchants, like my Wilmington grandfather, and if they had been, would they have set this afternoon aside? Or would they have disregarded the Sabbath, as we and almost all the other German Jews I knew in Richmond did? Thalhimer's stayed open late, and so did all the other stores downtown, since Friday was payday, when most of their customers shopped. And so did we, lots of times. The Sabbath meant nothing to us.

I walked along, reading only the English inscriptions on the gravestones because, of course, I could read no Hebrew whatsoever. They framed a world of meaning that I could not even say I'd lost because it never was mine to begin with.

I wondered, as I am forever doing, how and why I still knew myself to be a Jew. Strayed as I am from all observance, all ritual. But yet, this is who and what I am. I thought of Mr. Law proclaiming, "I'm a Geechee!" and I said to myself, *Maybe this* is *a tribal thing, after all.*

I laughed softly, thinking what Rabbi Goldburg and all my other religious instructors had ever so carefully coached me to say, if and when a gentile referred to us Jews as a "race." I was dutybound to explain that we were most definitely *not* a race, but a religion. Heaven forbid the Christians should think of us as a different race; we had enough trouble on our hands as it was.

But look at where we lay buried: on the other side of that chain-link fence from the other whites. Next to the "Colored." What is the difference, I asked myself, between a race and a tribe?

As I walked out of the cemetery, I remembered the day Rhoda told me she was part Cherokee: "It's not something I'm proud of," Rhoda had said, when I embarrassed her by whooping with glee.

"Being a half-breed is nothing to brag about. And don't you ever forget it, you hear?"

Silenced by her shame, I could think of nothing to say on that day long ago. But her remark came back to me now. Black, white, and Cherokee. The blood of three races pumped through Rhoda's heart. But one of those races was a tribe. What was the difference? I wondered. Was it strictly a matter of DNA? Was it hair, was it skin, was it noses?

And where did this place me? Whence came my own off-white sensibility, the feeling that I stood partway between white and black and Jewish? I had no clear answer, but I knew that in that divided graveyard, a fresh awareness of my braided origins had been bestowed on me.

IN THE AIR, on my way home, I opened the book Mr. Law had given me as a memento of our time in Savannah. It was about the Butler family of Georgia, whose five generations had created one of the most powerful slave-holding dynasties in the South. The book described the world of the Low Country into which Westley Law himself had been born, a past from which we southerners, black and white, were still struggling to create a future.

On the title page, he had written an inscription in his elegant, old-fashioned hand. "To Friend Gunst. Let us march on 'til Victory is won!"

nineteen

Now that I knew Rhoda's maiden name, I could look for members of the Cobin family who might still be living in Charleston or nearby Summerville.

I made my pilgrimage to Charleston in October, when the heat had lifted and the breeze from the water was fresh. I checked into the venerable Francis Marion Hotel and then went for a walk downtown. Eventually, I came to the old city market, a long arcade lined with tourist shops. One of these was devoted—I think the better word might be "consecrated"—to Confederate memorabilia and *Gone with the Wind;* Charleston was the city of Rhett Butler's birth, and he vowed to return to it when he left Scarlett at the end of the movie. "I'm going back to Charleston," he said. "I want to see if somewhere there isn't something left in life of charm and grace."

One of the sites I knew that was left, and which I wanted to find, was the slave market; it stood a little ways away from this arcade. As I wandered in that general direction, I was thinking of the billboard I had driven by on the way into town from the air-port. It was a huge replica of the Confederate flag with the legend underneath: "Our Proud Heritage. Long May It Wave."

I did not make it to the site of the former slave market. My eye was caught by a display of sea-grass baskets spread out on a cloth on the ground. These baskets are woven by men and women who still use the same designs their ancestors brought with them from Africa. They are beautiful and very strong, longleaf pine needles, sweetgrass and bulrushes, sewn with strips of palmetto leaf. But now that the coastal land is being bought up by developers for golf courses and gated communities, it's getting harder for the basket weavers to gather their materials.

I spied one basket unlike any other I had seen. It was larger than the others, and deep, with graceful U-shaped curves woven into its side. I bent down to admire it and to compliment its maker, a robust woman with shining eyes. We introduced ourselves and struck up a conversation. She told me that her name was Jery Taylor and that she lived in the town of Walterboro, a little ways south of Charleston.

"It's near Beaufort," Mrs. Taylor said, "just across the sound from St. Helena Island. Do you know of St. Helena?"

"Only a little. It's where the abolitionists started a school for free people, right? In 1862?"

The light in Jery Taylor's eyes got even brighter. "Yes!" she said. "So you've read a bit about our part of the world?"

"Yes, but just a beginning. I really want to visit the island. I know that Dr. King spent time there. He loved St. Helena."

"Indeed he did. It's a powerful place, and full of spirits. You should go there. Visit the Penn Center, where the old school was."

Mrs. Taylor saw me gazing at her basket and seemed to read my thoughts. "Now this one is very special," she smiled. "I call it my elephant-ear basket, because of those curves I wove into the side."

"Is it a traditional form?" I asked. "I haven't ever seen one like it."

"And you never will!" she answered. "Because this is my own design. I went to Ghana last year on a cultural exchange and I took it with me. The women who wove baskets there said they'd never seen one like it, either."

"Was it wonderful, going to Ghana?"

"Oh, yes." Mrs. Taylor beamed. "It was like coming home. Especially the way people talk. My grandmother was the one who taught me how to weave baskets, and she spoke Gullah. It's very close to the way people talk in West Africa, so when I was in Ghana I felt as if I was hearing her voice again."

I told Mrs. Taylor that I had lived in Jamaica for two years, and that Gullah is said to be very close to patois.

"Well," she said, "we're all branches from the same tree." And then she gave me a curious look. "Have you been here before?"

"Only once, a long time ago."

"So, tell me what brings you back to Charleston now."

As usual, I was carrying Rhoda's picture in my satchel. I handed it to Mrs. Taylor and explained who Rhoda was. "She was born in Summerville," I said. "I'm hoping to locate some of her family there."

Jery Taylor stared at me for a good long moment. Then she said quietly, "I have a feeling that you will. You know . . . the ancestors want to be found."

I remembered that little scrap of notebook paper on which Rhoda had written those few sentences for me, about her growing up. "I was *found* in Summerville S.C.," it said. That word seemed to be something of a blessing now.

I was thinking that I needed to build some sort of altar to Rhoda's spirit back in my hotel room. I would set her picture on it and light a candle. I was gazing at Jery Taylor's elephant-ear basket and thinking how it had crossed the ocean with her to Ghana and then come back home.

"Mrs. Taylor," I said, "could I buy that basket?"

She smiled up at me from her chair. "I think you may just need to have it with you," she said. She lifted the basket and we both held it for a moment. Then she set it back on its blanket and took my hands in hers.

"Good luck," she said, wrapping the basket for me. "I want to know what happens with Rhoda." We exchanged addresses and promised to keep in touch.

That night, I made my little altar. After I had placed Rhoda's picture beside the basket and lit a candle, I sat down on the bed and opened the Charleston phone book. It included Summerville, which is a twenty-minute drive away. Only two Cobins were listed; one was a Reverend George Cobin and the other was named David.

It was after ten o'clock, too late to call now; I would phone the two Cobins in the morning. I wanted to talk to Jonathan, tell him about my day and receive the encouragement he always gives me. I called and told him about my encounter with Jery Taylor, describing her basket and the altar I'd made, which I was looking at as we spoke. I said I would call Summerville in the morning, hoping to reach the two Cobins whose numbers were in the book.

Jonathan didn't miss a beat. "Don't call. Don't waste any time. Just *go*. Get in the car and drive straight to Summerville. Something is going to happen."

I was so nervous and excited in the morning that once I got to Summerville, I had to drive around for a while, to calm down. I needed to see the town, to catch whatever I could of Rhoda's spirit, and see if anything was left of what had been there in her time; after seeing that empty lot in Savannah where her house once stood, I knew not to get my hopes up.

But Summerville was unchanged—as much as that can be said of any place on earth. The pristine Greek Revival houses that were built for Charleston's planters were still there, lovingly kept up beneath their sheltering canopy of pines. But I did not see one black person. Summerville was a white town, as it had always been. The African American residents of the area lived on its outskirts, in the small family-centered settlements one finds throughout the rural South.

It was time to make my two phone calls. I went to the visitors' center in the center of town, where I figured there had to be an indoor telephone. The first call I made was to David Cobin. No one answered. I had only one other number now. On the seventh ring, just as I was beginning to give up, Reverend George Cobin picked up the phone.

He listened politely while I tried to breathe evenly and recite my story about Rhoda and Julia and Sam. "I'm very sorry," he said, after I was done. "I wish I could be of help. But none of those names ring a bell with me."

He paused for a moment, considering. "But that's not to say they weren't members of our family, and I just don't know of them. To tell you the truth, I'm not the expert in these matters. The one you want to speak with is my cousin, Juanita Hill. She's the family historian. She lives just down the road from us. Juanita's the one who keeps all the records, and plans our family reunions. Hold on . . . let me get her number for you."

"Thank you, Reverend Cobin," I breathed. "I appreciate your help."

He came back with Juanita Hill's number. "I wish you luck," he said. Saying a silent prayer, I dialed. She was there.

"Mrs. Hill," I said, trying to speak slowly, "Reverend Cobin gave me your number. My name is Laurie Gunst. I'm from Richmond, Virginia. I was raised by a lady named Rhoda Cobin, and she was from Summerville."

Then I floundered, searching for the right way to say what I had to say. My dread of mammy-itis was rising. So I bumbled my way through what must have been quite a confusing story for Mrs. Hill; I couldn't bring myself to describe Rhoda as a servant, so I used words like "mother" and "raised."

"Is Rhoda still living?" Mrs. Hill asked.

"Sadly, no. She was born in 1894 and she passed away in 1986. She left Summerville for Charleston when she was very young. So I'm pretty sure there isn't anyone still living who would remember her." Deep breath. "But she told me that her mother's name was Julia and her father's name was Sam. Do those names mean anything to you, Mrs. Hill?"

There was a very brief moment before she answered, and when she spoke I could hear the catch in her voice. "Samuel Cobin was my grandfather Ransom's brother," she said, so softly I could hardly hear.

I began to cry. "Where are you calling from?" Mrs. Hill asked.

"The visitors' center in Summerville."

"You just sit tight. I'll be there in fifteen minutes." She heard the sound of my crying. "Miss . . . I'm so sorry, but I've forgotten your name. What is it again?"

"It's Laurie, Mrs. Hill. Laurie Gunst."

"Well, Miss Gunst, I hope you won't think this is rude . . . but I just have to ask . . . " She faltered.

"Oh, it's perfectly all right, Mrs. Hill." Now I was laughing, because I knew what she was thinking. "I know I didn't explain my relationship to Rhoda very well. Yes, I'm white."

I could hear her laughing, too. "Forgive me for asking," she said. "I'm just a little confused."

"Of course. I didn't make myself very clear. I didn't want to say that Rhoda worked for my family. She did, but it wasn't . . . she was . . . "

"I understand."

☙

I WAS PACING up and down in the parking lot when Mrs. Hill drove up. She was with her daughter and granddaughter: three generations of Rhoda.

When she unfolded herself from the front seat—a short, plump woman with copper skin and high cheekbones and a wide, generous mouth—I saw that the resemblance was faint. But it was still there.

I ran to shake her hand, trembling with the sensation of seeing Rhoda again, come back to life. Mrs. Hill gently waved aside my proffered hand and hugged me instead.

She introduced me to her daughter, Shujuan Shannon, and Shujuan's little girl, Faith, who was two. We started chattering like birds on a wire, tripping over each other in our excitement as we pushed open the door to the visitors' center and found our way to chairs in the lobby.

Mrs. Hill had brought the pamphlet from the most recent Cobin reunion, with the family tree, and I had many pictures of Rhoda as well as the one of Willie Lloyd. Names and dates and stories began tumbling from our lips as we passed pictures and papers back and forth.

"We've traced our family back as far as Virginia," Mrs. Hill said. "That was where we started out, on a tobacco plantation in the eastern part of the state. Our ancestors . . . this would be Rhoda's grandparents . . . came here in 1862."

"Do you know why they came down here from Virginia?" I asked.

"We're not sure. But Butch—he's my nephew who lives in Philadelphia and has done most of the genealogical research—thinks it may have been on account of the war."

I wondered if these Cobins might have been free people of color, but then I realized: Had they been free, they surely would not have moved farther south in the midst of the war. I figured that whoever owned them had fled with his slaves from Virginia; 1862 was the year when the Union general George McClellan was fighting (and failing) to capture Richmond.

Mrs. Hill was pointing to the Cobin family tree. "Here they are, Rhoda's grandparents. Robert Cobin, Sr. and his wife, Mildred. They had ten children. One of them was my grandfather Ransom, and Rhoda's father Samuel was another. See, here's Samuel. Born in 1862."

Mrs. Hill let the paper with the Cobin family tree drift down into her lap. She took my hands. "Oh, this is such a miracle, you turning up like this! Out of a clear blue sky! We didn't know anything about Rhoda. All we had was her name in the family tree. And now here you are, bringing her back to us."

I told them all the stories Rhoda had told me about her life, hoping that these stories would build a bridge for us to walk across together—a bridge that would link us, somehow, across the abyss of race and place and time.

I couldn't help but notice that Shujuan, Mrs. Hill's daughter, was giving me a quizzical look. "Tell me something," she said. "From the way you describe Rhoda and you, I'm wondering . . . I mean, it all just sounds so . . . odd. Did you actually know your real parents when you were growing up?"

I had to laugh, but sadly. "No offense," Shujuan went on, "but it sounds like Rhoda was closer to you than they were."

"Yes," I said, "in many ways, she was. I did know my own parents. They were there the whole time I was growing up. But they were kind of . . . distant. My mother nursed me when I was a baby, but after that she pretty much turned me over to Rhoda."

Shujuan gave me a pitying look. Suddenly, in a flash of hurt and pain, I saw how this arrangement I had always thought of as so very normal—given the protocol of the privileged white South—must look to other people, to a mother like Shujuan, who neither could nor would be inclined to turn her own child over to the care of someone else. Her daughter was meanwhile trundling up and down, listening to our intense grown-up patter and picking up on our energy, as children never fail to do. I watched Faith run to her mother, who swept her up into her arms and bestowed a tender kiss on the top of Faith's head. I wondered why my mother had not wanted to do that to me, had let Rhoda be the one to cherish me instead. Did she envy Rhoda for the love I gave her in return? How many times must I have opened my arms and begged to be lifted into Mother's lap before I learned to turn to Rhoda instead?

Shujuan broke into my thoughts. "What is your background?" she asked. "Your family's, I mean."

I hesitated, afraid that maybe Shujuan did not harbor fond feelings for Jews. But how could I deny who I was?

"We're Jewish. My mother's side of the family came originally from Holland, from Amsterdam, and Daddy's grandfather was from Germany. Both sides have been in the South for a long time, in Virginia and North Carolina."

"Interesting," Shujuan said, with a cool, appraising look.

Faith suddenly decided that she needed to check me out. She squirmed from her mother's lap, walked over, and gave me one of those wise-eyed Old Head stares.

"Mama!" she said, her velvety brown eyes gazing deep into mine.

We three grown-ups laughed. "Looks like she recognizes you," Shujuan said.

❧

WE SPENT THE next two days driving around Harleyville and Ridgeville, the African American settlements where the Cobins lived. The railroad runs along a street of homes, and one of our first stops was the depot where Rhoda and her older sister, Lizzie, had seen the "colored" troops on their way to Cuba almost a century ago.

I got out of the car and stood beneath a huge tree next to the depot, imagining Rhoda as a little girl of four. How she tugged on Lizzie's hand and begged to go back home because she was scared of all the men and horses.

"This is a barbecue place now," Mrs. Hill said. "But unfortunately it's only open weekends."

We drove on, out of town, past flat autumn fields stippled with cut-over soybeans and corn. They made me think of the places where Daddy and I used to work his dogs. Mrs. Hill pointed out a tall sycamore tree where her grandfather's house had stood.

"Rhoda would have known this place," she said.

Shujuan piped up from the backseat, where she was sitting with Faith, "Speaking of old places, let's see if Son is home."

Mrs. Hill explained that his given name was David, but everyone in the family called him Son. He was over seventy and lived in a trailer beside the house where he was born, a cypress wood cabin with a crumbling brick chimney. If I had thought that Juanita bore a faint resemblance to Rhoda, I felt as if I were seeing Rhoda herself when Son Cobin stepped off his front porch to greet us. I thought I might faint.

"Nice to meet you," Son said, holding out his hand. "Everything all right?" He saw me gasping for breath.

"Yes, sir, thank you. It's just that you look so much like someone

I used to know. She was a distant relative of yours."

Juanita explained who I was, why I had come to Summerville. I asked Son if I could take his picture, but he firmly refused.

"No, thank you." He shook his head. "I don't like them things. They take away too much of a person." He gave me a slow smile. "But you can take all the pictures you want of that old cabin."

A tethered goat observed me nonchalantly as I walked around the cabin, clicking away, knowing I was walking in Rhoda's footsteps. I looked at the iron cauldrons in Son's yard, which were planted with camellias but that I knew must once have held boiling water at hog-killing time. Rhoda used to tell me about those days, how she'd help out. I felt her presence strongly in this yard.

As we got ready to go, Son stood in the driveway with us and pointed to a row of ancient pecan trees next to his house. Their trunks were as hollow as drums.

"Do you know, they are still bearing?" he said. "You look at those trees and you tell yourself, they've got to be dead. But they aren't. And as long as they keep bearing, I just can't bring myself to cut them down."

☉

MRS. HILL IS a retired teacher, and as we wended our way along the back roads from Son's place, we talked about the history of the neighborhood.

"I want to show you something," Juanita said. She slowed down and then pulled over to the shoulder of the road in what looked to me like the middle of nowhere. Barely visible in the tangle of brush vines from which it had been only slightly cleared, was a solitary grave with a soiled, tattered Confederate flag stuck into the earth.

"They only found this a year ago," Juanita said. "It belongs to a white man named Harley who used to own all this land. That's the family Harleyville is named after." We had gotten out of the car and stood looking at the flattened grave. "Old man Harley and his kin fathered a lot of our own people around here," Juanita said. "So I guess we're all mixed in together."

I told her what Rhoda had said, about being part Cherokee. Juanita nodded. "We've got that in us, too." Then I remembered something I had just read. "Ralph Ellison said that there's really no such thing as a white southerner," I said.

"Hah!" Shujuan cackled. "Try telling that to these rednecks cruising around in pickup trucks with the stars and bars."

⟡

BEFORE I WENT back to Charleston, Shujuan wanted me to meet the oldest member of the Cobin family, eighty-three-year-old Ella Mae Cobin Kelly, known as Aunt Dilcey. Ella Mae's father was Ransom Cobin, and Ransom was the brother of Rhoda's father, Sam. Ella Mae was therefore Rhoda's first cousin.

"But she wouldn't have known Rhoda," Mrs. Hill said, "because Rhoda left Summerville well before Aunt Dilcey was born. Still, you need to meet her. She's quite a character."

I had a feeling that Aunt Dilcey was going to be the "rootified" member of the Cobin family. The one who kept the hoodoo fires burning around these parts. I was about to confide my story of Rhoda's spell over me when Marvin Gaye came on the radio, singing "Let's Get It On."

All of a sudden, I flashed on my memories of Jamaica, of Homer and the few other black men I've slept with since then. I blushed, glad that Juanita and Shujuan couldn't read my thoughts. Here I was, riding around through the autumn fields and pine woods of South Carolina, past old man Harley's long-forgotten grave, cruising along with the living family members of Rhoda Cobin Lloyd and meeting others of her relations whose skin was even lighter than my own.

Suddenly I grasped what Juanita Hill had meant, as we stood gazing down at that grave: that "We're all mixed in together." And what Rhoda meant when she told me she was part Cherokee, but that this wasn't anything to be proud of. I realized, as I never had before, that I myself would almost certainly have been one of the white women who "went with" a black man—had I been born and raised in this rural, secret South, instead of in the well-defended fortress of white Richmond, where I was all but certain not to meet a black man from my own class. But had I been a country girl, with black boys down the road sweet as sugar, I would have been rolling into the ditches with them by the time I was twelve or thirteen.

We were almost at Aunt Dilcey's house. If I was going to tell Juanita and Shujuan the story I was waiting to relate to them, of Rhoda having maybe worked roots on me as an infant, it had better be now.

"You all," I said, "before we get to Aunt Dilcey's, I have to mention one small thing." Then I told them the story, as Sophia Norrell had told it to me. "I have no idea whether this is true," I concluded.

"Well," Juanita offered, "I can't say yes, but I can't say no. I do know that there have always been people in the family who knew about roots, and even though I'm not one of them, I know some who are. Dilcey is old enough to have come up in a time when just about everyone had the knowledge and grew up with those ways."

We pulled into Dilcey's yard. Shujuan called out her name and then led us inside the front room, its walls pitch dark from the smoke of an ancient woodstove. Dilcey was sitting deep in an old armchair, her eyes rheumy with age. She was wearing pants for warmth underneath a green polka-dot dress and a ragged sweater pinned together over her sagging breasts. Her head was tied in a black kerchief. Dilcey held herself like the matriarch she was, and when Juanita introduced us and I bent to shake her hand, I felt that I should bow instead.

But Dilcey was not given to formality. After Juanita explained that I had known a Cobin by the name of Rhoda long ago, Dilcey gave a little cackle of a laugh, showing that she had not one tooth left.

"Never knew a Rhoda," Dilcey rasped. "Knew her uncles, though. Gone from here long time now. Would you all like some cake?"

"Oh, don't trouble yourself, Aunt Dilcey," Shujuan said.

"Ain't no trouble! I can still get around, you know." Dilcey lifted her chin and raised herself up in her chair. "Went to the store yesterday. Drove myself. Know just where them police boys are, how to outrun 'em! Got me a boyfriend, too!" She gyrated her bony hips and gave me a sly, sweet smile.

"I believe you," I said.

"Yep, I ain't too old! See that picture over there?"

Juanita said that this was Dilcey's husband. He was wearing a military uniform.

"Good-lookin', weren't he? I knew it!" Dilcey said ominously. "Knew what kind of trouble a handsome man like him could get himself into, all them girls in them army camps. I followed him around, made sure none of 'em could get their hands on him!"

We helped Dilcey up from her chair and walked outside for a group photograph. As everyone lined up in the yard, I showed Dilcey the picture of Rhoda. She shook her head.

"Fine-lookin' woman! Wish I'd known her."

To which I silently answered, *You do know her, Dilcey. You know her real well.*

☙

JUANITA'S NEPHEW, SAMUEL "Butch" Lewis, had done census research on the Cobin family in Charleston, and he faxed several Xeroxed pages to Juanita for me. I drove back up to Harleyville the day before I left Charleston to get them. Butch had located Rhoda's mother, Julia, in the census of 1910 and found that she was a widow, living at 95 Drake Street in Charleston and working as a laundress. Rhoda and her older sister, Lizzie, were living with their mother. Rhoda was sixteen.

"You remember when I showed you how to iron?" Rhoda's ghost whispered. "Now you know who taught me."

Juanita Hill gave me the census record to take home. As we said goodbye, I thanked her yet again for spending this time with me, and asked her to be sure to thank Shujuan as well. "This has been one of the most wonderful times of my life," I said. "And I know Rhoda knows that she has been found."

Juanita hugged me again. "The Cobin reunion is going to be in Savannah this year," she said. "I'll be sending you all the information. It's the Fourth of July weekend."

"I'll be there," I said.

Q

THE FOLLOWING MORNING, I had just enough time to go to the Charleston library to look up Julia Cobin's death certificate. I suspected that she was already ill by the time the census was taken, because I knew that Rhoda and Lizzie would soon be orphans and would leave for Savannah not long after their mother's death.

The certificate rolled out of the microfilm machine, stark white script on greasy black paper. Julia Cobin died of stomach cancer, just after midnight on the 28th of September, 1911. She was thirty-two. Rhoda was seventeen. Her name was on the bottom of the page as the nearest kin.

I did the numbers and realized that Julia was not born in slavery; she was born in 1879 and was seventeen years younger than her husband, Sam. He was the one who remembered slavery. But the South into which Julia Cobin was born was not so very different from the one her husband had known. Slavery endured in many forms, long after its abolition. And what mattered to me now was what had mattered to Rhoda then: her mother's soul and spirit. Julia Cobin had passed along her courage to her daughter.

I descended the library steps with the copy of Julia's death certificate fluttering in my hand. I walked the short distance to Drake Street; number 95 was no longer there. But nearby stood an old red-brick building that took up most of a block. On the front was a historical marker. THE SEIDENBURG CIGAR FACTORY, it said.

So this was where Rhoda worked as a girl child, after her family moved to Charleston. Where she and the other "colored girls"—as Rhoda would have said—sat in long rows, rolling the pungent leaf. Here was where she learned to hate the stink of tobacco. In a factory owned by Jews.

Once again, I heard the echo of Claudine's voice and her unforgettable remark. *Negro's always singin' an' workin' . . . Jew's always eatin' an' countin' his money.* But I heard Rhoda's voice, too, as I stared out at the clouds from my seat in the plane back to New York. I was on my way home to my husband, and I knew what she would say had she been next to me.

"You all take good care of each other now. You hear?"

At the Cobin family reunion in Savannah; July, 2001. Left to right: Westley W. Law, me, Juanita Hill, and Cobin family member Gary Duggins.

Juanita Hill and I at the family picnic.

epilogue

CARRIE JEFFERSON SMITH and I know that we won't find the crossroads named Niggerfoot on any map of Virginia. But we both know roughly where it is; she was born in Ashland, not far away, and she used to hear her people talk about how the place got its name. They said a man was lynched there and then his foot was nailed to a barn door. Some said it happened during slavery and others said it wasn't that long in the past; the barn was old, sure, but not that old. Carrie's Aunt Mahalia, who's almost eighty now, said the man had taken up with a white woman and she got scared when it looked like her husband was about to find them out. She betrayed her lover and saved herself.

I don't think I would ever have gone back to that crossroads if Carrie hadn't come up with the idea of the two of us going to look for Niggerfoot. She broached it on a shimmering-hot summer night when she was visiting Mother and Daddy in Richmond. I was there, too, because Mother had just fallen and broken her hip. She was in great pain, and there seemed to be nothing I could do to relieve it. Carrie called from Washington, where she was visiting her sister, and when I told her what had happened, she said, "Tell Evelyn that I'm on my way. I'm leaving now. I'll be there in a couple of hours."

When I climbed the stairs to tell Mother, she moaned. "Oh, God, Laurie. I just don't think I'm up to seeing anyone. Even Carrie."

"I know. But she's coming, all the same. She loves you and she wants to see you."

Mother pushed herself into a sitting position, grimacing from the pain. "Do me a favor, will you?" She reminded me of Granny. "Hand me my comb and compact. They're on my dresser."

I brought them to her and she looked into the compact mirror. "Jesus," she groaned. "I look like the wrath of God."

"No, you don't," I answered, giving her a kiss. "You're just pale, that's all. The pain has worn you down."

"Comb my hair for me, okay?" I pulled it through her tangles gently. Her hair was still beautiful, thick as ever and iron gray. She lay back on her pile of pillows. "Wake me when Carrie gets here."

When I heard Carrie's truck pull into the driveway, I raced outside and we fell into each other's arms. "I'm so glad you're here," I said.

"How is Evelyn?" Carrie asked.

"She's in right much pain. But I know she will be so happy to see you."

Carrie and I went upstairs; Mother had heard the truck, and she was already awake. Carrie bent to embrace her and then sat down gingerly on the edge of the bed.

"How bad is the pain?" she asked tenderly.

"Worse than childbirth!" Mother said, managing a wan smile nevertheless.

The three of us began to giggle, manic with relief.

❧

THAT NIGHT, CARRIE and I fixed supper for Daddy and the three of us ate together at the kitchen table, the setting for so many other occasions in our lives. Carrie and Daddy reminisced about her father, Theodore, and her aunt, Elizabeth: Both had been dead for more than twenty years.

"Whenever I am in this house, Mr. Gunst," Carrie said, "it's as if they're alive again. I am never here that I don't see them. It's like they haven't died."

Carrie still addresses my father as "Mr. Gunst," but my mother has been "Evelyn" to her since she was a little girl. After we had taken a tray upstairs to Mother—she ate dinner for the first time since she had fallen—Carrie and I stood at the sink doing the dishes. This was when, out of the blue, she proposed the pilgrimage to Niggerfoot.

"You and I need to make this journey," she said. "Together. We need to find that crossroads. Draw a new map for ourselves."

"Okay," I said. But the idea scared me, to tell the truth. It made me sad, and anxious, and ashamed. Carrie and I were only very slowly getting to be friends, and ours was certainly a complicated relationship. In some ways, we were like sisters, united by the love my mother had for each of us. Yet, Mother's love for me had been so conditional, so full of betrayals, that I was aware of how much less constrained her love for Carrie was. Maybe it was the fact of Mother's aging that drew Carrie and me together now; we both knew that she would soon be gone, and unless Carrie and I found a way, we might lose one another when Mother was no longer there. If we were ever going to find a path into each other's hearts, we'd best start searching now.

WE ARRANGED TO meet in Richmond later that summer, when Carrie still had vacation time left from teaching at the university. The morning of the day that Carrie was to arrive in Richmond, I went to the Virginia Historical Society to look up Niggerfoot. When I asked the librarian if there were any materials on the place, I was embarrassed to use the word.

"I believe we do have some," she answered briskly. "I'll bring them to you."

There were two references to Niggerfoot, one in a book on old houses in Hanover Country and the other in the 1893 issue of the *Virginia Historical Magazine*. The book referred to the farmhouse at the crossroads as "Negro Foot Farm" and said, "No one seems to be able to identify the origin of the name. In nearby Powhatan County there is a place name, Negro Arm. It is not known if there is any correlation between the two."

The reading room was quite warm, with May sunlight streaming in through an enormous window that framed a towering magnolia tree. But I shivered slightly nonetheless, and when I read the 1893 Virginia Historical Magazine, I felt even colder, much as I did that day in the Lower Cape Fear Historical Society when I came to Harry Hayden's gleeful account of the Wilmington massacre. The magazine article was a lighthearted piece on curious Virginia place names by a turn-of-the-century antiquarian who couldn't resist being clever.

The Rev. Frank Stringfellow, an Episcopal clergyman of Virginia, tells me of a remarkable series of names recording the fate of some negro offender. In traveling from the Appomattox in Chesterfield county, we pass Skinquarter Creek, where the criminal was hung and flayed, his skin being displayed. . . . . Negro Arm Road in Powhatan, Negro Foot in Hanover, and Negro Head Run in Orange, show where other portions of the body were put up *in terrorem*.

But the author disagrees with the Reverend Stringfellow's opinion of what these names depict.

It is safe to assert that this is wholly untrue," he says, "and that no such barbarous punishment ever took place in Virginia. Under the Virginia, as under the English law, ears might be cut off, but we find no provision for feet.

I copied the page at the Xerox machine and showed it to Carrie when she arrived that afternoon. We exchanged incredulous looks at the kitchen table. "Oh, well," Carrie sighed, shaking her head. "Like we say: Denial isn't only a river in Africa."

We set out on our pilgrimage the following morning, going upstairs before we left to say good morning to Mother. She was still in bed, gazing out the window at a scarlet cardinal at the feeder on the sill.

"Where are you all off to?" she asked, flashing us one of her still-girlish grins, which was disconcerting because her dental implants had fallen out and she had no front teeth now.

Carrie bent down to give her a kiss. "Actually, Evelyn, we're going to look for Niggerfoot," she said.

Mother's expression changed to a frown. "Mmm, mmm, mmm," she murmured, with a combination of love and dismay. "You two . . . I have never . . ." Her voice trailed off and I knew she was wishing that Carrie and I hadn't gone and spoiled her morning reverie with that awful word. But then her Inner Hostess, her perfect southern woman, rose to the occasion. "Well . . . be sure and take some sandwiches. There's a beautiful ham in the ice-box. And give Mahalia my love."

Carrie's Aunt Mahalia lived in Ashland and we stopped to pick her up. I had not seen Aunt May since Carrie's wedding at our house almost twenty years before. But she still looked so much like her late brother, Carrie's father Theodore, that I told her so as we embraced. "And you're the spitting image of your daddy!" May exclaimed. I smiled ruefully because Daddy used to be handsome but now that he was ancient, it was hard for me to hear that I looked just like him.

May would spend the day with us. She said she knew just about where Niggerfoot was, and she said the word straight up. But Carrie and I weren't quite ready to go there yet; she said we ought to take some "cultural time" and go to see the house where she grew up and the one where Grandma Carrie lived.

We drove the short distance from Ashland, past fields buzzing with insects in the late spring sun, till we reached the little settlement where Carrie was born. Her mother's tiny cinder-block house had been pretty much empty since Dot died, and the previous winter it had been badly damaged by an ice storm. When we stepped inside, I was overwhelmed by sadness. The floors were buckling and the ceilings were about to come down, but Dot was still present. Her little china knick-knacks were placed here and there around the living room, and a snapshot, curled from the damp, was tacked to the wall in the kitchen: Dot smiling brightly, wearing a frilly red blouse, her Gypsy beauty refusing to yield to the cancer that was already growing in her lung. When I gently handed the photograph to Carrie, she began to cry. May put a steadying arm around her shoulder. "Let's go on outside, honey," May said.

The three of us walked down the sandy, pine-shaded path that led from Dot's house to Grandma Carrie's place. It was a very old cabin, weather-beaten and leaning like someone sinking to their knees. Its windows were empty, open to the vines that snaked their way in. We peered inside. There was still the old woodstove in the kitchen, and Carrie pointed to the empty place beneath the window where her grandmother's bed used to be. This was where Carrie had spent so many childhood nights, looking up at the stars and wondering what she would grow up to be.

Grandma Carrie's roses had gone wild in the front yard, and they were fragrant with tiny pink blossoms. As luck would have it, I had brought a bottle of ice water and some Dixie cups, and May magically produced a pair of scissors from her capacious purse. So we clipped as many blossoms as we could, pricking our fingers and sucking them afterward, swatting at gnats and fretting about the ticks we knew were lurking in the damp grass. But we were having a joyful time all the same, imagining how glad Grandma Carrie would be to know that we were there, reveling in her roses. Soon, we had a cup full of them for Carrie to take home.

"I'm famished," May said. "What did you bring for lunch?" We walked back to the car and broke out the ham sandwiches, which I told her were Mother's idea. It was so hot that we opened all four doors to catch the breeze. May and I sat in front and Carrie was in the back, and for a while we all chewed so intently that no one said much of anything except "Mmm." But then May looked out to the hazy blue field across the road, with its young tobacco plants already a good foot tall.

"When I was a little girl," she said softly, "I knew the man who owned all this land. Hill Carter. My daddy worked for him, just like every other colored man for miles around. Every morning, Carter would drive his truck down this same road we're looking at now. He'd slow down a little, but he'd never stop. My daddy and all the other men would run beside that truck and jump in the back. Just like they were dogs."

The shame I'll never lose stole over me, hot and familiar. I knew May didn't intend me to hear her story and apply it to myself. But I couldn't help doing just that. It came with the territory.

As if she had read my thoughts, May changed the subject. "Tell me, Laurie. How is your mother? Never a days goes by that I don't think of her."

"And she sends you her love, too. She's doing all right, I guess. Her mind isn't what it used to be, though. She forgets what happened five minutes ago. But she remembers everything from the distant past. So we talk about old times, which I love to do anyway. I have a feeling that if I live to be her age, my memories will be where I'll go to live, too."

May smiled. "I'm getting there myself." And then she said, "You know, there's something I've always wondered about your mother. Long as I've known her, which is ever since Lizzie and Theodore started working for you all, I've never understood how she got to be the way she is. You know what I'm saying?"

"I do, May."

"I remember when Lizzie went into the hospital with her sugar. Your mother paid every single one of those bills. She didn't make a big fuss over it, either. She just went and did it. Well, we were not accustomed to being treated in that way by the white people we worked for, Laurie. And I never forgot what your mother did." May paused for a moment. "So, I just always wondered. Your mother being the way she is, did she have a lot of friends? What I mean is, wasn't she kind of lonely in her life? Because there must have been so few people she knew who saw things like she does. . . . "

I reached across the car seat and took May's hand. "Thank you," I said. "Almost no one sees that side of her. She is one of the loneliest women I've ever known. And especially with my father. He's a good soul, you know, and he means well. But he never had the heart for things that Mom does. They just don't see the world the same way."

"Amen," said Carrie, from the backseat. She leaned forward and touched my shoulder. "I guess we'd better head for Niggerfoot. Before it gets to be too late."

The crossroads turned out to be harder to find than we'd thought. May kept saying she knew it was just down this road or that, but we drove around for what seemed like ages. It was as if we were looking for a place that might have existed only in our dreams (or nightmares). And we were nervous, too, suddenly quiet like birds when they know a hawk's on the wing. I stopped to ask directions from a scrawny old country woman in a faded calico dress who was standing by her mailbox. She got a kick out of saying the old name for the place, I could tell.

"Niggerfoot's just over that rise," she grinned. "You all'll see the old store and the barn soon as you start coming down the hill. Store's been closed for years, gas pumps, too. Hope you're not running low."

We topped the rise and, sure enough, there were the barn and the store, riding like two old boats in a rolling green sea of fields. Suddenly, I was a little girl again, here with my father and our dogs, smelling the bird blood and chicken livers. And something else: the scent of the past, which I often do think I can smell. For me, it has the pungent, mysterious odor of a drawer in an antique chest. Or the earth in the woods beneath a rotting log—the one you can't resist rolling over, so you can see all the bugs wriggling out.

I pulled up by the barn and we three sat there, staring. "Well," Carrie murmured, "this *is* the place. Most definitely."

Being here was anticlimactic, as I might have known it would be. There was no monument, no black-and-white Virginia historical marker on the roadside to tell us what happened here. No one wanted to recall such an event—no one white, anyway. But we did. On this late spring afternoon with the evening shadows gathering, we had come to pay our respects. To the ghosts who haunt this place. To the spirit of the man we knew was tortured here, no matter what that book in the library said. He was still here, on this southern road. Remembered by a few old people now, but forgotten by most. The world speeds on, heedless of the past.

These roads of ours can lead us to the scenes of terror, but they can also lead us home. To where our mothers and fathers raised us, and if they were black, did everything within their power to love and shield us from the worst and bitterest truths, like the one this crossroads whispers of. Some of our roads lead to sanctuary, and some to shame. They are so often the same road.

After we took May home, Carrie and I drove slowly to Richmond. I took the two-lane instead of Route 95; I couldn't handle the trucks and the traffic speeding by at eighty miles an hour. We were both still back in another time, and we needed to stay there for a while. So we didn't say much. I sneaked a glance at Carrie. She was holding her grandmother's roses in the Dixie cup, gazing out the window at the rolling green fields.

"Well," I offered, "I guess we found it."

Carrie turned to look at me. She did not smile, but her face was serene. "We did, girlfriend," she says. "We surely did."

Dr. Carrie Jefferson Smith, as she is today.

Mother and I in 1990.

OTHER DIED IN September 2002 at the age of ninety-two. Her death was not a peaceful one. She struggled for weeks. My sister Susan, who was living in Santa Fe, came to say goodbye. She had become so estranged from Mother and Daddy that she had not seen them for over twenty years. The one exception was my wedding, to which she came because I begged her to and because she and Jonathan are very fond of one another. She was gentle with Mother, but it was very hard for her to be there. My brother, Dickie, lived in Richmond and he was often at the house, but his schizophrenia had returned with redoubled force and he was intent on denying the reality of Mother's impending death.

It was my sister Mary and I and Mary's three daughters who kept a constant vigil at her bedside.

"I'm ready now!" she kept crying out, writhing in agitation. "Please, please, let me go!"

I held her as the morphine took effect, allowing her to fall into a restless half-sleep from which she would awaken only to discover that she had not died. My father couldn't bring himself to enter the room and say goodbye. He was ninety-seven, very frail, and so terrified of losing her that he stayed in his room across the hall with Glenda, his ever-loyal mistress. By then, she had become so much a friend not just to him but also to Mother, to Mary, and to me that even though the past would never be forgotten, Mary and I were nevertheless trying to let it be bygone.

I sang to Mother, the spirituals Rhoda had given me. By the time she was only days away from dying, she could not see me anymore, but I knew she still heard. Her eyelids fluttered when I came to this verse from "Swing Low, Sweet Chariot": "If you get there before I do, tell all my friends I'm coming there, too." The ghost of her girlish smile flickered across her face and then was gone.

She was naked beneath the sheet and kept tugging it down to uncover her body. At first we women, modest for her, kept trying to pull the sheet back. But we soon gave that up. I stared down at the withered husk of her body, her belly and breasts still beautiful with the imprint of the lives they had labored to bring forth. I thought about how I had been nourished by her blood, her bones. I grieved for myself, too, in that moment, lamenting that I had never allowed myself this; I will die without knowing the grief and bliss of mothering a child.

Carrie Jefferson came two days before the end to say goodbye. She and I sat on either side of Mother's bed, holding hands over her still form. Carrie bowed her head on Mother's breast and said, "Thank you, Evelyn." And then, unable to choke back her tears, "Thank you . . . for my life."

Sixty-one days later, my father followed Mother to the grave. They had been married for seventy-two years. They are buried side by side in Richmond's Hebrew Cemetery, where four generations of their families lie.

⚬

CLAUDINE LEAKE IS now ninety-four; she was born in 1910, the same year as Mother. She recently moved to a nursing home in

Richmond. We are still devoted, talk often on the phone, and I visit her when I return to town. She is blind now, but her spirit is undimmed. When I asked her if she remembered making her remark about Negroes and Jews, she frowned.

"Oh, Lord. You been holdin' on to that all these years?"

"Are you kidding, Deanie? How could I ever forget it? It changed my life. For the past fifty years, I've been wandering around repeating it to myself and wondering if it really *was* a saying, or if you made it up."

"Aw, wasn't no sayin'! 'Course I made it up. I was just in an awful mood that day. Must have had my monthlies."

☙

CARRIE JEFFERSON SMITH is associate professor of social work at Syracuse University. Her field is kinship care: developing strategies for children who are at risk to stay within their extended families instead of going into foster homes. She has been awarded numerous grants to further this work and has won honors for her teaching.

Our friendship continues to deepen. As Carrie likes to say, when we talk about our braided pasts, our shared roots in Virginia: "The fruit don't fall too far from the tree."

☙

SOPHIA NORRELL BEAL is seventy-eight. She lives in downtown Richmond, in assisted-living housing that was once a Civil War hospital. It has been renovated, "but only slightly," Sophia says. The building is next to the Hebrew Cemetery where my parents are buried.

Sophia and I are in close touch, and we visit whenever I am in town. Shortly after Mother died, Sophia told me that Mother had come to see her, in the middle of a night when Sophia was feeling desperately lonely and sad. Mother appeared in the doorway of Sophia's bedroom and smiled, and Sophia knew this was a sign that everything was going to be all right.

So far, Sophia is the only member of the family who has been visited by my mother since her death.

acknowledgments

WHEN I AM asked how long it took me to write *Off-White*, I never know what to answer; in one way or another, I've been working on it for most of my life. I began writing drafts of the book a decade before my parents died, and friends kept asking me how I could do this while they were still alive. How, they wondered, could I bring myself to tell the truth about the living? But to me, the deeper question was: How could I even know what was truth? For memoir—like its sister, memory—is a moving target. As I researched my family's past and returned endlessly to my own, my vision—along with my writer's sense of what mattered most about my story—kept shifting like the patterns in a kaleidoscope. Part of me wanted to write a commemorative family saga, and as I watched my parents moving toward their deaths, this urge to create a record of their remarkable lives as southern Jews became almost overwhelming. But the other part me knew that this book had to be primarily my own story, my journey to becoming "off-white."

Three women in particular partnered me along the way.

Ellen McGrath, coach and friend, guided me in the work of confronting my past and healing its wounds. When I faltered, she lent me her good faith and abundant courage till I could regain my own.

Laura Golden Bellotti worked with me on the manuscript at a critical time when I was otherwise very much alone, without an agent or a publisher. Her brilliant editing and generous heart kept me going.

And finding Susan Schulman, my agent, was like coming home.

☙

I AM GRATEFUL to others who opened many a door. Philip Gerard, Beverly Tetterton, and Melton McLaurin, in Wilmington. John Finney, in Savannah.

The Cobin family of Summerville—with special thanks to Juanita Johnson Hill, Gary Duggins, and Samuel "Butch" Lewis, the family historian, who kindly shared his research with me.

Thanks to Lynn Brennan and Jerry Jenkins of Richmond, for their unwavering faith in this project. To Jack Spiro and Saul Viener. And to my New York memoir-writing friends, Elaine Savory and Mariette Bermowitz, for our hours of talk and sisterhood.

My sisters, Susan and Mary, and my brother, Dick, stood with me while I delved into our shared and often painful past. Their love and courage sustain me.